CorelDRAW!

Richard Feldman

NOW!

You're Only Seconds Away from Great Results

Quick Access to the Power of CorelDRAW!

Step-by-step Instructions to Professional Results

Master Tasks, Don't Memorize Commands

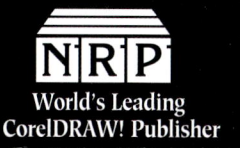

NRP
World's Leading
CorelDRAW! Publisher

CorelDRAW! Now!

By Richard Feldman

Published by:
New Riders Publishing
201 West 103rd Street
Indianapolis, IN 46290 USA

All rights reserved. No part of this book may be reproduced or transmitted in any form or by any means, electronic or mechanical, including photocopying, recording, or by any information storage and retrieval system, without written permission from the publisher, except for inclusion in brief quotations in a review.

Copyright © 1993 by New Riders Publishing

Printed in the United States of America 1 2 3 4 5 6 7 8 9 0

Library of Congress Cataloging-in-Publication Data:

```
Feldman, Richard, 1956-
    CorelDRAW! Now! / Richard Feldman.
      p.   cm.
    Includes index.
    ISBN 1-56205-131-8 : $24.95
    1. Computer graphics. 2. CorelDRAW!. I. Title
  T385.F449   1993                             93-33012
  006.6'869--dc20                                  CIP
```

Publisher
Lloyd J. Short

Associate Publisher
Tim Huddleston

Acquisitions Manager
Cheri Robinson

Acquisitions Editor
Rob Tidrow

Managing Editor
Matthew Morrill

Marketing Manager
Gregg Bushyeager

Product Director
Cheri Robinson

Senior Editor
Nancy E. Sixsmith

Production Coordinator
Lisa Wagner

Production Editors
John Kane
Lisa Wagner

Editors
Judy Richardson
Steve Weiss
Lisa Wilson
Phil Worthington

Technical Editor
Deborah Miller

Book Design
Roger S. Morgan

Production
Rich Evers
Dennis Clay Hager
Julie Pavey
Michelle M. Self
Alyssa Yesh

Proofreaders
Ayrika Bryant
Mitzi Foster Gianakos
Sean Medlock
Linda Quigley
Ryan Rader
Marcella Thompson
Dennis Wesner
Donna Winter

Indexers
John Sleeva
Suzanne Snyder

Acquisitions Coordinator
Stacey Beheler

Editorial Assistant
Karen Opal

Publishing Assistant
Melissa Lynch

About the Author

Richard Feldman is president and owner of Slides Plus Inc., a full-service audiovisual production company specializing in slide, multi-image, video, and multimedia production. He has been a CorelDRAW! user for three years.

He also is a contributing author of *CorelDRAW! Special Effects*, from New Riders Publishing.

Dedication

This book is dedicated to my friend Charlie, my computer mentor and a fine writer in his own right; and to my wife, Karen, whose confidence in me has always greatly exceeded my actual abilities.

Acknowledgments

To say that this book would not have been possible if not for the enormous help of others is somewhat clichéd, but absolutely appropriate.

I'd first like to thank my friends and family, who encouraged me to take on this assignment and thought I'd be crazy not to.

Thanks to everyone at New Riders Publishing, whose efforts probably will make my writing sound literate: Lisa Wagner, John Kane, Stacey Beheler, Judy Richardson, Steve Weiss, Lisa Wilson, and Phil Worthington.

And finally, a special thanks to Cheri Robinson, who held my hand over long-distance phone lines and led me through this project.

Trademark Acknowledgments

New Riders Publishing has made every attempt to supply trademark information about company names, products, and services mentioned in this book. Trademarks indicated below were derived from various sources. New Riders Publishing cannot attest to the accuracy of this information.

Corel is a registered trademark, and CorelCHART!, CorelDRAW!, CorelMOSAIC!, CorelMOVE!, CorelPHOTO-PAINT!, and CorelTRACE! are trademarks of Corel Systems Corporation.

Microsoft Windows is a registered trademark of Microsoft Corporation.

Trademarks of other products mentioned in this book are held by the companies producing them.

Warning and Disclaimer

This book is designed to provide information about the CorelDRAW! computer program. Every effort has been made to make this book as complete and as accurate as possible, but no warranty or fitness is implied.

The information is provided on an "as is" basis. The author and New Riders Publishing shall have neither liability nor responsibility to any person or entity with respect to any loss or damages arising from the information contained in this book or from the use of the disks or programs that may accompany it.

Contents at a Glance

Introduction	1
1. Getting Started	9
2. Drawing Lines and Curves	19
3. Drawing Rectangles and Ellipses	33
4. Setting and Manipulating Text	43
5. Moving, Duplicating, and Transforming Objects	71
6. Using Outlines and Fills	87
7. Arranging and Aligning Objects	117
8. Working with Graphic Styles	139
9. Special Effects	159
10. Managing Files	193
11. Printing Files	205
12. CorelTRACE!	213
13. CorelCHART!	227
14. CorelPHOTO-PAINT!	245
15. CorelMOVE!	259
Index	277

Table of Contents

Introduction 1

1 Getting Started 9
Exploring the CorelDRAW! Screen 9
Setting Defaults 10
- Status Line 10
- Print 10
- Page Setup 11
- Grid 11
- Rulers 12
- Color Palette 12
- Edit Wireframe 12
- Preferences 12
- Curves 14
- Display 14
- Mouse 15
- Roll-Ups 15
- Dimension 15

Examining the Toolbox 15
Using the Menu Bar 16
- File Menu 16
- Edit Menu 16
- Layout Menu 17
- Effects Menu 17
- Text Menu 17
- Arrange Menu 17
- Display Menu 17
- Special Menu 17
- Roll-Up Menus 18
- Help Menu 18

Understanding Image Terminology 18

2 Drawing Lines and Curves 19
Drawing Lines 19
- Freehand Mode 19
- Bézier Mode 22

Drawing Curves 23
- Freehand Mode 23
- Bézier Mode 24

Editing Line Color and Thickness 25
- Using the Toolbox 25
- Using the Pen Roll-Up Menu 26

Editing Nodes and Control Points 28
Drawing Dimension Lines 30

3 Drawing Rectangles and Ellipses 33

Creating Rectangles 33
Rounding Corners 35
Converting Objects to Curves 36
Creating Ellipses and Circles 37
Drawing Arcs and Wedges 39

4 Setting and Manipulating Text 43

Entering Text 43
    Entering Text on the Screen 43
    Entering Text with the Artistic Text Dialog Box 44
Pasting Text 45
Selecting Text Attributes 46
    Fonts 47
    Alignment 47
    Font Size 47
    Style 48
    Edit Text 48
    Edit Text Spacing 49
Editing Text 52
Changing Individual Character Attributes 53
Entering Paragraph Text 56
Using Spell Checker 57
    Creating a Personal Dictionary 58
Using the Thesaurus 59
Using the Symbol Library 60
    Tiling Symbols 62
Fitting Text to a Path 63
Using the Straighten Text and Align to Baseline Commands 67
Copying Text Attributes 68
Using Special Characters 70

5 Moving, Duplicating, and Transforming Objects 71

Opening Files 71
Moving Objects with the Mouse 72
Using the Move Command 73
Moving Objects with the Keyboard 74
Stretching Objects with the Mouse 74
Stretching Objects Using the Stretch & Mirror Command 76
Mirroring an Object 77

    Mirroring an Object Using the Stretch & Mirror Command 77
        Rotating Objects with Using the Mouse 78
        Rotating Objects Using the Rotate & Skew Command 79
        Skewing Objects with the Mouse 80
        Skewing Objects Using the Rotate & Skew Command 81
        Duplicating Objects 81
        Cloning Objects 83
        Using Transformation Commands 85

6   Using Outlines and Fills 87

    Setting Outline Width and Color 87
    Using the Calligraphic Outline Pen 89
    Filling Objects with a Solid Color 89
    Working with Color Palettes 91
    Adding Colors to the Palette 92
        Rearranging the Color Palette 93
    Using Fountain Fills 94
    Creating a Preset Fountain Fill 96
    Creating Custom Fountain Fills 97
    Using Bit-Map and Pattern Fills 100
        Two-Color Patterns 100
        Creating a Pattern 101
        Using a Full-Color Pattern 104
        Filling with Bit-Map Textures 104
        Using PostScript Textures 107
    Setting Defaults 107
    Using the Fill Roll-Up Menu 108
        Fountain Fills 108
        Two-Color Patterns 109
        Full-Color Pattern 110
        Bit-Map Texture Fills 110
    Copying Styles 112
    Practical Uses 114

7   Arranging and Aligning Objects 117

    Aligning Objects 117
    Aligning to Guidelines 119
    Grouping Objects 120
        Editing Objects within a Group 122
    Changing Grid Origin 123
        Adjusting the Grid Size 124
    Changing the Order of Objects 125
    Combining Objects 127
        Conserving Memory 127
        Combining Objects that Overlap 128

	Breaking Apart an Object	129
	Creating Window Masks	130
	Welding Objects	132
	Working with Layers	133
	Displaying Layers	134
	Adding Layers	134
	Moving Objects between Layers	135
	Adding Objects to Layers	135
	Reordering Layers	136
	Distinguishing between Layers	136
	Using the MultiLayer Option	137
	Locking a Layer	137
	Printing Layers	138
8	Working with Graphic Styles	139
	Adding Pages to a Document	139
	Copying Objects between Pages	141
	Creating a Master Layer	142
	Hiding a Master Layer	143
	Deleting Pages	143
	Working with Paragraph text	144
	Using Multiple Text Frames	144
	Formatting Paragraph Text	147
	Formatting Columns	150
	Using Templates and Styles	152
	Creating a Template	152
	Using Supplied Templates	154
	Applying Styles	155
9	Special Effects	159
	Using the Envelope Effect	159
	Adding a Preset Envelope	163
	Copying an Envelope Shape	164
	Enveloping Paragraph Text	166
	Editing Perspective	167
	Aligning Vanishing Points	168
	Copying Effects	169
	Creating an Extrusion	170
	Extruding by Specific Value	171
	Controlling Color	172
	Rotating an Extrusion	172
	Dynamic Linking	173
	Separating Objects	174
	Controlling Lighting	175

Using the Contour Command 176
Using the Blend Command 179
    Creating a Simple Blend 179
    Blending Objects along a Path..181
    Splitting a Blend Group 182
    Fusing a Blend Group..182
    Controlling Color 183
    Creating Multiple Objects 183
    Creating Airbrush Effects 185
Working with PowerLines 188
    Applying PowerLines 189
    Adjusting Nib Shape 191
    Adjusting Image Controls 191
    Saving Custom PowerLines..192

10 Managing Files...193
Sorting Files 193
Using Keywords and Notes 194
Importing and Exporting Files 195
    Exporting Files (Vector Based) 196
    Exporting Files (Bit-Maps)..198
Using Object Linking and Embedding....................................199
    Embedding Objects 200
    Linking Objects 200
Using CorelMOSAIC!...200
    Opening a File...200
    Creating a Library 201
    Searching for Files 202
    Copying Files to a Library 202
    Creating a Catalog 203

11 Printing Files 205
Preparing Your Printing Device...205
    Print Setup 205
    Print Dialog Box 205
    Options Dialog Box 207
Printing a File 209
    Printing Tips 210
Batch Printing 211

12 CorelTRACE!...213
Tracing an Image...213
Using the Tracing Options 216
    Tracing with the Pick Tool..216
    Tracing with the Magic Wand 217

Using the Silhouette Method 218
Setting the Custom Tracing Options 219
Tracing a Text Object 220
Importing a Traced Image 221
Tracing Multiple Files..224

13 CorelCHART! 227

Exploring the CorelCHART! Screen 227
    The CorelCHART! Toolbox 227
    The Text Ribbon 230
    Anatomy of a Chart 231
    The Chart Menu Bar 232
Exploring the Data Manager 233
Creating a Chart 234
Exploring Chart Types 239
Importing a Chart with OLE 242

14 CorelPHOTO-PAINT! 245

Exploring the Photo-Paint Screen 245
Exploring the Toolbox 246
    Selection Tools 248
    Display Tools 249
    Painting Tools 249
    Drawing Tools 250
    Retouching Tools 250
Exploring the Roll-Up Menus 251
Exploring Image Enhancement 252
Exploring the Effects Menu 255

15 CorelMOVE! 259

Exploring the CorelMOVE! Screen 259
    The Toolbox 261
    The Control Panel 262
    Menu Bar Controls 265
Creating a Simple Animation 267
Using CorelSHOW! 275

Index 277

New Riders Publishing

The staff of New Riders Publishing is committed to bringing you the very best in computer reference material. Each New Riders book is the result of months of work by authors and staff, who research and refine the information contained within its covers.

As part of this commitment to you, the NRP reader, New Riders invites your input. Please let us know if you enjoy this book, if you have trouble with the information and examples presented, or if you have a suggestion for the next edition.

Please note, however, that the New Riders staff cannot serve as a technical resource for CorelDRAW! or CorelDRAW! application-related questions, including hardware- or software-related problems. Refer to the documentation that accompanies your CorelDRAW! package for help with specific problems.

If you have a question or comment about any New Riders book, please write to NRP at the following address. We will respond to as many readers as we can. Your name, address, and phone number will never become part of a mailing list or be used for any other purpose than to help us continue to bring you the best books possible.

> New Riders Publishing
> Paramount Publishing
> Attn: Associate Publisher
> 201 West 103rd Street
> Indianapolis, IN 46290

If you prefer, you can fax New Riders Publishing at the following number:
> (317) 581-4670

We welcome your electronic mail to our CompuServe ID:
> 70031,2231

Thank you for selecting *CorelDRAW! Now!*

Introduction

Personal computers have revolutionized the way we work. Communications, word processing, and information management are just a few of the areas that have been drastically affected by the PC. Graphics production is no exception. Programs that initially replaced a few traditional drawing tools have grown into complete production studios in a box. Case in point—CorelDRAW! 4.0. The current release of the program enables even the novice artist to produce graphics on a professional level. Plus, CorelDRAW! comes with all the tools you need to incorporate graphics in slides, flyers, brochures, posters, or even computer-based multimedia presentations.

If you have any experience with the earlier releases, it all looks pretty familiar. If you're completely new to computer graphics, CorelDRAW! might as well be a control panel screen on the space shuttle. First and foremost, though, this is not the space shuttle! Although it is extremely powerful as a graphics tool, it still is easy to use. Second, no one learns the program in one sitting. Compare learning the program to learning to play the piano. You don't expect to play like a concert pianist after only one lesson, so don't expect to master CorelDRAW! in the first practice session.

But don't get discouraged. This book is here not only to help you get up and running faster than by using the manual, but to help you gain a better understanding of the program. And if that's not enough, it offers practical user tips, shortcuts, and recommendations to help you create graphics on a professional level.

Good luck!

Overview of CorelDRAW! 4.0

Right now several software programs that attempt to be all things to all people are on the market. These all-in-one packages offer an array of programs (such as word processing, spreadsheets, and databases) of limited power. That is not the case with CorelDRAW!. Although some of the Corel modules are not especially awesome, a good deal of them could go head-to-head with any stand-alone package available.

When you open the box you get the following:

- **CorelDRAW!.** The heart and soul of this collection, by itself worth the price of admission. It is a *vector-based* (or *object-oriented*) drawing program. What that means is that images are made up of lines and shapes that can be filled with color. Although this might sound rather simplistic, the graphics you can produce are anything but simple. First, you have 750 type fonts at your disposal, along with more than 18,000 high-quality clip-art images and more than 5,000 drag-and-drop symbols. Second, you have a collection of special effects tools that enable you do things like create 3-D objects, alter the perspective of objects, and morph the shape of one object into another. Third, you have DTP (desktop publishing) capabilities, like creating documents up to 999 pages long or creating page templates for a newsletter or flyer (43 professionally designed templates are included). And that barely skims the surface.

- **CorelMOSAIC!.** An exceptional utility that displays, organizes, and manages your graphics files. You can display CorelDRAW! files, as well as files in other formats, such as PostScript and Photo-CD files. CorelMOSAIC! enables you to batch operations (like printing a number of different files at once), or create libraries of files that are compressed, freeing up space on your hard disk.

- **CorelCHART!.** If you need to create charts for presentations, this module can easily handle the job. It offers the basics: bar, line, and pie charts, as well as many different 3-D and more specialized types. You even can create pictographs, wherein a stack of coins or dollar bills represents a bar of the chart. Included are over 80 financial functions you can use to ensure that data is accurate.

- **CorelTRACE!.** CorelTRACE! enables you to take digitally scanned images and convert them so that they can be brought into CorelDRAW! and edited like a typical object. You can scan a company logo so that it can appear on a newsletter, for example. Version 4.0 now comes with *OCR (Optical Character Recognition)*, which means you can scan text from a page, bring it into a document in CorelDRAW!, and treat it as text.

Features of *CorelDRAW! Now!*

- **CorelPHOTO-PAINT!**. If you can imagine your grandmother riding a surfboard in Hawaii, you can create it in Photo-Paint. This module comes with powerful photo retouching tools with which you can create photo-realistic images. The interface is similar to all the other modules, so the learning curve is greatly reduced. The special effects filters can sharpen or blur images, posterize them, or even re-create them as a Van Gogh painting. It also can create CMYK color separations that then can be viewed on-screen for complete accuracy.

- **CorelMOVE!**. This is a completely new module that enables you to add movement to your presentations. You can choose from an extensive library of professionally designed actors, or create your own by using CorelDRAW! tools. This is hardly a high-end animation program, but it does enable you to create some interesting animation programs.

- **CorelSHOW!**. Using the Show module, you can assemble objects you create and combine them in a multimedia presentation. You can combine charts, graphics, and animations with sound and full-motion video to create dazzling on-screen presentations. User cues enable the viewer to add input and branch to different parts of the presentation, making it a truly interactive medium.

Features of *CorelDRAW! Now!*

Features designed into this unique book include the following:

- Referenced step-by-step instructions for performing each essential task
- Tips and insights you can use to improve your efficiency
- Common problems and solutions

Installation

Hardware Requirements

CorelDRAW! 4.0 has the following system requirements:

- An IBM or compatible 386 or 486 or a PS/2 computer
- A minimum of 4M of RAM
- Microsoft Windows 3.1
- A hard drive
- A color monitor of VGA resolution or better
- A mouse or digitizing tablet

Introduction

4M is the minimum RAM needed to run the program, but 8M is recommended. Even at 8M, a permanent swap file probably would be required. (Consult the Windows manual for information on swap files and virtual memory.)

Optional Hardware

Although it is not required, a CD-ROM drive is an investment worth considering. Of the 750 fonts that come with the program, most of them are contained on CD discs. The CDs also contain most of the clip art for the drawing module, as well as animations, sound files, paint files, and chart templates. Access to this sort of resource definitely expands your ability to create professional-looking artwork.

User Requirements

As powerful as this drawing program is, you don't need a great deal of experience to get up and running. All you need is a basic understanding of DOS—the ability to work with directories, copy and move files, and pretty much turn the computer on and off. Well, you also should have some experience working under Windows (but you don't have to be a power user or whatever). With Windows, you simply need an understanding of how to use the interface. If you spend any time working with other Windows programs, you probably know enough to get going. If not, you might want to review the *Basics* chapters of the Windows manual.

Installation and Options

If you have a CD-ROM drive, use the first CD disc to install the program. It is much faster and easier than the floppies. Otherwise, start with Disk 1 of the floppies.

1. Insert Disk 1 into the proper drive.
2. From the Windows Program Manager, click on Run from the File menu.
3. Type the drive letter that contains the disk, followed immediately by **:setup**. Press Enter.
4. You are greeted by the welcome screen; click on Continue.
5. In the registration screen, type your name and enter the serial number for your copy of the program (the number is located in the software license agreement envelope with the floppy disks). Click on OK.

Installation   5

6. The next screen is for Full or Custom Installation. If you have tons of hard disk space, click on Full Install, and the program puts every module on your drive. However, chances are that space is something of a premium, or that you don't want to install all the modules right now.

   You can go back to the installation program later and install anything you skip during the initial installation.

   Click on Custom Installation.

7. The destination directory is COREL40. Leave it as is and click on Continue.

8. You now are presented with the program installation options, as shown in figure I.1.

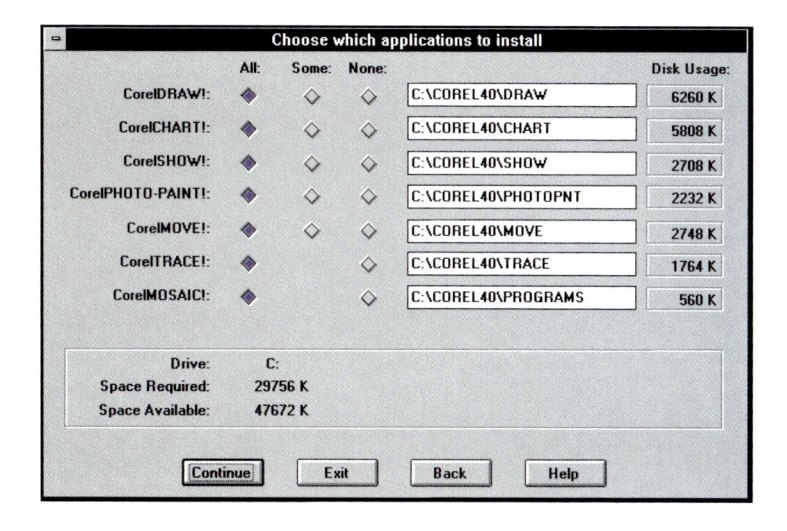

Figure I.1
The program installation options.

9. Each module of the program is listed, as well as the disk space required to install it. Click on the box for CorelDRAW! under Some. You are presented with the options for the Draw module.

10. The box for Program Files and On-line Help should be checked.

    It is strongly recommended that you install On-line Help for any module you install.

11. SAMPLES takes about 400K of disk space. If you have the room, you should install them. The reason is that they are high-quality images created with the program, and you can learn much by examining them to see how they were created.

12. SYMBOLS takes up about 1.6M of disk space, and is worth having. If you want them, but are concerned about space, click on the Customize button. From the Customize menu you can select the symbol sets you want to install.

Look on page 371 of the clip-art manual if you want to see what the symbol sets include.

13. If you install from the floppies, you have the option of copying some clip art to your hard drive. It takes up about 3M of space, another good reason to have a CD-ROM. If you have room, install the clip art.

14. Click on Continue to return to the application options.

15. If you plan to install Chart, Show, Photo-Paint, or Move, select the All option for each. If space is scarce, click on None for all four—you can always install them later.

16. If you don't have a scanner, or don't have the need to convert bit-map files (like TIFF) for use in CorelDRAW!, select None for CorelTRACE!.

17. It is recommended that you install CorelMOSAIC!. It is a powerful and useful program, and it uses only about 560K of memory.

18. After all the selections are made, click on Continue.

19. You now are prompted for which filters, fonts, and drivers you want to install.

20. For filters, select All if you have enough space (you never know when you're going to need to import or export in a strange format). Otherwise, select Some and remove the filters for file formats you are sure you won't work with.

21. Select All for fonts.

22. If you have a scanner, select Some and select your scanner from the list.

23. When your selections are complete, click on Continue.

24. Follow on-screen instructions. Insert the proper disks when prompted.

25. After the program is installed, you are prompted to have changes made to your AUTOEXEC.BAT file. Let the program do so. Your original AUTOEXEC.BAT file is saved as AUTOEXEC.COR.

26. You are prompted to install SHARE.EXE. CorelDRAW! 4.0 needs this to be loaded on your system, so let the program install it.

Installation

27. After the installation is complete, a program group and icons for all installed applications are created.

28. You should reboot your computer so that any changes made to your system during installation take effect.

Installing Additional Fonts

If you have a CD-ROM drive you can install any or all of the over 750 TrueType fonts that come with the program.

1. From the Program Manager, select **R**un from the **F**ile menu.

2. Type the letter for your CD-ROM drive, followed immediately by **:fontinst**. Press Enter.

3. At the welcome screen, click on **C**ontinue. You then are prompted for where you want the actual font files to reside. If you want to access them from the CD, just click on **C**ontinue. If you want them on your hard drive, enter the path and directory. Click on **C**ontinue.

Accessing fonts from the CD is slower, but saves space on your hard drive. Loading them to your hard drive speeds up access, but can use up much needed space. In either case, be conservative as to how many fonts you install. The more TrueType fonts that are loaded, the slower Windows and certain Windows applications run.

4. The TrueType Fonts Selection dialog box appears, as shown in figure I.2.

5. You choose a font group by checking its box. To see what fonts a group contains, see page F1 of the clip-art manual.

6. To load specific fonts, select Assorted, and click on Customize. You now can add individual fonts by name. The fonts are displayed in the clip-art manual beginning on page F5.

7. After all selections have been made, click on **C**ontinue.

8. When font installation is complete, click on OK.

8 Introduction

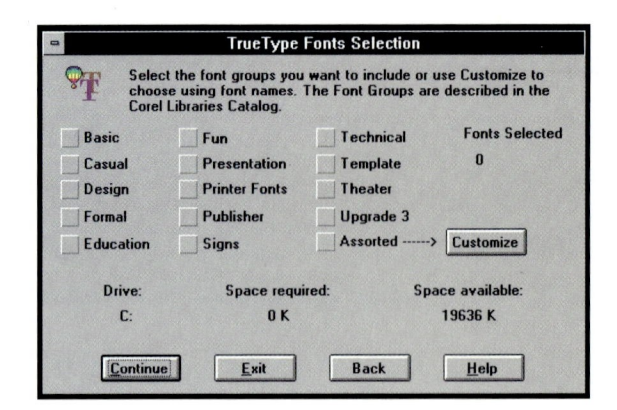

Figure I.2
The TrueType Fonts Selection dialog box.

You now are ready to begin learning the programs. Remember, you can return to the installation program and install any items that were passed over during the initial installation process.

Chapter 1
Getting Started

Before you can use CorelDRAW! successfully, you must have a basic understanding of the way the program works. This chapter introduces you to CorelDRAW!. After you work through the tasks of this chapter, you will be ready to create professional-looking drawings.

Exploring the CorelDRAW! Screen

Think of the CorelDRAW! screen (see fig. 1.1) as your drawing table. On it are all your drawing tools, as well as a drawing surface.

- **Title bar.** This tells you the program you are working in—in this case, CorelDRAW!—and the name of the file you currently are working on. Because you have just started the program and no file is loaded, the name UNTITLED.CDR is displayed.

- **Menu bar.** This contains the eight drop-down menus, as well as the on-line help directory. Click on each to see the options each menu offers. The options will be discussed later in this chapter and throughout the book.

- **Status line.** This displays important information about what currently is happening on the drawing screen.

- **Rulers.** You can display optional rulers to help you position objects on the screen.

- **Toolbox.** This allows you quick access to the tools you will use most often.

- **Editing window.** This is your workspace, where all your drawing will happen.

FEATURES COVERED

This chapter looks at:

- Setting defaults
- The CorelDRAW! screen
- The toolbox
- The menu bar
- Input terminology

Chapter 1: Getting Started

> **Printable page area.** Consider this the live area of your drawing. Normally, only that which falls in this area will be printed.
>
> **Vertical/horizontal scroll bars.** These enable you to scroll the image on the screen from left to right, or up and down.
>
> **Color Palette.** This allows you quick access to add or change colors in your drawing.

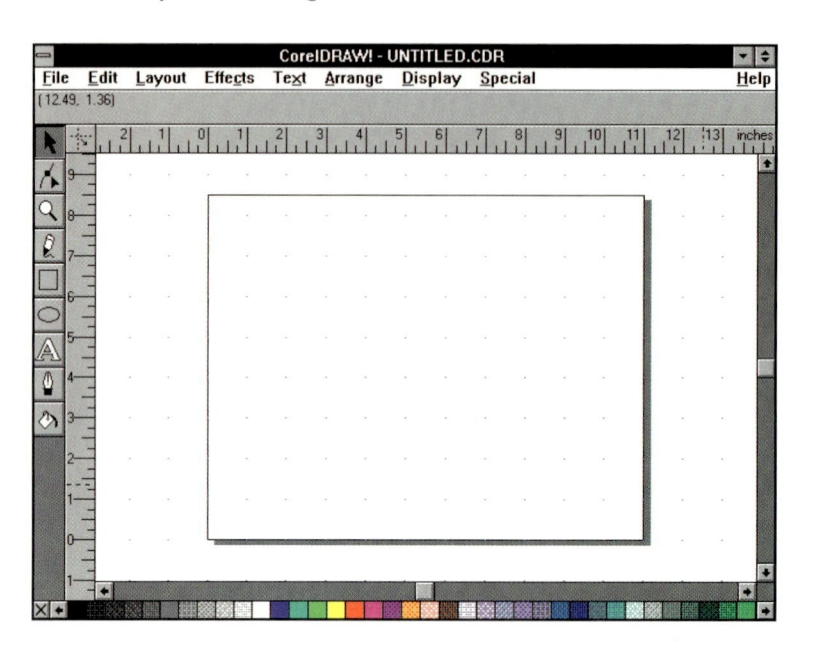

*Figure 1.1
The CorelDRAW! screen.*

Setting Defaults

Before you get started, there are a number of settings you can make to customize the screen area and the way the program performs certain functions. I will make recommendations for you to start with, and when you feel more comfortable with the program, you can change them to whatever works best for you.

Status Line

From the Display menu, click on Show Status Line. As you will see, the status line displays important information about what is happening on-screen, and should always be displayed.

Print

Select File from the menu bar, then choose Print Setup to display the Print Setup dialog box. The Default Printer box should be marked, and the printer configured for Windows should be listed.

Page Setup

From the menu bar, select **L**ayout, then choose Page **S**etup. CorelDRAW! 4.0 offers extensive options for page layout. You can click through the options to get an idea of what is available, but use the following settings for now. Set Paper Size for Letter. Click on the **L**andscape box. Set Page Layout to Full Page. Click on the Paper Color box to reveal color selections, and click on white. Click on the Show Page **B**order box so that it contains a check mark.

Grid

Using the grid enables you to draw with more precision. From the **L**ayout menu, click on Gr**i**d Setup. The Grid Setup dialog box appears (see fig. 1.2).

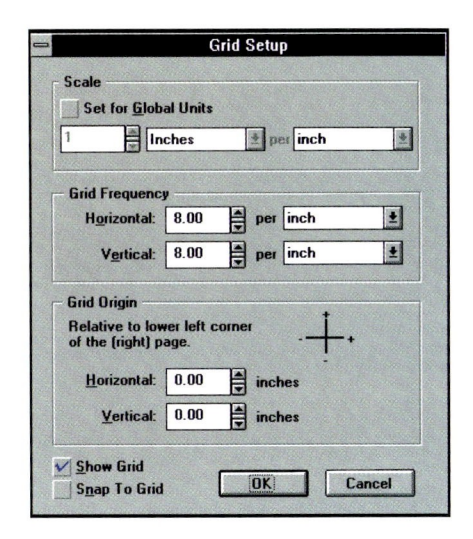

Figure 1.2
The Grid Setup dialog box.

The options in the Grid Setup dialog box include the following:

- **Scale.** This option enables you to specify the scale used in your drawing. To set the scale, click on the check box for Set for **G**lobal Units, then choose the scale you want (1 inch equals 1 mile, for example). For now, leave this section unchecked.

- **Grid Frequency.** This option controls the spacing of the grid lines. You can work in millimeters, picas, and points, but choose inches for simplicity. In the Grid Frequency section, click on the unit box arrow and choose inches for both V**e**rtical and H**o**rizontal. Using the up/down arrows, adjust the frequency numbers to 8 per inch.

- **Grid Origin.** This option refers to the point at which the grid coordinates are 0,0. This can be dead center in the screen or anywhere you want, but it probably is best to be the lower left corner of the drawing page. Set **H**orizontal and **V**ertical both to 0.

Click on the box to the left of **S**how Grid so that a check mark appears. This gives you a visible display of the grid on the screen. You will not see eight grid lines per inch—that would be too confusing to look at. Be assured the grid is there.

When you click on the S**n**ap To Grid check box, objects adhere to the nearest grid line, making it easy to align objects. Leave this box unchecked for now.

Click on the OK button to save the settings. Look on the left side of the status line and you will see that Snap to Grid is activated.

To activate or deactivate Snap To Grid mode, the shortcut is to press Ctrl+Y. Try it now.

Rulers

From the **D**isplay menu, select Show **R**ulers. This displays vertical and horizontal rulers in the units chosen earlier: inches. Displaying the rulers reduces the working area of your screen, and that might be a concern if you are working on a small monitor. Start off with the rulers showing, and remove them later if you feel you need the room.

Color Palette

From the **D**isplay menu, select **C**olor Palette. This reveals an additional menu. Your choices are **N**o Palette, **C**ustom Palette, PANTONE **S**pot Colors, PANTONE **P**rocess Colors, and **T**RUMATCH Process Colors. For now, choose **C**ustom **P**alette. Color Palette options are addressed in Chapter 6, "Using Outlines and Fills."

Edit Wireframe

When you are working on a drawing, you have two options of how to view objects. You can view them in full color as they will appear when printed, or as a Wireframe model, in which all objects are represented by a thin black outline. You will want to work in full-color view to start. From the **D**isplay menu, make sure there is no check mark next to **E**dit Wireframe. If there is, click on it to return to full-color view.

Preferences

From the **S**pecial menu, select Pr**e**ferences (or use the shortcut—Ctrl+J). As you can see, there are a number of options you can adjust here.

- **Place Duplicates and Clones.** As you'll learn shortly, this is a command to make a duplicate or clone of an object. What you are setting here is the relative position of the copy from the original. If you set it at 0 and 0, the copy will be placed directly on top of the

Setting Defaults   13

original. Although you may want to do this at times, there is an easier method that will be discussed later. For now, set it Horizontal = 0.10, Vertical = –0.10 inches. This will place the copy down and to the right 1/10 of an inch. It will come in handy if you want to make a drop shadow of an object quickly. More on that later.

- **Nudge.** One way to move an object on-screen is by using the arrow keys, which is called *nudging*. This setting is how much an object moves with each press of the arrow key. Set nudge at 0.010 for now. Remember, you can change this to whatever works for you, and as often as you find necessary.

- **Constrain Angle.** There are certain commands, such as rotating an object, for which you want to control the motion of that object. This will set that control at set intervals. Set it for 15 degrees for now; constrain is discussed at length later on.

- **Miter Limit.** Generally, when two lines meet to form an angle, you want them to meet at one point to create a clean, sharp corner. The miter setting enables the edges of the lines to meet. The corner point can extend far beyond the actual line if you are working with extremely small angles. Set the miter at 10 degrees.

Later on, when you've learned the basics of line drawing, draw two lines at a sharp angle, say 15 degrees, the lines 1/8 of an inch thick. Go to Miter Limit, change the value, and watch what happens.

- **Undo Levels.** As you are working, you might accidentally move the wrong object or color a line the wrong color. Undo enables you to do just that—back up and undo the operation you performed. Undo Levels enables you to set the number of operations you may undo. The maximum is 99, but set it to 20—that should be more than enough.

- **Auto-Panning.** Checkmark the Auto-Pan box. This will automatically scroll the page whenever you move an object beyond the visible portion of the working area of the printable page.

- **Cross Hair Cursor.** This option will turn the screen cursor (the movable arrow) into a cross hair that extends to the height and width of the screen. It is annoying to look at and not really necessary, so make sure the box is left unchecked.

- **Interruptible Display.** You might be working on a graphic that is somewhat complex, and every time you make a change it takes a long time for the image to completely redraw. You have to wait until this finishes before you resume control of the cursor and issue another command. By checking this box, the screen redraw will stop at the click of the mouse button (after drawing the current object), giving you access to all your tools quickly.

14   Chapter 1: Getting Started

- **3.0 Compatibility Message.** If you do not plan to open files that were created in CorelDRAW! 3.0, then you can disregard this and leave the box unchecked. If you do plan to open 3.0 files, check this box. Then, when you access one of these files, the program will prompt you to change it to CorelDRAW! 4.0 format.

Curves

Clicking on the Curves button brings up the Curves Dialog Box. The default setting for each option is 5 pixels and should be left at that. I will not go into what each setting does now because it is technical stuff and won't do you much good right now. It is covered adequately in the manual, so you can refer to it later when you have become comfortable with the program.

Display

Click on Display to bring up the Preferences - Display dialog box. The options here include the following:

- **Preview Fountain Steps.** This is the number of steps used to represent a fountain fill (or color gradation) of an object. If the object was to go from black to white, for instance, this would represent the number of gray stripes displayed to give a gradated appearance. More steps yields a smoother look, less steps saves time by redrawing faster. For now, set it at 20.

- **Greek Text Below.** This setting affects how certain text is displayed on the screen, and has no impact on output. Text that appears smaller on the screen than the value specified here will appear on-screen as small rectangles. If you are working with a lot of small text, this speeds up screen redraw time. Set it at 9 pixels.

- **Preview Colors.** 256-Color Dithering is the default value and will be set automatically if your hardware supports it. Windows Dithering is your option if your graphics adapter supports just 16 colors.

- **Optimized Palette.** As you will learn, you have the option of viewing a file full-screen, without menus, tools, palettes, and so on. If you check this option, CorelDRAW! optimizes the colors it uses when displaying a full-screen image. Up to 256 colors with no dithering (dot patterns) will be used, assuming your hardware can support this. If it can, check the box.

- **Show Font Sample in Text Roll-Up.** This is a little ahead of the game, but it enables you to view how text will look when you edit it using the Text roll-up menu. More on this later.

Examining the Toolbox 15

Mouse

Click on the button marked **m**ouse to bring up the Preferences - Mouse dialog box. The options listed refer to the right, or secondary, mouse button. For now, choose 2x zoom. When the right mouse button is pressed, the screen will zoom in on the area where the cursor was when the button was pressed. As you become more familiar, you may prefer one of the other options.

Roll-Ups

Click on the **R**oll-ups button to access the Preferences - Roll-Ups dialog box. *Roll-ups* are like additional menus that can be brought up on-screen to remain active as long as you need them. You will use roll-up menus to control operations like special effects. What you can set here is the way they will be displayed on-screen. The choices are show none, show all, show them as they appeared when you last exited the program, or how they currently appear now. I would mark appearance on exit. Then, when you return to the program, whatever roll-ups were active when you exited will still be active. This seems the most practical approach.

> *Checking show all affects system resources by slowing the system down considerably.*

Dimension

Dimension lines are used in technical drawings to show size and distance. The Dimension Preferences dialog box enables you to format dimension lines. Dimension settings are addressed in Chapter 2, "Drawing Lines and Curves."

Examining the Toolbox

The toolbox allows you quick access to the tools you will use most often. They are the following:

> **Pick tool.** This is the most frequently used tool. It enables you to select an object or group of objects and transform them (by moving, rotating, duplicating, and so on). To access this or any tool in the toolbox, just click on the icon.

> *Because the Pick tool is used most often, there is a shortcut to access it. Whenever any drawing tool is selected, pressing the space bar will activate the Pick tool. Press the space bar again and you'll return to the previously selected tool. You will find it handy to switch back and forth between the Pick tool and the drawing tools in the toolbox.*

Chapter 1: Getting Started

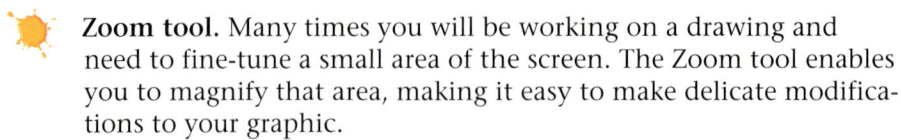

Shape tool. When you want to change the basic shape of an object, use the Shape tool. As you will see, its effect varies for different types of objects.

Zoom tool. Many times you will be working on a drawing and need to fine-tune a small area of the screen. The Zoom tool enables you to magnify that area, making it easy to make delicate modifications to your graphic.

Pencil tool. The Pencil tool enables you to do just what you'd think—draw lines and shapes. It can draw straight lines automatically, freehand curves, Bézier curves, dimension lines, and closed objects (polygons) that then can be filled with a color.

Rectangle tool. Almost every object is composed of a few basic shapes. This tool enables you to draw rectangles and squares.

Ellipse tool. Another basic shape is the ellipse. This tool enables you to draw ellipses and circles.

Text tool. Use this tool to add text to a graphic. It also enables you to access the symbol library that is included in CorelDRAW!.

Outline tool. This tool enables you to adjust the attributes of a line or an object's outline (that is, its color or thickness). It also can add arrow heads and tails to a line, or change it from solid to dashed.

Fill tool. This tool enables you to adjust the fill attributes of an object. You can choose a uniform color, a fountain fill, a two-color pattern, a full-color pattern, a bit-map texture, or a PostScript texture.

Using the Menu Bar

A great deal of commands are accessed through the menu bar. This section takes a fast look at them and touches on a few of the most basic commands.

File Menu

The File menu contains a couple of important commands. Open enables you to bring up a previously created CorelDRAW! file. Save enables you to save a file to disk. If you make changes to a file and want to retain the unchanged version, you would use Save As to save the new file with a different name. After you are done working on a drawing and have saved it, the New command will clear the screen so you can start afresh.

Edit Menu

The Edit menu also contains a number of important editing commands, many of which are more easily accessed using hot keys. Undo (Ctrl+Z) enables you to do just that—back up and undo the operation you performed. If you remember when you were setting preferences, you can undo up to 99 steps. **R**edo reverses the Undo step you have just taken. **R**epeat (Ctrl+R) enables you to apply the command you just completed on another object. Cu**t** (Ctrl+X), **C**opy (Ctrl+C), and **P**aste (Ctrl+V) enable you to bring objects to and from the Windows Clipboard. De**l**ete (Del key) removes a selected object from a drawing. **D**uplicate (Ctrl+D) copies a selected object to the drawing. And Select **A**ll selects every object in the drawing.

Layout Menu

The **L**ayout menu has commands for setting up the options for the drawing page area. Among these commands are controls to set the page size and style, display a grid on the screen, and add pages to a document.

Effects Menu

The Effe**c**ts menu is where you find the powerful tools for changing the shape and color of an object. The options here enable you to make simple adjustments to an object, such as rotating or stretching it, as well as more drastic reconstructions, such as changing the perspective or modifying it into a 3-D object.

Text Menu

The Te**x**t menu gives you access to the text controls of CorelDRAW!. Edit Te**x**t (Ctrl+T) is used fairly often, so I would commit this hot key to memory right away. You can access the Text **R**oll-Up menu, the Thesa**u**rus, the Sp**e**ll Checker, and Fit Text to Path, a command that enables you to fit text to a path (have the text sitting on the edge of a circle, for instance).

Arrange Menu

The commands of the **A**rrange menu affect how objects are arranged. You can move objects in specific increments, align them with one another, change the order in which they appear, group them together, and combine them into one object.

Display Menu

Many of the **D**isplay menu's commands should be familiar from setting the defaults earlier. Show **P**review (F9) enables you to view your drawing in full-screen view, without any of the CorelDRAW! interface showing.

Special Menu

The **S**pecial menu gives you access to the Pr**e**ferences menu, which you worked with earlier. From the **S**pecial menu you can create custom fill patterns, arrows, and symbols, or extract and merge text from your word processor into a CorelDRAW! document.

Roll-Up Menus

Some of the menus include a command line for a roll-up menu (Text **R**oll-Up, **B**lend Roll-Up, and so on). Roll-up menus are additional menus that can be brought up on-screen, and will remain active as long as you need them. You will use them to control operations like special effects.

Help Menu

On the far right of the menu bar is the **H**elp menu. Selecting it accesses Corel's on-line Help file. It is rather extensive, and is a good way to get quick advice.

Understanding Input Terminology

You should be familiar with the following terms for working with images on-screen:

- **Mouse button.** This refers to the primary mouse button. It usually is the left mouse button, pressed with the index finger, but Windows enables you to swap mouse button operation as an aid to left-handed users. Whenever you see an instruction for the mouse button, we are referring to the primary mouse button.

- **Secondary button.** This refers to the secondary (or right) mouse button. It generally is pressed with the middle finger, but as stated previously its operation can be swapped.

- **Click on.** Position the cursor on a designated item and quickly press and release the mouse button.

- **Double-click on.** Position the cursor on a designated item and quickly press and release the mouse button twice in succession.

- **Drag.** Position the cursor on a designated item, press and hold the mouse button, move the cursor to the desired location, and release the mouse button.

Chapter 2
Drawing Lines and Curves

*L*ines and curves are defined by nodes. A node *is a point that defines the shape of a line or curve. A straight line, for instance, requires only two nodes, with the line running between them. A node can act as a handle that enables you to alter the line or curve. This chapter teaches you to create lines and curves of various types, as well as how to edit their size, shape, and color.*

Drawing Lines

Probably the most basic element in drawing is the line. CorelDRAW! offers a number of options for drawing lines of different types.

Freehand Mode

Working in Freehand mode is much the same as working with pencil and paper. The program tracks the movement of the cursor across the screen and positions nodes to form the shape of the drawing.

1. Using your mouse, place the cursor on the Pencil tool in the toolbox, and click and hold the mouse button until the fly-out menu appears (see fig. 2.1). Then click on the freehand pencil.

2. Look at the vertical and horizontal rulers as you move your cursor around the screen. A small dashed line moves along the rulers, indicating the exact position of the cursor. Place your cursor on the grid point 1 inch from the left side of the drawing page and 7 1/2 inches from the bottom of the drawing page and click. This sets the starting node of the line.

In this chapter, you learn about the following operations:

- Drawing lines
- Drawing curves
- Selecting line color
- Using the Pen roll-up
- Editing nodes
- Drawing dimension lines

Chapter 2: Drawing Lines and Curves

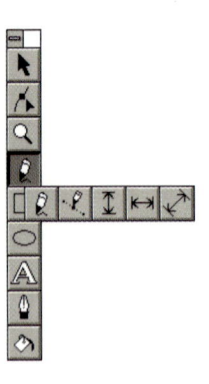

Figure 2.1

The Pencil tool's fly-out menu.

3. Place your cursor on the grid point 9 inches to the right and 1/2 inch down from the first point, and click the mouse button. In Freehand mode, you can draw a straight line between any two points using this click, move, and click again method.

4. Place your cursor 1 inch in from the left of the page and 6 inches from the bottom of the page and click. Hold down the Ctrl key, and try to repeat the process in step 3. Notice how the line does not dip down, but remains perfectly horizontal (see fig. 2.2).

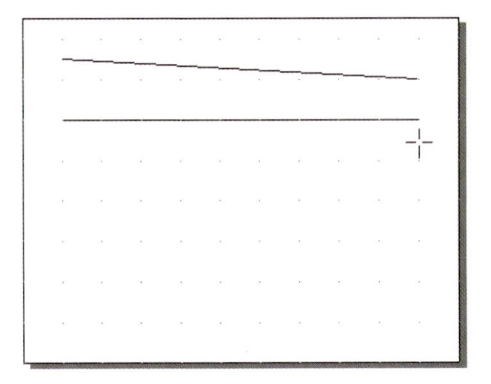

Figure 2.2

Using the Ctrl key to maintain a perfectly horizontal line.

TIP

To constrain the angle of the line to a multiple of the angle in the Constrain Angle setting in the Preferences menu, press and hold down the Ctrl key (see the section "Setting Defaults," in Chapter 1, "Getting Started"). This control is useful when you want to draw straight horizontal and vertical lines. You must hold down the Ctrl key until the mouse button is released for the Constrain to be in effect.

You can create multisegment lines in Freehand mode by following these steps:

1. Place your cursor 1 inch in from the left and 4 inches from the bottom and click. This marks your starting point.

Drawing Lines   21

2. Now move your cursor 3 inches to the right and 1/2 inch down and double-click. This ends the first segment of the line, and starts the second segment at the same point.

3. Move your cursor 1 inch up and 3 inches to the right and double-click again.

4. Then move your cursor 1/2 inch down and 3 inches to the right and click once. This single click ends the line (see fig 2.3).

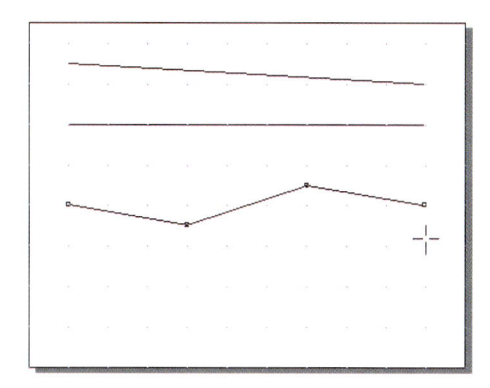

Figure 2.3
Creating a multisegment line.

Before you go on to the next section, save your work. Choose Save from the File menu, and the Save Drawing dialog box appears (see fig. 2.4). Name the file by typing **FREELINE** in the File Name box. Then click on OK and the file is saved to disk.

> *You should make and select a directory before doing this. The original default is to save to the CorelDRAW! directory (or to the last directory accessed), and saving a file to an application directory probably is not a good idea.*

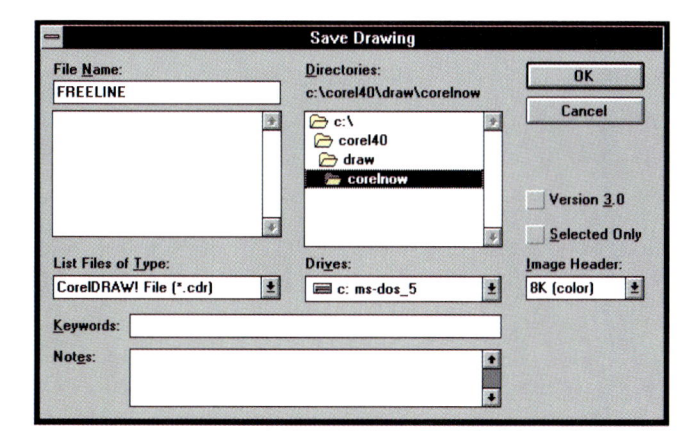

Figure 2.4
The Save Drawing dialog box.

Now you can start a new drawing. Choose New from the File menu. The screen area will clear and the title bar will display UNTITLED.CDR.

Chapter 2: Drawing Lines and Curves

Bézier Mode

In Bézier mode, you draw lines by placing nodes in the path you want the line to form. Bézier mode enables you to draw with more precision. To draw a line in Bézier mode, follow these steps:

1. Click on the Pencil tool to reveal the fly-out menu, and choose the Bézier pencil. A message will appear on the status bar to indicate that you are in Bézier mode.

2. Place the cursor on a grid point 5 inches in from the right edge of the page and 7 inches up from the bottom of the page and click. This sets the first node of the line.

3. Move the cursor down 3 inches and 1 1/2 inches to the right of the first node and click again.

4. Move the cursor 3 inches to the left and click again.

5. Return the cursor to the first node and click.

6. Press the space bar to discontinue Bézier mode.

By placing the final node on top of the first node, you create a closed shape (in this case, a triangle), as you can see in figure 2.5. As you will see later, this enables you to fill the triangle with a color or some other fill.

Figure 2.5
A triange drawn in Bézier mode.

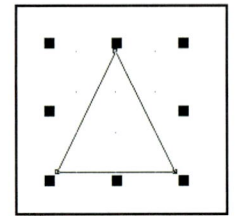

7. Choose **S**ave from the **F**ile menu. Name this drawing BEZLINE. Click on OK, then choose **N**ew from the **F**ile menu.

8. Now try your hand at a little more complicated shape. Using the Bézier pencil, try to replicate the star shown in figure 2.6.

You probably won't create a perfect star the first time, so delete it and start again. To do so, select the Pick tool from the toolbox, and click anywhere on the drawing. The object is surrounded by eight black boxes, signifying that it is selected. Press the Del key to remove the object and start again.

9. When you're happy with the drawing, save it as BEZLINE2.

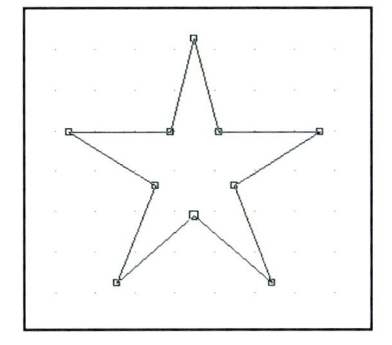

Figure 2.6
Creating a star by using the Bézier pencil tool.

Drawing Curves

As with lines, CorelDRAW! offers options for drawing curves of different types.

Freehand Mode

Drawing curves in Freehand mode is like drawing with a pencil on paper. Pressing the mouse button is the equivalent of pressing a pencil point to paper. Releasing the mouse button is like lifting the pencil from the page.

1. Click on the Pencil tool and select the Freehand pencil from the fly-out menu.

2. Place the cursor on the left side of the drawing page.

3. Click and hold the mouse button and drag the cursor to the right. The program will plot the path of the cursor and place nodes to form the shape of the curve. Release the mouse button to stop drawing the curve (see fig. 2.7).

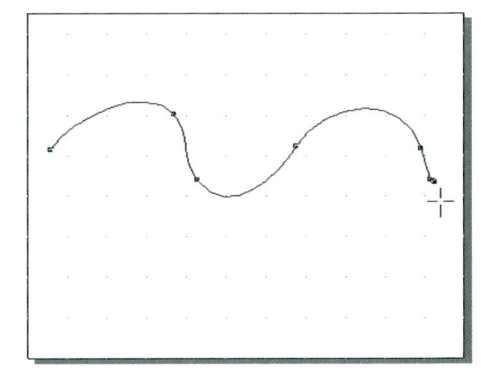

Figure 2.7
Drawing curves in Freehand mode.

4. You can go back and erase part of the curve you are drawing if you want to. Click and drag the cursor to draw a freehand curve. Holding down the mouse button, press and hold the Shift key while you

retrace the curve just drawn. You will see portions of the curve disappear. At any point you can release the Shift key and continue drawing the curve.

You can extend a curve by using the Autojoin feature. First, use the Pick tool to select the curve that you want to extend. Then select the Pencil tool and start drawing from either end node of the curve you want to extend.

Bézier Mode

Using the Bézier pencil enables you to draw curves with exacting precision.

1. Select the Bézier pencil.
2. Move the cursor to the starting point of the curve (on the left portion of the page).
3. Click the mouse button, and a node will appear. This node is the starting point of the curve.
4. Move the cursor to the right about 6 inches.
5. Press and hold the mouse button. The end node is created and positioned.
6. Continue to hold down the mouse button and move the cursor around. The cursor no longer is drawing the line, but is adjusting the control point of the curve. By moving it, you control the height and slope of the curve. When you are satisfied with the shape of the curve, release the mouse button (see fig. 2.8).

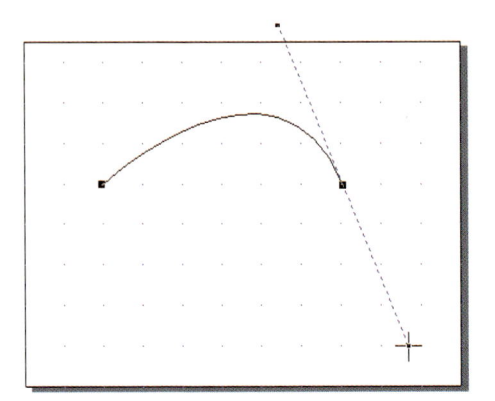

Figure 2.8
Creating a curve in Bézier mode.

7. At this point you can press the space bar to disconnect the Bézier pencil, or move the cursor to another position to continue the curve.

Editing Line Color and Thickness

So far, all the lines and curves have been drawn with the default color (Black) and thickness (Hairline—0.2 points). Both color and thickness can easily be edited, and your choices are almost unlimited.

Using the Toolbox

Use the Outline Pen tool to edit the attributes of a line or curve.

1. You need an object to edit. Choose Open from the File menu. In the Open dialog box, double-click on BEZLINE2.

   You might be prompted to save any work that is on-screen. Click on Yes to save, or No to clear the screen.

2. Although there is only one object on-screen, you must select it before you can edit. Click on the Pick tool, then click anywhere on the object to select it.

3. Click on the Pen Outline tool to bring up the fly-out menu (see fig. 2.9). To edit the color quickly, you can click on one of the seven color boxes (black, white, or five shades of gray). To access the color palette, click on the Outline Color tool. The Outline Color dialog box appears, as shown in figure 2.10.

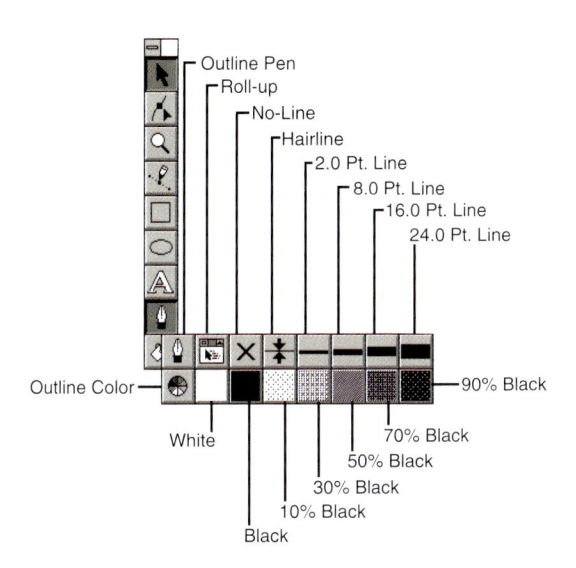

Figure 2.9
Toolbox with Pen Outline fly-out menu.

4. Choose Custom Palette from the Show list box of color palette options, then check the check box next to Show color names. You now can scroll through the palette and see what colors are available. Double-click on Blue.

Chapter 2: Drawing Lines and Curves

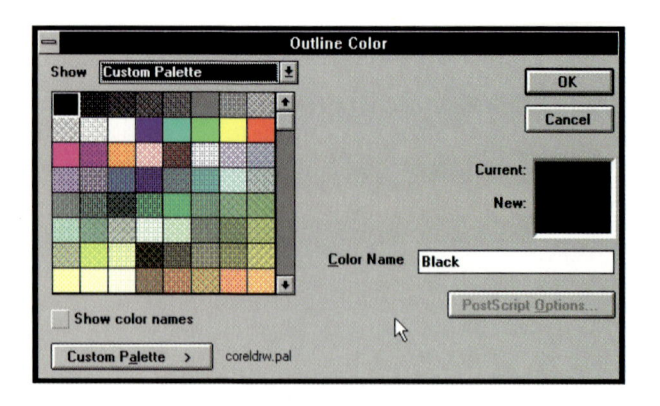

Figure 2.10
The Outline Color dialog box.

Here's a shortcut to change the color of a line. Click on the object with the Pick tool to select it. Place the cursor on the new color in the Color Palette at the bottom of the screen, and click the secondary mouse button. If you do not want the line to be visible, click on the X at the far left of the Color Palette with the secondary mouse button.

5. Now you need to thicken up the line (see fig. 2.11). Select the Pen Outline tool, and click on the Pen Outline icon; the Outline Pen dialog box appears. Click on the menu arrow for width and change it from inches to points. Increase the width value from 0.2 points to 8.0 points. Click on OK.

Figure 2.11
Thickening up the line.

Using the Pen Roll-Up Menu

One of the great features of Corel is the roll-up menus. Roll-up menus help speed up your work by giving you access to a number of tools, and by staying active on the screen as long as you need them.

1. Click on the Pen roll-up from the Outline Pen menu (see fig. 2.12).

2. Open a new file. Using the Pencil tool, draw a 6-inch horizontal line in the middle of the page, and select it (press the space bar).

Editing Line Color and Thickness 27

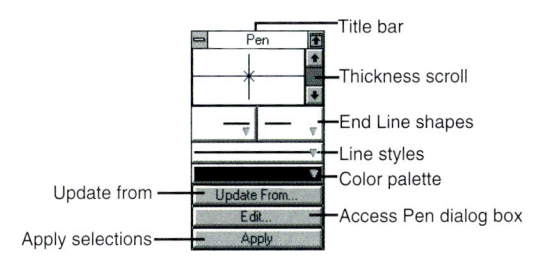

Figure 2.12
The Pen roll-up menu.

When you draw an object and change to the Pick tool, the object just drawn is selected. Pressing the space bar activates the Pick tool, thus selecting the object.

3. If you want to change the position of the roll-up, just click on the title bar and drag it to another spot on-screen.

4. Click on the up arrow of the Thickness scroll. The new thickness is displayed visually and by value. Set it at about 6.5 points.

5. Click on the left End Line Shape box, and select a shape for the back end of the arrow.

6. Click on the right End Line Shape box, and select a shape for the point end of the arrow.

7. Click on the Line Styles box. You can leave the line solid, or you can choose one of the dashed styles.

8. Click on the orange box in the Color Palette box. If the color you want is not displayed, click on MORE, and the Color Dialog box will appear, giving you access to the entire palette.

9. Click on Apply. The image now reflects all the changes, as does the Pen roll-up menu (see fig. 2.13).

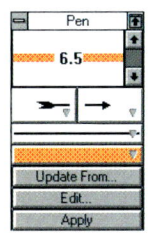

Figure 2.13
The Pen roll-up menu after changes.

Corel enables you to set default line attributes before you start drawing, saving you the trouble of editing each object after it is drawn. Using the Pick tool, click on an empty area on-screen so that no object is selected. Choose an attribute from a menu, or select attributes from a roll-up and the Outline Pen dialog box will appear (see fig. 2.14). Then choose the type of object you want these attributes to apply to, and the attributes will be applied automatically.

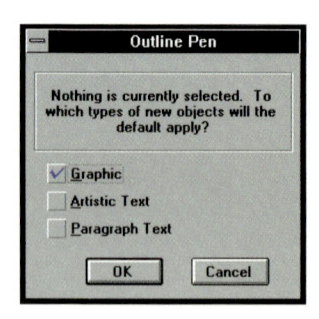

Figure 2.14

The Outline Pen dialog box.

When you are done using a roll-up menu, double-click in the upper left corner to close it (just like any window). If you want to keep a roll-up menu handy, click the up arrow in the right corner to roll it up. It now is there whenever you need it, and uses very little of your valuable screen space.

Editing Nodes and Control Points

After an object has been drawn, you can go in and make subtle or not-so-subtle changes to its shape by using the Shape tool.

1. Open a new drawing. Using the Freehand Pencil tool, create a zigzag line consisting of five node points from left to right (see fig. 2.15). Remember to double-click at the three inner nodes to create a multi-segment line.

Figure 2.15

Creating a zigzag line with five node points.

2. Select the Shape tool.

3. Click on and drag one of the nodes, and see how it affects the shape of the line. Notice how the node becomes filled in when it is selected.

4. Double-click on any node to access the Node Edit roll-up menu (see fig. 2.16).

Figure 2.16

The Node Edit roll-up menu.

Editing Nodes and Control Points   29

5. Click on the first segment of the line, and select To **C**urve from the Node Edit roll-up menu. Now click on the center of that segment, and drag the cursor up and to the left (see fig. 2.17).

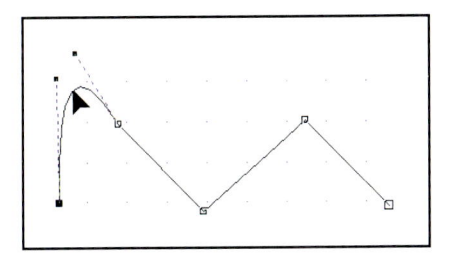

Figure 2.17
Using the Node Edit roll-up menu to convert a line to a curve.

You can edit the shape of a curve segment by dragging any point along it, or by dragging one of its control points (the small black squares on the end of the dashed lines).

You can select all the segments of a curve at once to change their attributes. Place the cursor above and to the left of the segments, then click and drag the cursor around all the segments. This is called marquee-selecting—*notice the dashed bounding box. When you release the mouse button, all nodes and segments within the bounding box are selected. You can select the entire group or a section of it.*

6. Marquee-select all the segments of the line. Click on To **C**urve.

7. Select the center node of the line by clicking on it or drawing a small bounding box around it.

8. To make this a round corner, you could adjust its two control points. Instead, click on S**m**ooth (see fig. 2.18).

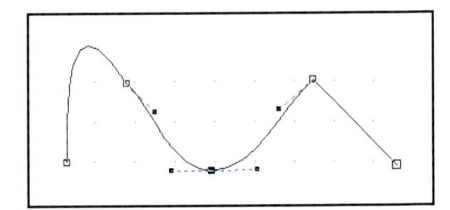

Figure 2.18
*Using the S**m**ooth feature to make rounded corners.*

9. Pull one of its control points to the side so that the curve looks a little lopsided. Notice how the other control point reflects its movement but not its length. Click on S**y**mmet, and move one of the control points. Notice how the other control point reflects its movement and length.

10. Select C**u**sp. Now when you adjust a control point, it affects only the segment on that side of the node.

NOTE: *The Stretch and Rotate commands were not discussed by design, but will be covered in Chapter 5, "Moving, Duplicating, and Transforming Objects."*

11. To edit the entire line so that it is one smooth curve, select all segments and click on S**m**ooth.

TIP: *To return the line to its former state, you could edit each node individually, but there's an easier way. Choose **U**ndo from the **E**dit menu. The program has reversed the last command, in this case, S**m**ooth. As we set the Undo default for 20 steps, you could reverse an additional 18 steps if you wanted to. Also, notice that **U**ndo displays the previous step it will undo—**U**ndo Move, **U**ndo Duplicate, and so on.*

Drawing Dimension Lines

One of the new features of CorelDRAW! 4.0 is the capability to draw dimension lines. *Dimension lines* are used in technical illustrations to show the size of objects or the distance between them. This is demonstrated by adding dimension lines to the triangle created earlier.

1. Open the BEZLINE.CDR file. You now will indicate the dimensions of this object on the drawing.

TIP: *When you click on the **F**ile menu, you will notice up to four file names listed at the bottom of the menu. The program remembers the last four drawings you worked on, and lists them here. When you have 50 or 100+ files in the directory, this can be a real time-saver. If the file you need is one of these four, just click on it to open.*

2. The object is a little small on-screen, so you'll want to zoom in on it. Select the Zoom tool, then click on the + icon (zoom in) in the fly-out menu. Place the cursor above and to the left of the object, and click and drag it down and to the right so that it is completely surrounded by the bounding box. Let go of the mouse button, and the object fills the screen. To return to normal view, click on the full page icon in the Zoom fly-out menu.

TIP: *When you set the default settings, the secondary mouse button was set for 2X zoom. Place the cursor anywhere on the page and press the secondary mouse button. The result is a 2X zoom in on the spot where the cursor sits.*

3. From the Pencil tool fly-out menu, select the Vertical Dimension Line tool.

Drawing Dimension Lines 31

4. Position the cursor 1/2 inch to the right of the triangle, even with its base. Click the mouse button. Holding the Ctrl key, move the cursor up to align with the top of the triangle, and click. This sets the dimension line. Next, slide the cursor down to about the middle of the line, move it to the right 1/4 inch, and click. This sets the extension line and adds the dimension value.

5. Select the Horizontal Dimension tool by clicking on its icon. Place the cursor 1/2 inch below the triangle, flush left with its corner, and click. Holding the Ctrl key, move the cursor flush right with the triangle and click again. Slide the cursor to the middle of the line, move it up 1/4 inch, and click.

6. Select the Angular Dimension tool. Position the cursor on the lower left corner of the triangle, and click. Move the cursor to the upper corner of the triangle, and click. Slide the cursor to about the middle of the line, move it about 1/2 inch away from the triangle, and click (see fig. 2.19). If you move it 1/4 inch as you did the other lines, the type overlaps on the triangle.

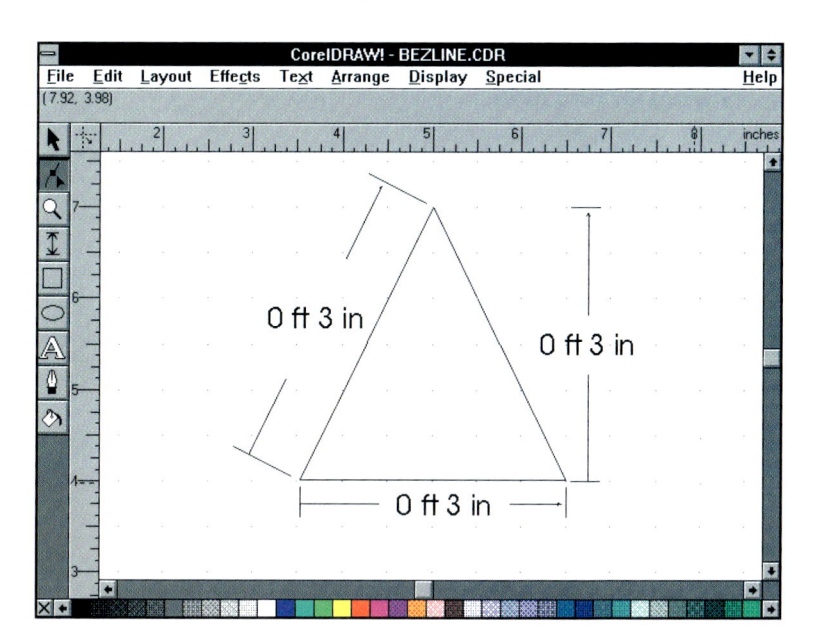

Figure 2.19
A triangle with dimensions labeled.

7. Save this as a new drawing. Choose Save As from the File menu, and type **BEZLINE3**.

Use Save As when you make changes to a drawing but want to keep the original version as well. The Save command overwrites the original file.

NOTE

Chapter 2: Drawing Lines and Curves

It is a good idea to name files with six letters and two numerical digits (for example, abcdef01). This way you could have 100 versions of the same file, named 00–99.

Chapter 3
Drawing Rectangles and Ellipses

Almost every object is composed of a few basic elements, such as rectangles and ellipses. In CorelDRAW!, rectangles and ellipses are primary objects, or predefined shapes. What this means is that they retain certain characteristics even when edited. You can nullify these characteristics when necessary, by converting objects to curves.

Creating Rectangles

The basic process for drawing a rectangle is by clicking and dragging to define two opposite corners of the rectangle.

1. Select the Rectangle tool from the Toolbox.

2. Place the cursor in the upper left portion of the drawing page. Click and hold down the mouse button, and drag the cursor down and to the right. The first mouse click defines one corner of the rectangle. As you move the cursor around the screen, you can see how it changes the shape of the rectangle.

3. Position the cursor in the lower right portion of the page and release the mouse button. This defines the position of the second corner and the size and shape of the rectangle (see fig. 3.1).

The alternative method for drawing a rectangle is by defining its center point first, then setting one of its corners.

1. Using the Pick tool, select the rectangle you've drawn and delete it by pressing Del.

2. Place the cursor in the center of the page. Click and drag the cursor as you did for the previous rectangle, but hold down the Shift key while doing so. This causes

FEATURES COVERED

This chapter covers the following operations:

- Creating rectangles and squares
- Rounding corners
- Creating ellipses and circles
- Drawing arcs and wedges

Chapter 3: Drawing Rectangles and Ellipses

the rectangle to be drawn from the center out, instead of corner to corner (see fig. 3.2).

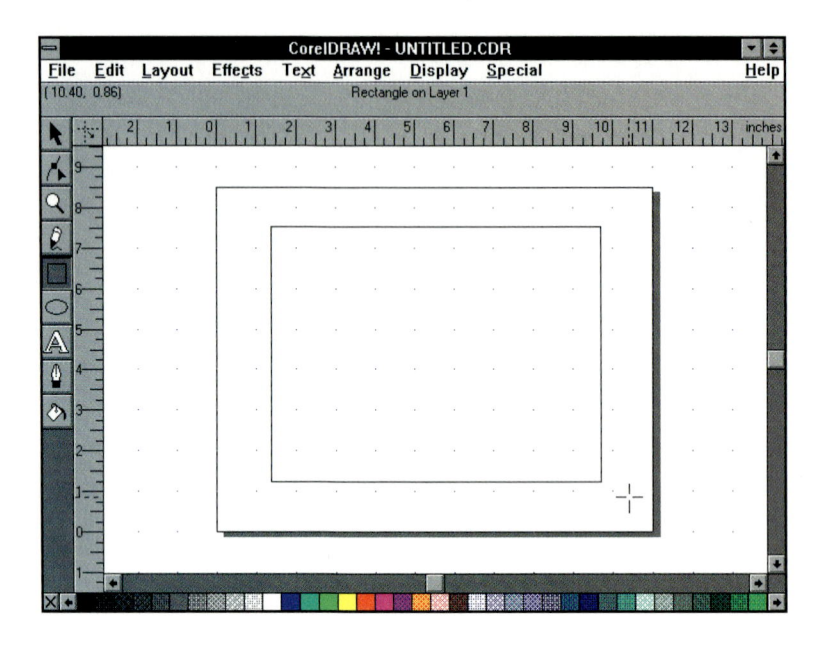

Figure 3.1
Defining the size and shape of the rectangle.

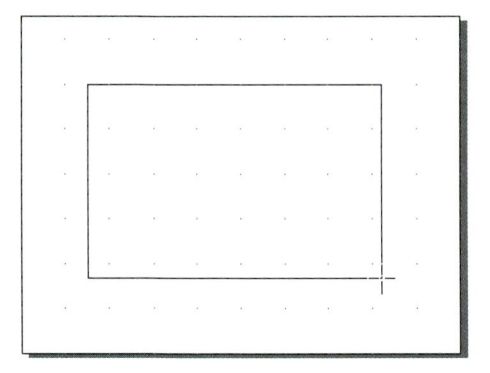

Figure 3.2
Drawing the rectangle from the center out.

3. When the rectangle is the size and shape you want, release the mouse button and the rectangle is drawn.

You must hold down the Shift key until after you release the mouse button. Otherwise, the center point you defined will become one corner of the rectangle.

There no doubt will be times when you need to draw a rectangle that is a perfect square. You can use the grid points and rulers to measure the sides, but CorelDRAW! makes it easier than that.

Rounding Corners   35

With the Rectangle tool, click and drag the cursor as you did to draw the first rectangle, but hold down the Ctrl key. This *constrains* the shape of the rectangle to a perfect square (see fig. 3.3).

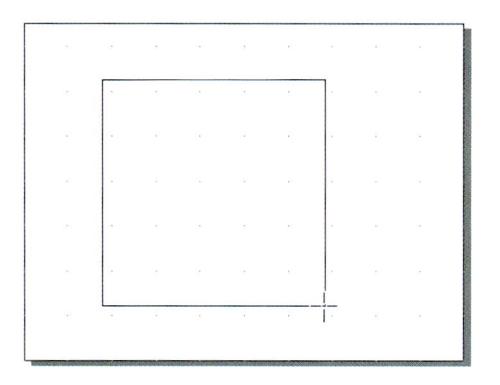

Figure 3.3
Constraining the shape of the rectangle to a square.

To draw a rectangle as a square from the center out, hold down the Ctrl and Shift keys while drawing.

Rounding Corners

When rectangles are drawn, their corners are square by default. You can make the corners round by using the Shape tool.

1. Using the Rectangle tool, draw a rectangle approximately 5 by 8 inches.
2. From the Toolbox, select the Shape tool.

   If you select the Shape tool right after drawing an object, that object will be selected and its nodes will be highlighted. If the object is not highlighted, just click anywhere on the object to select it. An object must be selected before you can edit it.

3. Click on the upper right node and drag it down about 1/2 inch. The upper right corner, as well as the other three corners, are rounded (see fig. 3.4).

   Here is an example of what is meant by a predefined shape, a term we used at the beginning of the chapter. The object is a rectangle: a four-sided polygon with opposite sides parallel and adjacent sides meeting at right angles. If you want to change the position of only one of the nodes, you first must convert the object from a rectangle to a curve.

4. Save this image as RCTNGL01.CDR.

Figure 3.4

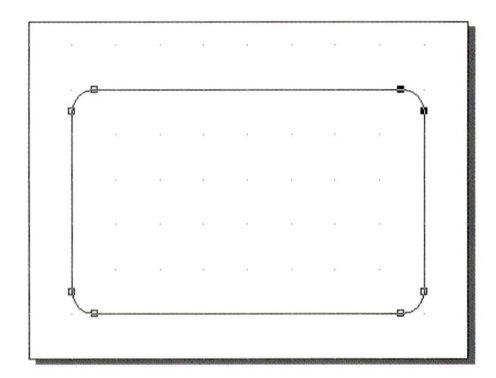

The rectangle with rounded corners.

Converting Objects to Curves

Objects such as rectangles, elipses, and text have special characteristics that control their shape. Converting them to curves removes these special characteristics.

1. With the Rectangle tool, draw a 5-by-7-inch rectangle in the center of the page.

2. Press the space bar to activate the Pick tool. The rectangle should be selected. If not, click on it with the Pick tool. Look at the status bar. It tells you that the selected object is a Rectangle, 7 inches wide and 5 inches high. (If the rectangle you've drawn isn't exactly 5 by 7 inches, it's okay for this example.)

3. From the menu bar, select the Arrange menu. From that menu, choose Convert To Curves.

4. Look at the status bar again. It now shows the selected object as a Curve. Although it looks exactly the same, it no longer carries the characteristics of a rectangle.

5. Select the Shape tool.

6. Click on the upper right node and drag it down 1/2 inch (see fig. 3.5).

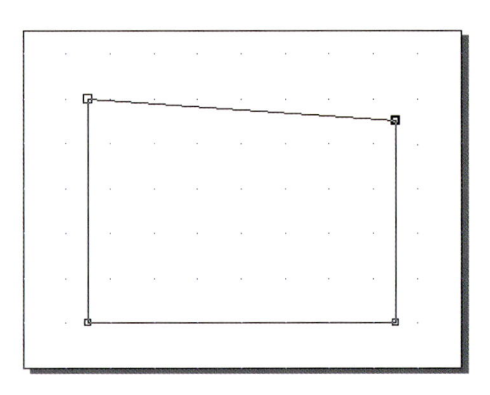

Figure 3.5

Using the Shape tool to drag the upper right node down.

Creating Ellipses and Circles 37

Now, instead of the corners becoming rounded, the Shape tool changes the position of the node.

7. With the Shape tool selected, double-click anywhere on the object to bring up the Node Edit roll-up menu. Because this object now is a curve, you can apply any of the functions of the Node Edit roll-up to this object.

8. Click on the top segment of the object, then choose To **C**urve from the Node Edit roll-up menu. Click on the middle of the segment and drag down about 1 1/2 inches.

9. Now click on the bottom segment of the object, then choose To **C**urve from the Node Edit roll-up menu. Click on the middle of the segment and drag up about 1 1/2 inches (see fig. 3.6).

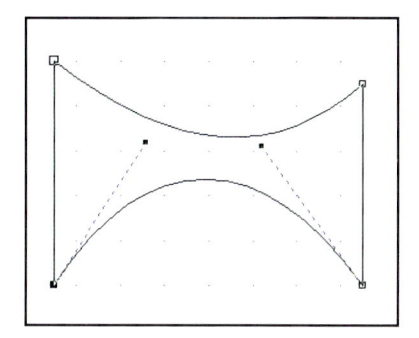

Figure 3.6
*Using To **C**urve on the sides of the rectangle.*

At this point you might decide that you prefer the object to be a rectangle. There is no Convert to Rectangle command. However, you can undo up to 99 previous actions performed.

You can access **U**ndo from the **E**dit menu, but it's easier to use the keyboard shortcut. Press Ctrl+Z to undo the last action performed. Continue to press it as you watch the screen. The point at which you want to stop is when the object returns to its original shape and the status lines shows the object as a rectangle, not a curve.

*If you go back too far, don't worry. CorelDRAW! has a R**e**do command. You can access it from the **E**dit menu, or use the keyboard shortcut Alt+Enter. It can return you back to where you made the first undo command.*

Creating Ellipses and Circles

The procedure for drawing ellipses and circles is basically the same as for rectangles and squares, except you use the Ellipse tool.

38   Chapter 3: Drawing Rectangles and Ellipses

1. From the Toolbox, select the Ellipse tool.
2. Place the cursor in the lower left portion of the page.
3. Click and drag the cursor up and to the right (see fig. 3.7). The movement of the cursor defines the height and width of the ellipse.

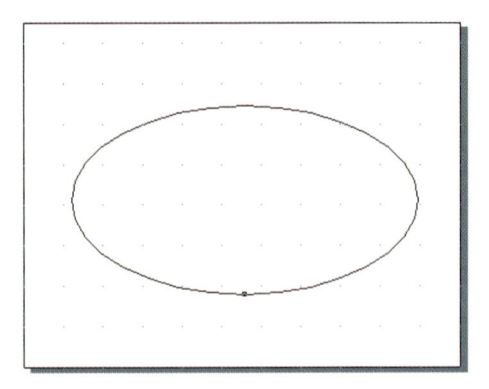

Figure 3.7
Drawing an elipse with the Ellipse tool.

NOTE
The ellipse you draw fits into an invisible rectangle. When you click and drag to create the ellipse, you actually are defining the opposite corners of a rectangle in which the ellipse fits.

As with the rectangle tool, you can define the center point of an ellipse and draw out from there.

4. With the Ellipse tool selected, place the cursor in the center of the ellipse you've just drawn. Click and drag the cursor while holding down the Shift key; this causes the ellipse to be drawn from the center out. You can move the cursor in any direction from center to create an ellipse. Move the cursor so that the new ellipse is similar in shape to the first, but slightly larger (see fig. 3.8).

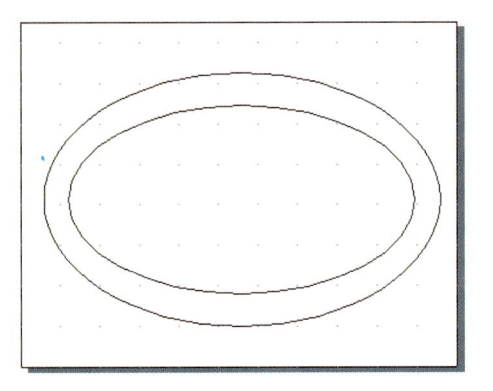

Figure 3.8
Drawing an ellipse from the center out.

In order to draw a circle, you need to constrain the shape of the ellipse. As before, you use the Ctrl key to constrain an object.

5. With the Ellipse tool selected, place the cursor in the center of the ellipses. Click and drag the mouse while holding down both the Ctrl and Shift keys. The Ctrl key constrains the ellipse to a perfect circle, and the Shift key causes the circle to be drawn from the center (see fig. 3.9).

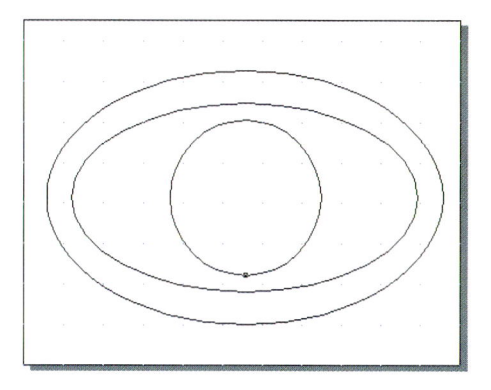

Figure 3.9

A circle within an ellipse within an ellipse, resembling an eye.

Drawing Arcs and Wedges

To understand what we mean by an arc or wedge, imagine that an ellipse is a pie. An *arc* is a line that follows the outside edge of the pie. A *wedge* is a slice cut out of the pie, or the remaining pie when a slice has been removed. To draw an arc or wedge, you first draw an ellipse with the Ellipse tool, then edit the ellipse with the Shape tool.

1. Select the Ellipse tool from the Toolbox.

2. Place the cursor in the center of the page. Hold down the Ctrl and Alt keys, and click and drag the cursor toward the upper right corner of the page. Release the mouse button when the circle is about 7 inches in diameter (see fig. 3.10).

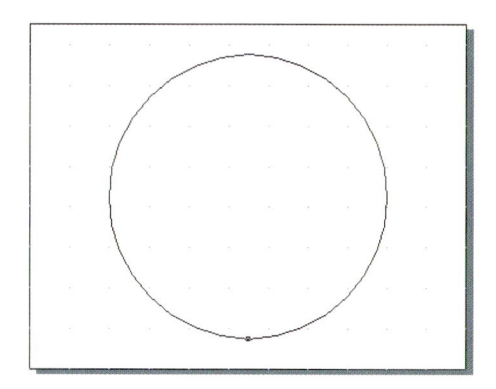

Figure 3.10

To draw a wedge, start with a circle.

Chapter 3: Drawing Rectangles and Ellipses

When the circle is drawn, you will see a node at the bottom point of the circle. The node appears on the bottom because you dragged the cursor up when you created the circle. If you drag the cursor down when creating the circle, the node will be on top.

3. Select the Shape tool from the Toolbox.

Click and drag the node to create an arc or wedge. If the cursor is inside the ellipse, a wedge is drawn. If the cursor is outside the ellipse, an arc is drawn.

4. Click on the node and, while keeping the mouse button pressed, move the cursor toward the center of the circle.

5. Rotate the cursor counterclockwise about one-third of the way around the circle, then release the mouse button. The resulting object is a wedge representing about two-thirds of the original pie (see fig. 3.11).

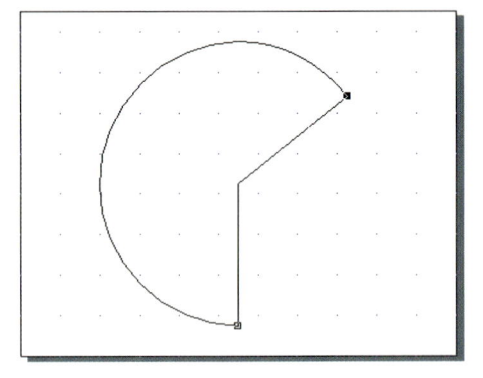

Figure 3.11
The circle is edited into a wedge.

6. Click on the node and, while keeping the mouse button pressed, move the cursor so that it is outside the edge of the wedge.

7. Rotate the cursor counterclockwise about halfway around the circle (the node would be at 12 o'clock), then release the mouse button. The wedge has changed to an arc (see fig. 3.12).

You can alternate back and forth between arc and wedge mode. Just click on the node and drag the cursor inside or outside the ellipse, then edit the node.

Drawing Arcs and Wedges 41

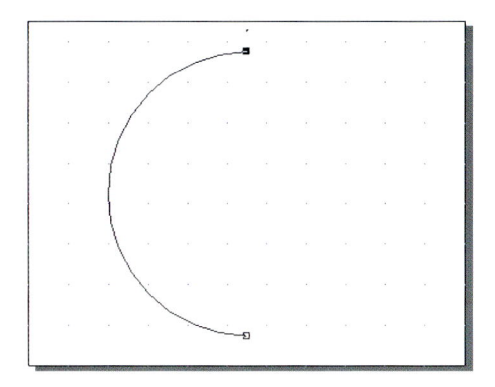

Figure 3.12
The wedge has become an arc!

Chapter 4
Setting and Manipulating Text

CorelDRAW! 4.0 comes equipped with an array of powerful tools for setting and manipulating text. The Text tool offers you two options—Artistic and Paragraph text—as well as access to the symbol library. You also can import text from supported word processor programs.

Entering Text

CorelDRAW! enables you to enter text in a number of ways. You can enter text in strings of up to 250 characters, called *Artistic text*. You can enter Artistic text directly on the screen or by using a dialog box.

Entering Text on the Screen

1. Click and hold the cursor on the Text tool to reveal the fly-out menu (see fig. 4.1).
2. Select the Artistic text tool.
3. Position the cursor in the center of the page (vertically), and about 1 inch in from the left side of the page.
4. Click the mouse button. Move the cursor away and you'll see a small, vertical black line. That is the text cursor.
5. Type the following (see fig. 4.2):

    ```
    As you enter text on the keyboard, it appears on the
    screen.
    ```

FEATURES COVERED

In this chapter, you will learn about the following:

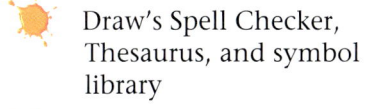

- Entering and pasting text
- Text attributes
- Entering, editing, and modifying text
- Draw's Spell Checker, Thesaurus, and symbol library
- Fitting text to a path
- Using special characters

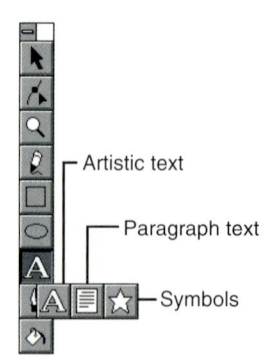

Figure 4.1
The Text tool fly-out menu.

- Artistic text
- Paragraph text
- Symbols

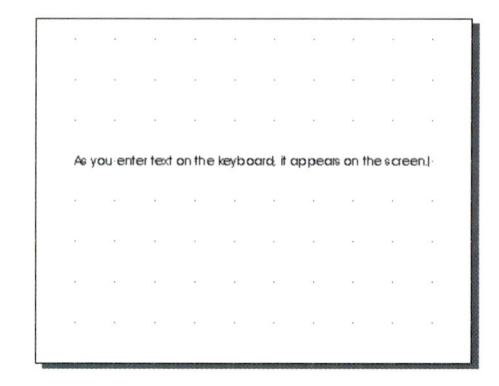

Figure 4.2
Entering text directly on the screen.

As you enter text on the keyboard, it appears on the screen.

Entering Text with the Artistic Text Dialog Box

1. Select the Artistic Text tool.

2. Position the cursor about 1 inch below the text on the screen, 1 inch in from the left.

3. Click on the mouse button to reveal the text cursor.

4. Instead of typing the text, access the Artistic Text dialog box. Press Ctrl+T to bring up the box.

*Many of the commands in CorelDRAW! can be accessed on-screen with the mouse, or on the keyboard with shortcut keys. In most cases, the method you use will be the one you are most comfortable with. Although the Text dialog box can be accessed with the mouse from the Te**x**t menu, I strongly suggest you get in the habit of using the keyboard shortcut—Ctrl+T.*

5. Enter the following text string in the dialog box (see fig. 4.3):

```
As you enter text on the keyboard, it appears in the dialog box.
```

Pasting Text

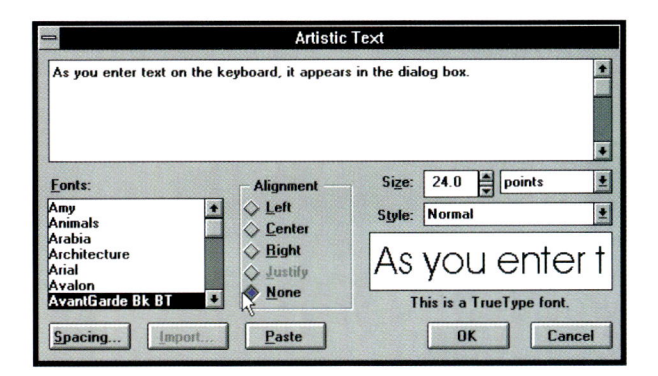

Figure 4.3
Text as it appears in the Artistic Text dialog box.

6. Click on OK. The dialog box disappears, and the new text is added to the page.

Pasting Text

Using the Windows Clipboard, you can copy text from other Windows applications and paste it into CorelDRAW!.

1. From the File menu, select New. You can save this file, but it is not necessary.

2. Click on the minimize arrow in the upper right corner to minimize CorelDRAW!. Click on the Program Manager icon if it is not currently displayed. From the Windows Accessories group, select Write.

3. The Windows Write program appears. Enter the following text string:

   `The text is being entered in another application, and pasted in CorelDRAW!`

4. Place the cursor just to the right of the text string, and click and drag the mouse to the left so that the entire text string is highlighted (see fig. 4.4).

5. Select Edit from the menu bar, then choose Copy. The text string is copied to the Windows Clipboard.

If you are not experienced using Clipboard, it is well worth your time to learn how to use it. Clipboard is covered in the Windows manual, and is relatively easy to master.

6. You now can close the Write program (it's not necessary to save the file) and return to CorelDRAW!.

7. Once in CorelDRAW!, select Edit, then choose Paste. The text string you copied appears on the page (see fig. 4.5).

46 Chapter 4: Setting and Manipulating Text

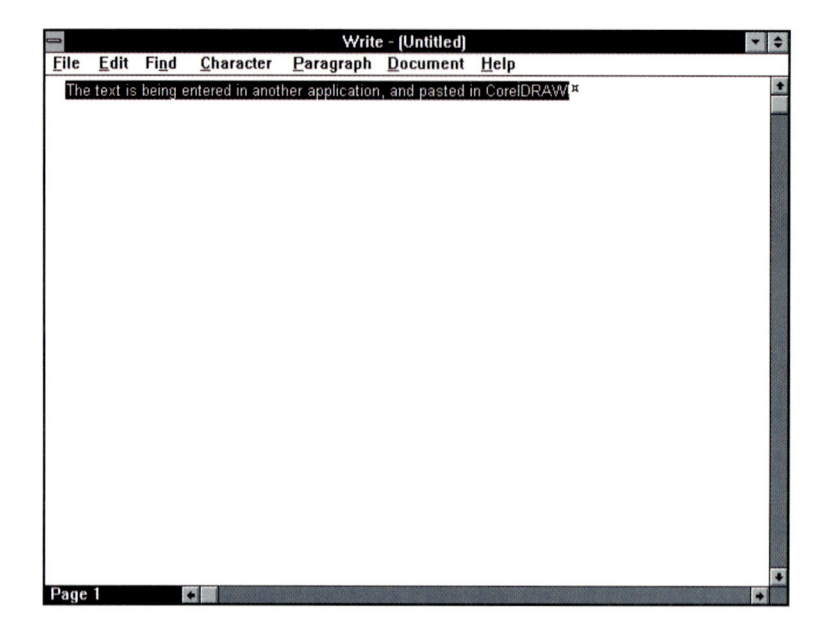

Figure 4.4
Entire text string highlighted by using the mouse.

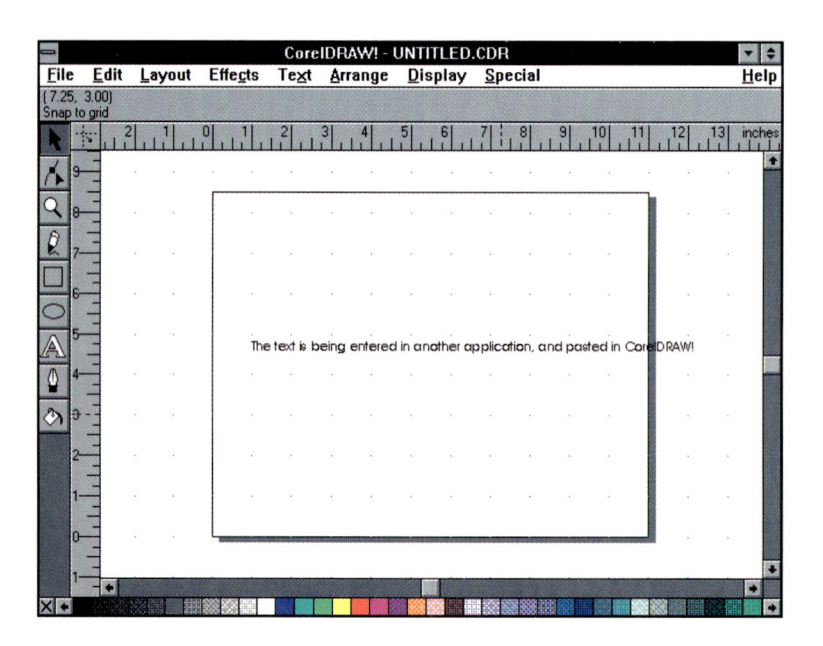

Figure 4.5
The copied text string appears on the page.

8. Save this file as TEXT01.

Selecting Text Attributes

The text string you imported to CorelDRAW! could use a little work. The type is on the small side, and it runs off the page. It's a simple task to edit the attributes of a text string.

Selecting Text Attributes

1. If TEXT01 is not currently the open file, select **O**pen from the **F**ile menu and choose TEXT01.
2. Use the Pick tool to select the text string.

   A text string (or any object) must be selected before it can be edited.

3. One method for selecting text attributes is the Artistic Text dialog box you used earlier to enter text. Press Ctrl+T to access it. The text string is displayed in the dialog box, as are a number of controls to change its attributes.

Fonts

All fonts that currently are available for use in CorelDRAW! are displayed in the **F**onts window of the Artistic Text dialog box.

1. You will use the font Toronto for this text string. Click on the down-arrow key (or use the slide) of the font window to scroll through the names until you see Toronto.

   *A shortcut for finding a font is to type the first letter of the font you are looking for on the keyboard—in this case, **T.** The list will jump to the first font that begins with T, Technical. From there you are just a few clicks away from the font you want.*

2. Click on Toronto to highlight it. A sample of the text string appears to the right, in the font that you have highlighted.

Alignment

For Artistic text, the Alignment options in the Artistic Text box are **L**eft, **C**enter, **R**ight, and **N**one. In left or right alignment, all lines of a text string will align flush left or right, respectively. In center alignment, each line of the text string will center within the text block. When **N**one is selected, the current alignment is maintained, but if individual characters are resized or moved, the text will not realign.

We want the text to align flush left, so click on the box next to **L**eft to highlight it.

Font Size

As mentioned, the type appears to be a little small, so bump it up in size. The size currently is 24 points, the default setting. Click on the up-arrow key of the Si**z**e box and increase the point size to 48.

48   Chapter 4: Setting and Manipulating Text

> *If you want the text to be 250 points, it will take a while to reach that number using the arrow key. To save time, place the cursor within the size box to the left or right of the displayed value. Click and drag the cursor across the value to highlight it. Now you can enter a new value from the keyboard and it will replace the existing value.*

Style

1. Click on the arrow key of the Style box. A drop-down menu lists all the styles available for the font you have selected. All styles will not be available for all fonts. Make this text string bold by choosing Bold. The dialog box should now resemble figure 4.6.

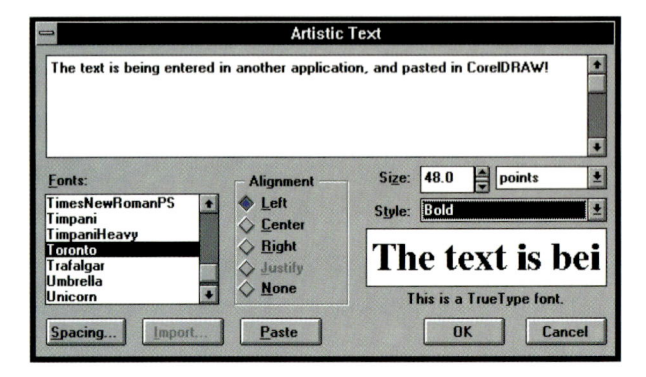

Figure 4.6
Choosing styles in the Artistic Text dialog box.

2. Click on OK. The changes have taken effect, but the text string is running off the side of the page.

Edit Text

The text string could use some improvement. It is very small and runs off the right side of the page.

1. To access the Artistic Text dialog box, press Ctrl+T.

2. Place the cursor on the text string in the dialog box and click on the space between the words *in* and *another*. This will place a text cursor in the text string, enabling you to edit the text.

3. Using the arrow key, make sure the text cursor is just to the right of the letter *n* in the word *in*, and press Del. There now should be no space between the two words.

4. Press Enter. The text string is now split into two lines.

5. Repeat this procedure with the words *and pasted* to split the string into three lines.

Selecting Text Attributes   49

*With this text string currently displayed, click on the Alignment boxes for **C**enter and **R**ight. The dialog box displays the text string centered, then flush right, giving you an idea of what these options look like. Choose **L**eft alignment before continuing.*

6. Click on OK (see fig. 4.7).

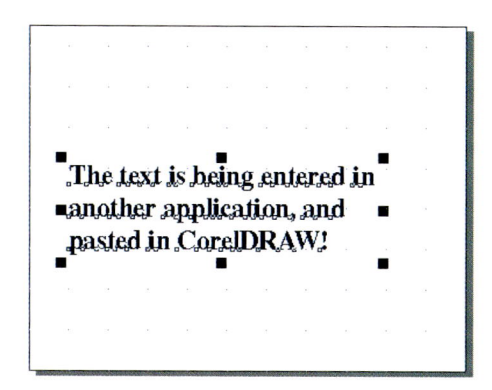

Figure 4.7

See how the text looks now?

Edit Text Spacing

In CorelDRAW! you can adjust the spacing of a text string two ways: visually adjusting it on-screen, or by numerical value through a dialog box.

1. Before you start, you will want to get in closer to the text. Click on the Zoom tool, and select the Zoom In tool from the fly-out menu (see fig. 4.8).

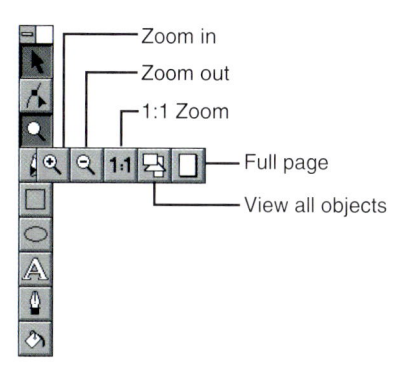

Figure 4.8

The Zoom tool fly-out menu.

2. Use the Zoom In tool to draw a bounding box around the text string, with about 1/2 inch of space on each side. The area inside the bounding box now fills the screen (see fig. 4.9).

50 Chapter 4: Setting and Manipulating Text

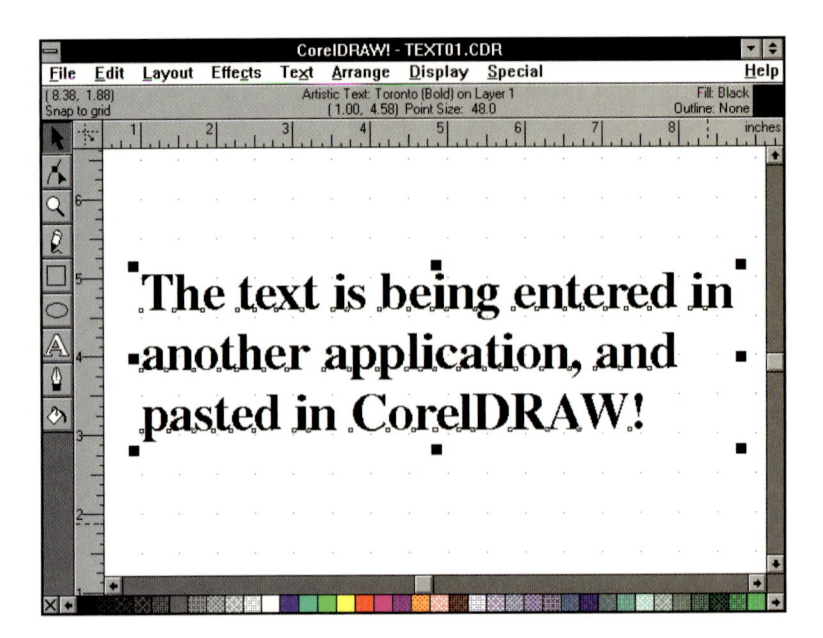

Figure 4.9

Using the Zoom In tool to enlarge the text string.

3. With the text string selected, select the Shape tool from the toolbox. Notice the change on-screen. The nodes on each letter have gotten bigger, the eight black rectangles surrounding the text have disappeared, and two arrows (one vertical, one horizontal) have appeared below the text. These arrows will enable you to edit the character and line spacing of the text.

4. Place the cursor on the horizontal arrow. The cursor changes to a crosshair. Click and drag the crosshair 1/2 inch to the left. Notice how this brings the characters within each word closer together, but does not affect the space between words.

If you hold down the Ctrl key when you drag the horizontal arrow, the space between words will change and the space between characters will not.

5. Click and drag the cursor on the vertical arrow, moving it 3/8 inch up. This reduces the space between lines (see fig. 4.10).

Selecting Text Attributes 51

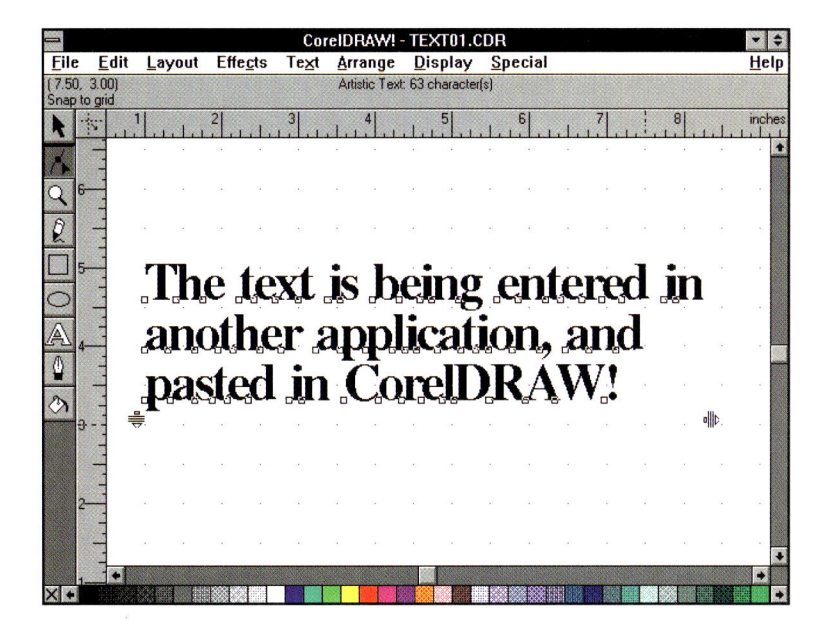

Figure 4.10
Reducing the leading.

The second method for adjusting spacing is by entering numeric values.

1. With the text string selected, access the Text dialog box (Ctrl+T) and choose Spacing. This brings up the Spacing dialog box (see fig. 4.11).

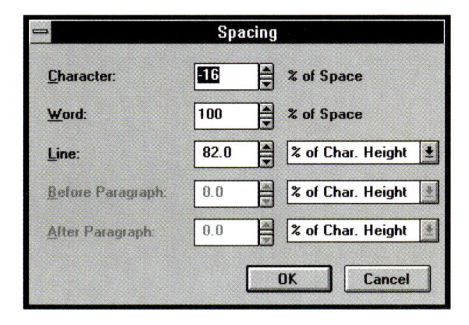

Figure 4.11
The Spacing dialog box.

The values displayed are that of the current text string, which means they reflect the changes we made. The default values are:

  Character: 0 % of Space

  Word: 100 % of Space

  Line: 100 % of Character Height

As you saw before, the space between words was unaffected by our changes.

52 Chapter 4: Setting and Manipulating Text

2. To adjust the numeric values, you can click on the arrow keys or highlight the value with the mouse and type in a new value. Set the **C**haracter Space % to -40, the **W**ord Space % to 200, and the **L**ine Space % to 100. Click on OK to close the Spacing dialog box. Click on OK again to close the Text dialog box. The text string now appears as shown in figure 4.12.

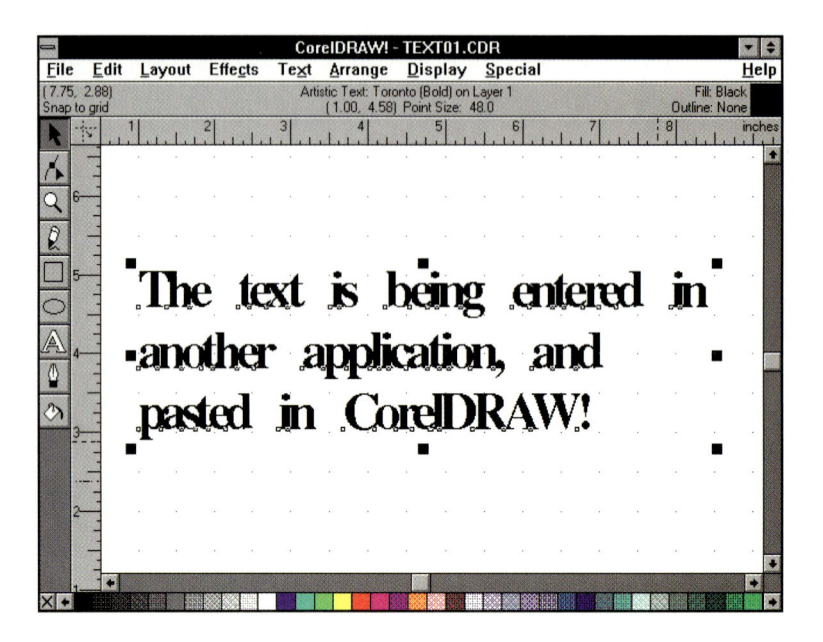

Figure 4.12

The text with more space between the words.

It is not recommended that you create text spaced in this fashion. These values are distorted to better display the outcome of space adjustments.

3. Save this file as TEXT02.

Editing Text

You can change the actual text of a text string on-screen or through the Artistic Text dialog box.

1. If TEXT01 is not the current file, open it now.

2. Select the text string with the Pick tool. Press Ctrl+T to bring up the Artistic Text dialog box.

3. Before you edit the text, return the spacing settings to the default values. Choose **S**pacing to access its dialog box. Enter these values—**C**haracter: 0, **W**ord: 100, **L**ine: 100.

4. Click on OK to return to the Artistic Text dialog box.

Changing Individual Character Attributes

5. Click on the text display box directly to the right of the word *CorelDRAW!*. The text cursor will appear, enabling you to add text or edit the existing text.

6. Type the following:

   `, and now we are adding additional characters to the text string.`

   As you type, enter the carriage returns as they appear in figure 4.13.

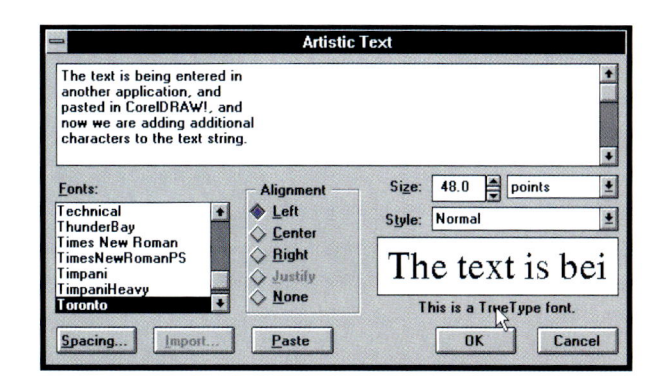

Figure 4.13
Enter the carriage returns as they appear in this figure.

7. Click on OK. The text string appears on-screen with additional text added.

It's not necessary to access the dialog box to add or edit the text string. You can do it directly on-screen.

1. Select the Artistic Text tool from the toolbox. Click on the space directly to the right of the word *adding*. This places a text cursor within the text string. With the Backspace key, delete the word *adding*, and type **editing**.

2. When you are done, click on the Pick tool to discontinue the text edit mode.

With the Artistic tool selected, you can click anywhere within a text string to place the text cursor. You then can move the text cursor throughout the text using the arrow keys.

Changing Individual Character Attributes

At times, you might want to edit only a portion of a text string, such as highlighting a word or phrase.

1. Select the text string with the Pick tool. Select the Shape tool.

54   Chapter 4: Setting and Manipulating Text

2. Place the cursor on the first node of the text string (for the letter *T* in the word *The*). Double-click the mouse to access the Character Attributes dialog box (see fig. 4.14).

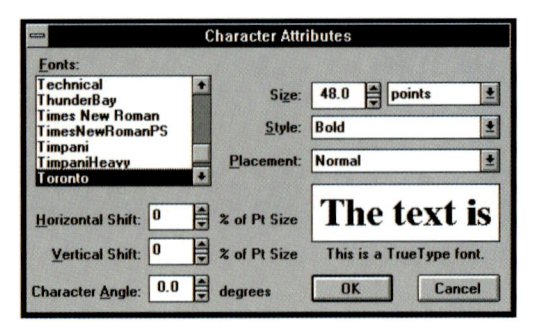

Figure 4.14

The Character Attributes dialog box.

3. This dialog box should seem familiar because it shares many of the same command functions as the Artistic Text dialog box. Using the Si*z*e window, increase the point size to 64.

4. Click on OK. The letter *T* now is 50 percent larger than the rest of the text string (see fig. 4.15).

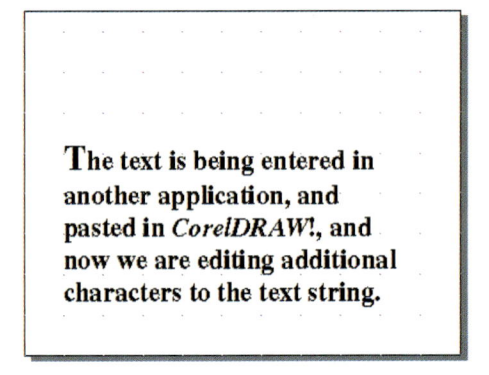

Figure 4.15

See how big the T is now.

5. With the Shape tool, click and drag the cursor to surround the nodes of the word *CorelDRAW!* with the dashed rectangle. The precise nodes are to the left of each letter.

When you need to pick more than one node with the Shape tool, or more than one object with the Pick tool, use this click and drag method to draw a surrounding rectangle. This rectangle is referred to as a highlight box, a bounding box, a marquee select, or a marquee box.

6. There now will be ten nodes highlighted—the nodes now are solid black (see fig. 4.16).

Changing Individual Character Attributes 55

Figure 4.16
Ten nodes all high-lighted solid black.

7. Double-click on any of the highlighted nodes to access the Character Attributes dialog box.

8. From the **S**tyle window, select Bold-Italic.

9. Click on OK. Click on the Pick tool on the screen away from the text string. This will unselect the object, removing the nodes and making it easier to read (see fig. 4.17). Select the Zoom In tool and draw a marquee box around the text string so that it fills the screen.

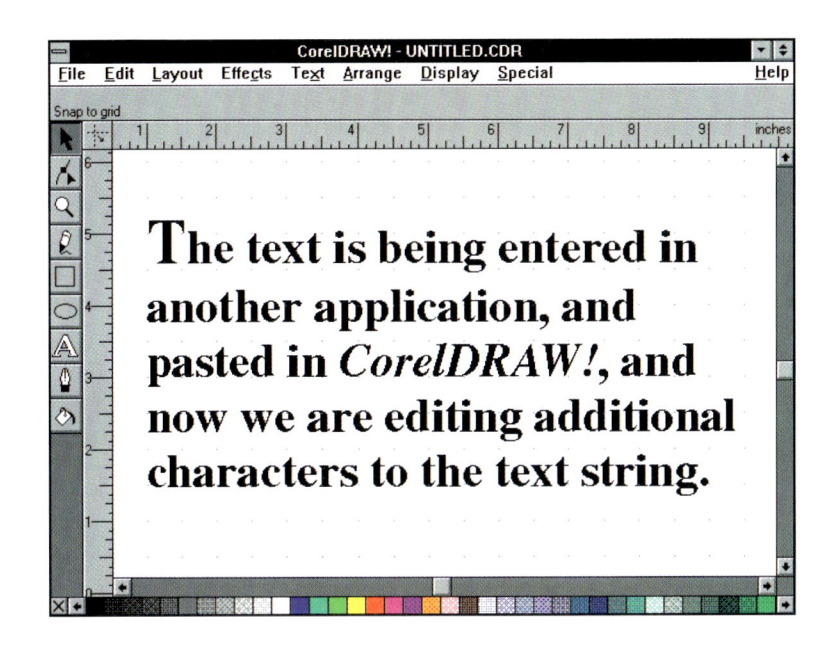

Figure 4.17
The text string in its finished form.

In this example you made minor changes to the text. You can select any character or group of characters, and apply a different font, make it subscript or superscript (reducing its size and placing it below or above the text line), or make it italic by entering the specific angle the character will slant.

10. Save this file as TEXT03.

56 Chapter 4: Setting and Manipulating Text

Entering Paragraph Text

When you need to add lengthy blocks of text to a file, instead of Artistic text you can add Paragraph text. With Paragraph text, you first create a frame that contains the text and then type it, and the program automatically formats it within the frame.

1. Choose New from the File menu to start a new drawing.

2. Click and hold the Text tool to reveal the fly-out menu, then click on the Paragraph Text tool.

3. You draw a paragraph frame the same way as you would a rectangle: by clicking and dragging the cursor. With the Paragraph Text tool, click and drag the cursor to create a frame about 5 inches square in the center of the page.

4. Now add the text directly to the screen. Type the following text four times in a row, and do not hit the return key while typing (see fig. 4.18):

    `The quick brown fox jumped over the lazy dog.`

Figure 4.18
The text string entered as Paragraph text.

In figure 4.18, two words are spelled incorrectly on purpose. As you enter the text you should intentionally spell a few words wrong. We will use this text shortly to demonstrate the Spell Checker.

5. Increase the text size to fill the frame you have created. Bring up the Text dialog box (Ctrl+T) and change the Size to 32 points. Click on OK. The text now fills the frame (see fig. 4.19).

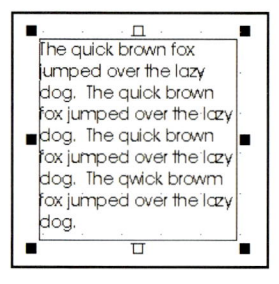

Figure 4.19
The text string fills the frame.

6. Save the file as TEXT04.

Using Spell Checker

The Spell Checker command enables you to select entire strings of Artistic or Paragraph text to check for spelling errors. You also can select individual words or enter a word into the Spell Checker to check for error.

1. If TEXT04 is not the currently opened file, open it now.

2. Using the Pick tool, click anywhere on the text string to select it.

3. Select Text from the menu bar, then choose Spell Checker to access the Spelling Checker dialog box (see fig. 4.20).

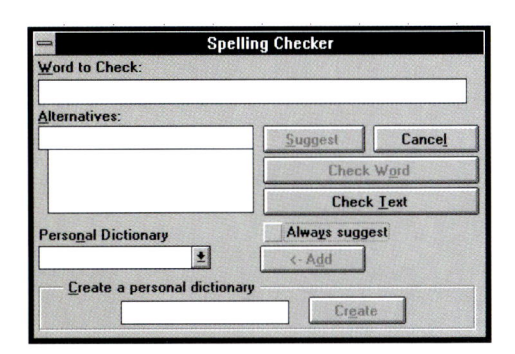

Figure 4.20

The Spelling Checker dialog box.

4. Click on the Check Text box. The program scans the text string and stops at a word it thinks is misspelled—for example, the word *qwick*.

5. To correct the spelling, click on Suggest. The Spell Checker displays suggestions for spelling the word correctly; in this case, the words `quick` and `wick` are displayed (see fig. 4.21).

Figure 4.21

The Spell Checker in action.

6. Double-click on the word `quick`, and the program replaces the misspelled word with the correct one. It then continues to scan the text string for other spelling errors.

*With the correct spelling highlighted, you can choose **R**eplace to correct the current word or Re**p**lace All to correct the current word and any repeat occurrences.*

7. If the program finds additional errors, follow the same procedure to correct them.

*The next time you access the Spell Checker, click on the Alwa**y**s Suggest box to check it. Now, when you scan text for errors, the program will list possible corrections without being prompted.*

8. Sometimes a word can be spelled correctly but not be in the program's dictionary (such as a proper name), so it displays it as a spelling error. If so, choose **I**gnore and the program will leave the word unchanged. If it appears more then once in the text string, choose I**g**nore All to skip the word and any repeat occurrences.

9. Save file as TEXT05.

Creating a Personal Dictionary

You can create a personal dictionary to hold words not found in the program's dictionary. These can include proper names, abbreviations, acronyms, and words specific to your industry.

1. Access the Spell Checker dialog box from the Te**x**t menu.

2. Click on the **C**reate a personal dictionary window; a text cursor appears. Enter a name for the dictionary, up to eight characters in length.

For this example, the dictionary is named "Personal". You might want to use your given name if the computer you work on is shared by others, so that each of you can have your own dictionary. If you work in foreign languages, you can name the dictionary in that language. Or you simply can have one personal dictionary and add all new words to it.

3. Choose Cr**e**ate to save the dictionary.

4. Click on the **W**ord to Check window; a text cursor appears.

5. Type **Leopold**. Choose Check W**o**rd.

6. A message box appears telling you the word has not been found. Click on OK.

7. The Spell Checker now displays the alternative spellings it has found (see fig. 4.22). The word is spelled correctly but is not in the dictionary.

Using the Thesaurus 59

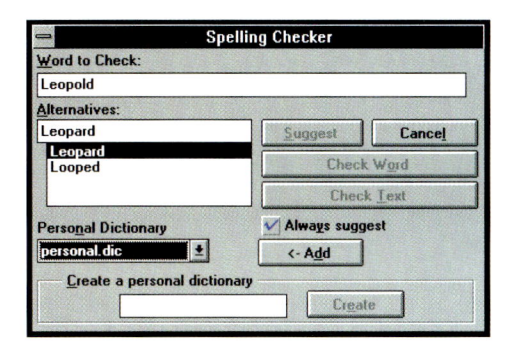

Figure 4.22

Spell Checker, unfamiliar with Leopold, thinks maybe you mean Leopard, or Looped.

8. Choose Add, and Leopold is added to the new dictionary.

9. Choose Cancel to close the dialog box. Now, check to see that it works.

10. Bring up the Spelling Checker dialog box again.

11. Click on the arrow of the Personal Dictionary window to display the dictionaries available. Click on personal.dic to make it active.

12. In the Word to Check window, type **Leopold**. Choose Check Word.

13. A message box appears, telling you that the word is spelled correctly. Click on OK. Click on Cancel to close the Spelling Checker dialog box.

Using the Thesaurus

The Thesaurus can help you find synonyms for selected words.

1. From the Text menu, choose Thesaurus to access the Thesaurus dialog box.

2. The Synonym for window has a text cursor displayed; type **Light**.

3. Choose Lookup. The dialog box displays a list of definitions and synonyms for the definition currently highlighted (see fig. 4.23).

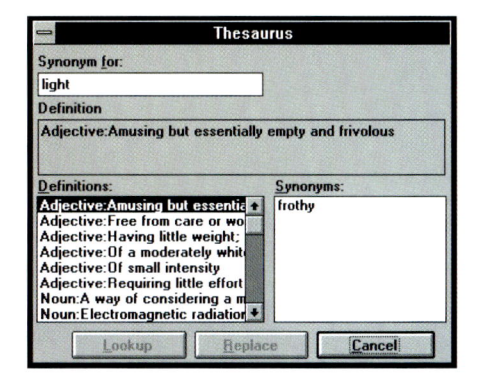

Figure 4.23

The Thesaurus dialog box.

Chapter 4: Setting and Manipulating Text

4. The synonym displayed for this definition is `Frothy`. If you click on another definition, it will be displayed in the **D**efinitions window, and the appropriate synonyms will be displayed in the **S**ynonyms window.

You can use the Thesaurus on words that are part of a text string currently displayed.

1. Open the file TEXT05 if it is not already open.

2. Select the text string by clicking on it with the Pick tool.

3. Select the Paragraph Text tool. (If you were working with Artistic text, you would use the Artistic Text tool.)

4. Place the cursor directly to one side of the word *quick* and click and drag the cursor over the word so that it is highlighted (see fig. 4.24).

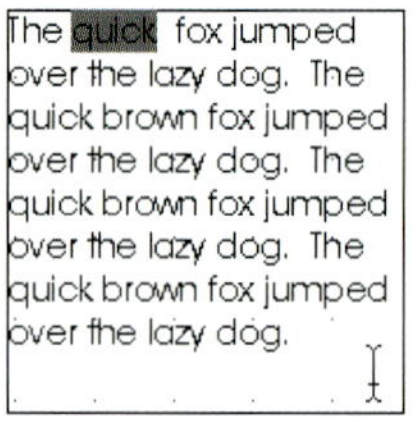

Figure 4.24
The word "quick" highlighted.

5. From the Te**x**t menu, choose Thes**au**rus. The Synonym **f**or window contains the word `quick`, and a list of definitions and synonyms is displayed.

6. From the **S**ynonyms list, choose `speedy`. It will appear in the Replace **w**ith: box.

7. Choose **R**eplace. The dialog box disappears and the synonym you selected replaces the original word in the text string (see fig. 4.25).

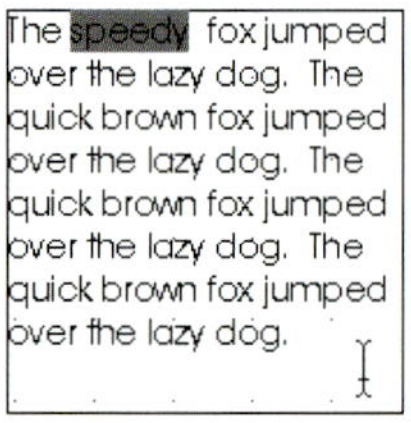

Figure 4.25
The word is replaced with its synonym.

Using the Symbol Library

CorelDRAW! 4.0 includes a library of over 5,000 symbols that you can import into your drawings.

1. Select **N**ew from the **F**ile menu.

Using the Symbol Library   61

2. Click and hold on the Text tool to reveal the fly-out menu. Click on the Symbols icon to access the Symbols roll-up menu (see fig. 4.26).

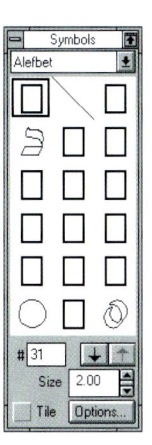

Figure 4.26
The Symbols roll-up menu.

3. The symbols are divided into sets by type. The name of the current set appears just below the title bar. To see a list of all the sets, click on the down arrow next to the current set's name.

4. Use the arrows to scroll down through the list of symbol sets. Stop scrolling when you see Science, and click on it. The Science set now is active and appears in the current set window.

5. Click on the down arrow just below the displayed symbols to scroll through the entire set of symbols. Use the up arrow to return to the top of the set.

6. Click on the very first symbol in the upper left corner of the set. It now has a box around it, and its number (#33) is displayed just below the symbol set.

7. To bring the symbol to the page, click and hold on it and drag the symbol to the drawing page. Release the mouse button and the symbol will be drawn to the page.

8. Click on the symbol in the upper right corner of the set (#35). Before you bring it to the page, you can edit the size at which it will be drawn.

9. Click on the up arrow of the Size window until the value is 3.00.

10. Click and drag symbol #35 to the page and release the mouse button (see fig. 4.27).

11. Save the file as SYMBOL01.

62 Chapter 4: Setting and Manipulating Text

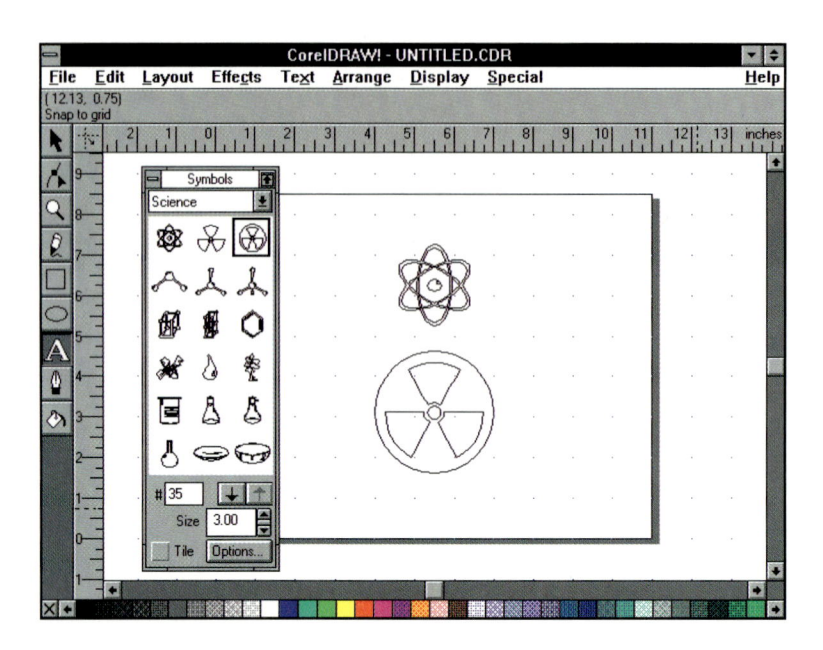

Figure 4.27
The symbol is drawn to the page.

Tiling Symbols

The Symbols roll-up menu has a Tile option, which enables you to create a pattern of symbols.

1. From the File menu, select New.

2. If the Symbols roll-up menu is not already on-screen, click on the Symbols icon from the Text tool fly-out.

3. Using the down arrow next to the symbol set name, scroll down to Sports & Hobbies. Click on it to make it the active set.

4. Click on the Bowling Ball symbol (#40).

5. Click on the Tile box to check it.

6. Using the down arrow, reduce the size to 0.80.

7. Click on the Options button. In the Options dialog box, set each grid option to 1.00. Click on OK.

8. Click and drag the Bowling Ball symbol to the page and release the mouse. The symbols now are drawn in a pattern (see fig. 4.28).

9. Save the file as SYMBOL02.

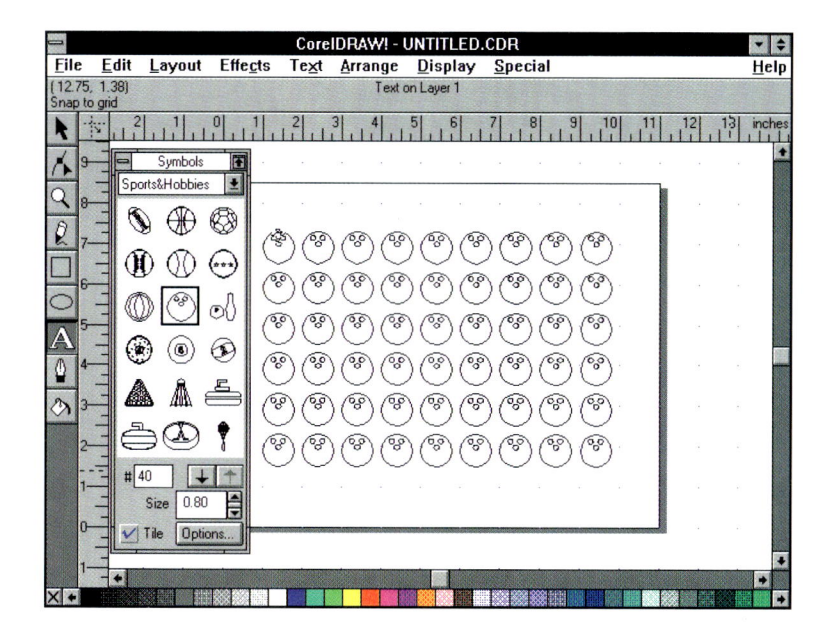

Fitting Text to a Path   63

Figure 4.28
The symbol is tiled into a pattern.

Fitting Text to a Path

One of the more powerful commands in CorelDRAW! is the capability to fit a text string to a path. The path can be a line, a curve, a circle, a rectangle, and so on.

1. From the File menu, select New.
2. Select the ellipse tool. Place the cursor in the center of the page.
3. With the Shift and Ctrl keys pressed, draw a circle approximately 6 inches in diameter.
4. Select the Artistic Text tool. Place the cursor in the center of the circle.
5. Click the mouse to set the text cursor and type the following: **Artistic Text Fitted to a Path**. Click on the Pick tool to leave Text mode.
6. The next step is to enlarge the text and center it. Press Ctrl+T to access the Text dialog box.
7. Increase the font size to 48 points, and choose Center alignment. Click on OK (see fig. 4.29).
8. From the Text menu, select Fit Text To Path. The Fit Text To Path roll-up menu appears (see fig. 4.30).

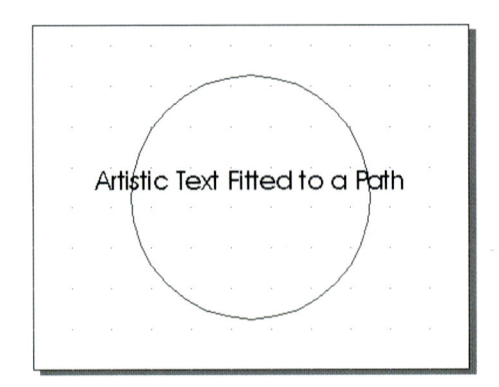

Figure 4.29
Text increased to 48 points and center-aligned.

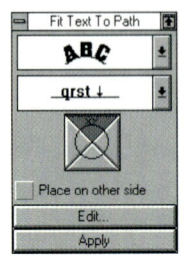

Figure 4.30
The Fit Text To Path roll-up menu.

9. For the roll-up to be active, the text string and a path must be selected objects. With the Pick tool, drag a highlight box completely around both objects. Release the mouse button, and the status line should show that two objects are selected. The roll-up has now become active.

Sometimes you will not want to select multiple objects with a highlight box, because the box may include unwanted objects. To pick a group of individual objects, click on the first object with the Pick tool. Then, hold down the Shift key and click on another object. You can continue and click on as many objects as you want, as long as you keep the Shift key pressed down.

10. You now can choose the options for the text. Click on the orientation arrow to reveal the drop-down menu (see fig. 4.31).

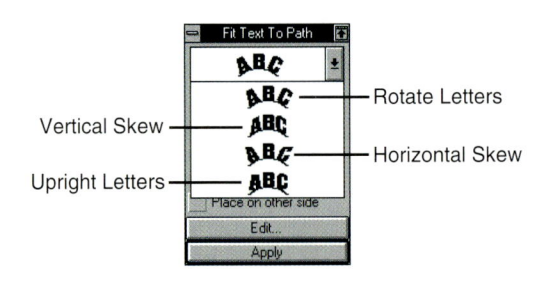

Figure 4.31
The drop-down menu displays text orientation options.

Fitting Text to a Path 65

11. Click on Rotate Letters. This will force the letters to follow the contours of the circle.

12. Click on the vertical alignment arrow to reveal the drop-down menu (see fig. 4.32).

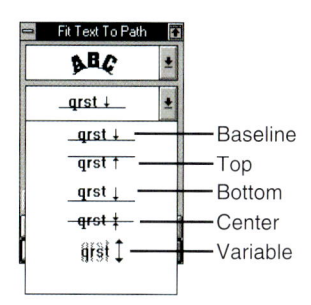

Figure 4.32
Vertical alignment options are shown.

13. Click on bottom.

14. The quadrant control enables you to place the text in one of the quadrants displayed when the path you are using is an ellipse or a rectangle. You can pick the quadrant by clicking on it. Click on the top quadrant if it is not already highlighted.

15. Click on Apply; the text is fitted to the upper quadrant of the circle (see fig. 4.33).

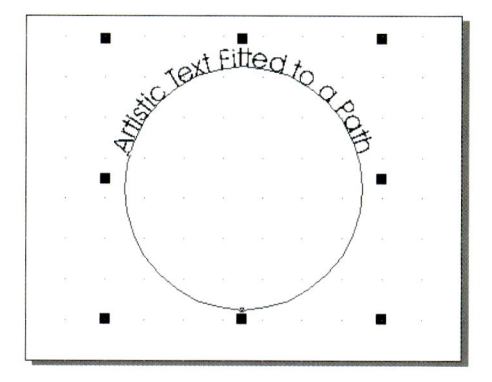

Figure 4.33
Text is fitted to the circle.

16. Now you will make the text float around the circle and rotate it slightly. Select Edit from the roll-up menu. The Fit Text To Path Offsets dialog box appears, as shown in figure 4.34.

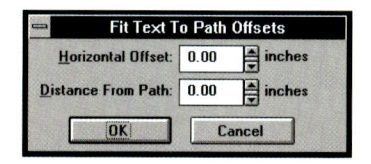

Figure 4.34
The Fit Text To Path Offsets dialog box.

66   Chapter 4: Setting and Manipulating Text

17. Set the **D**istance From Path to 0.50 inches. This will float the text 1/2 inch from the circle.

18. Set the **H**orizontal Offset to 1.00 inches. This will rotate the text 1 inch around the circle.

19. Click on OK, then click on Apply (see fig. 4.35).

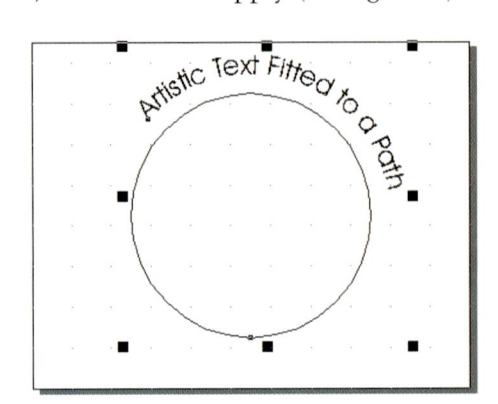

Figure 4.35
The text floats around the circle and has rotated 1 inch.

NOTE
*Notice that because you adjusted the **D**istance From Path, the vertical alignment has changed from bottom to variable. Variable alignment enables you to move the text string away from the path line.*

20. You also can place the text inside the circle. From the vertical alignment menu, select bottom.

21. Click on the bottom quadrant to select it.

22. Click on the Place on other side box to check it. This places the text on the opposite side of the path.

23. Click on Edit on the roll-up. Change both values to 0.00. Click on OK.

24. Click on Apply. The text is in the bottom quadrant and inside the circle (see fig. 4.36).

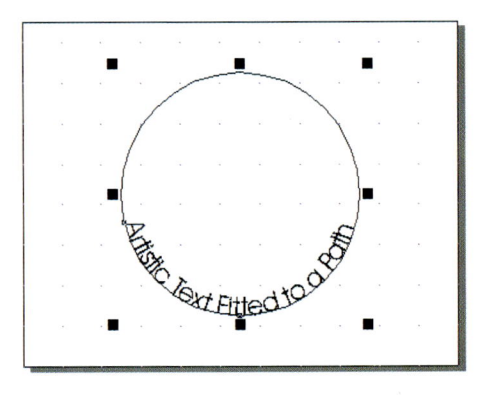

Figure 4.36
The text is fitted inside the circle.

25. Save the file as TEXT06.

Using the Straighten Text and Align to Baseline Commands

The **S**traighten Text command undoes changes that have been made to characters in a text string, such as rotating or shifting horizontally or vertically. The Align to Base**l**ine command aligns characters vertically to the baseline, but will not affect changes like rotation or horizontal shifting.

1. Select **N**ew from the **F**ile menu.

2. Select the Artistic text tool, and enter the following text in the center of the page: **CorelDRAW! 4.0**. Select the Pick tool to discontinue text mode, and highlight the text string.

3. Another way to edit text is by using the Text roll-up menu. From the Te**x**t menu, select Text **R**oll-Up. The Text roll-up menu appears as shown in figure 4.37.

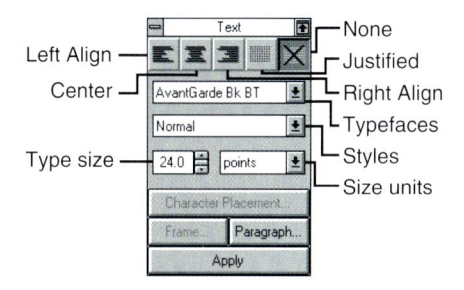

Figure 4.37
The Text roll-up menu.

4. Click on the center align box.

5. Click on the drop-down menu for typefaces and scroll down until you get to Switzerland. Click on Switzerland.

6. Click on the styles menu, and select Bold. Increase the type size to 72 points.

7. Click on Apply; the text edits take effect (see fig. 4.38).

8. Select the Shape tool. Place the cursor on the node for the letter *C* (the node to its left) and drag it up about 1/2 inch.

9. Select the node for the letter *D* and drag it down about 1/2 inch.

10. Double-click on the node for the *4* to bring up the Character Attributes box. Adjust the character angle to 20 degrees and click on OK.

11. Double-click on the node for the *O* and adjust the character angle to –20 degrees. Click on OK; the text string is somewhat jumbled now (see fig. 4.39).

68 Chapter 4: Setting and Manipulating Text

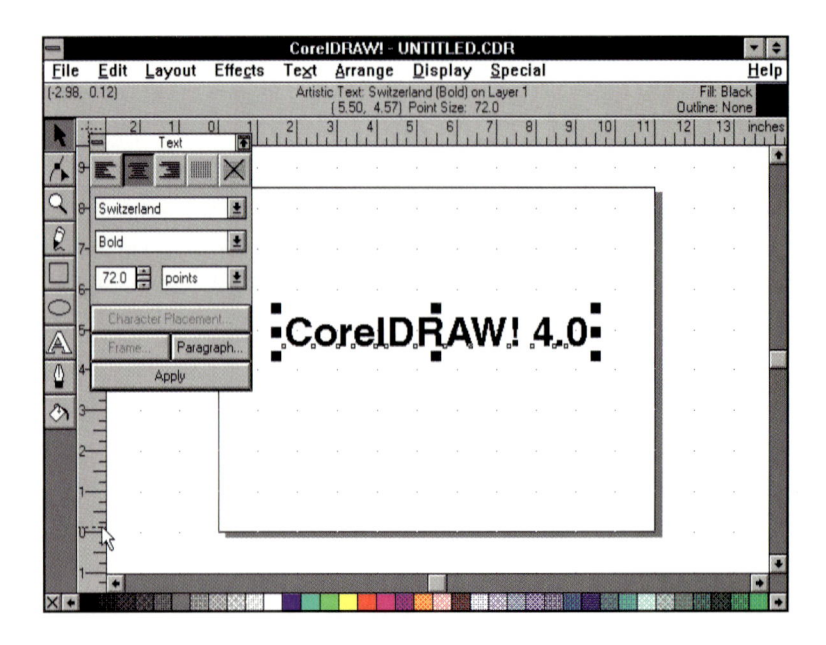

Figure 4.38
An Artistic Text string.

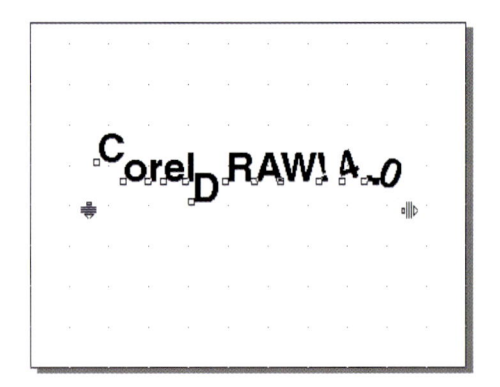

Figure 4.39
The text string in need of alignment.

12. From the Text menu, choose Align to Baseline. The *C* and *D* return to their original position, but the *4* and the *O* remain unchanged.

13. Press Ctrl+Z to Undo the Align to Baseline command.

14. From the Text menu, choose Straighten Text. Now the angle adjustments as well as the vertical changes have been edited.

Copying Text Attributes

If you have two or more text strings in a drawing, you can make changes in the attributes of one and then copy those attributes to any other text string.

1. Select New from the File menu.

Copying Text Attributes 69

2. Select the Artistic Text tool, and enter the following text in the top half of the page: **Copy Text Attributes**.

3. Using the Artistic Text tool, enter the following text in the bottom half of the page: **Copy From This Text**. Select the Pick tool to discontinue Text mode, and highlight the text at the bottom of the page.

4. Select either the Text Roll-up (from the Text menu) or the Text dialog box (Ctrl+T). Make the following changes—Typeface: Toronto; Center Alignment; Style: Bold-Italic; Size: 72 points (see fig. 4.40).

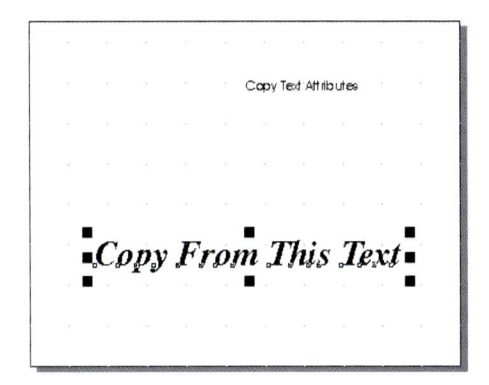

Figure 4.40
The text string with different text attributes.

5. Using the Pick tool, select the text string at the top of the page.

6. From the Edit menu, select Copy Attributes From. The Copy Attributes dialog box appears, as shown in figure 4.41.

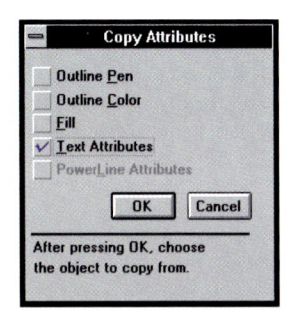

Figure 4.41
The Copy Attributes dialog box.

7. Choose Text Attributes, and click on OK.

8. The cursor now appears as the FROM arrow. Place the arrow on the text at the bottom of the page and click on it. The two text strings now have the same text attributes.

70 Chapter 4: Setting and Manipulating Text

Using Special Characters

To access the special characters, press Alt and type the character number shown on the CorelDRAW! Character Reference Chart. You'll find the chart on the last two pages of the *Quick Reference* booklet.

1. Select the Artistic Text tool and click on the center of the page.

2. Hold down the Alt key and type **0169**. The copyright symbol is drawn. Type **0174** with the Alt key down for the registered mark. Repeat this procedure for **0147** and **0148** (true quotes), **0189** (1/2), and **0163** (British pound). Figure 4.42 shows these special characters.

Figure 4.42
A sampling of special characters.

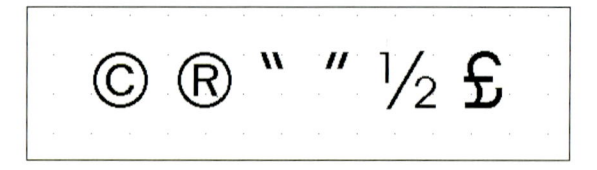

The special characters in this example can be accessed from any normal font. Dixieland, Greekmath, Musical, Geographic, and CommonBullets typefaces have their own set of special characters, as shown on the character reference sheet.

Chapter 5
Moving, Duplicating, and Transforming Objects

Creating an object is just the beginning step in constructing a good piece of art. You usually need to move, duplicate, and transform objects you have created to attain the look you want. These skills are ones you must master to create professional-looking artwork.

Opening Files

To edit an existing drawing, make the file active by using the Open command.

1. From the File menu, select Open. The Open Drawing dialog box appears, as shown in figure 5.1.

2. Use file BEZLINE2 for this example. Click on it once in the File Name list to select it. A thumbnail appears in the preview window.

3. To open the file, click on the OK button or double-click on the file name. Choose either method and open the file now.

This chapter covers the following operations:

- Opening files
- Moving objects
- Stretching objects
- Mirroring objects
- Rotating objects
- Skewing objects
- Duplicating objects
- Cloning objects

Chapter 5: Moving, Duplicating, and Transforming Objects

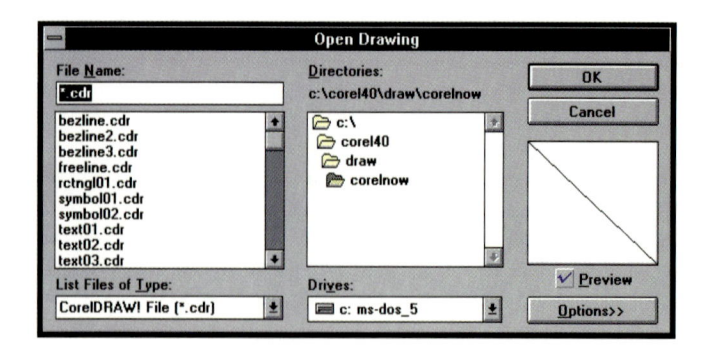

Figure 5.1
The Open Drawing dialog box.

> If you check **P**review, you can see a thumbnail drawing of the selected file before you actually open it.

> At the bottom of the **F**ile menu, CorelDRAW! lists the last four files you have worked on. If the file you are looking for is one of these, just click on it once to open it. This shortcut saves you the time and trouble of navigating through the Open Drawing dialog box.

Moving Objects with the Mouse

The simplest way to move objects on the page is by using the mouse.

1. Using the Pick tool, click on the object to select it.

2. Click and hold the mouse pointer on the object, and drag it to the right of the page. The cursor changes to an arrowheaded cross, indicating that an object is being moved. A marquee appears to show you the new position you have selected for the object. Place the marquee on the right side of the page and release the mouse button (see fig. 5.2).

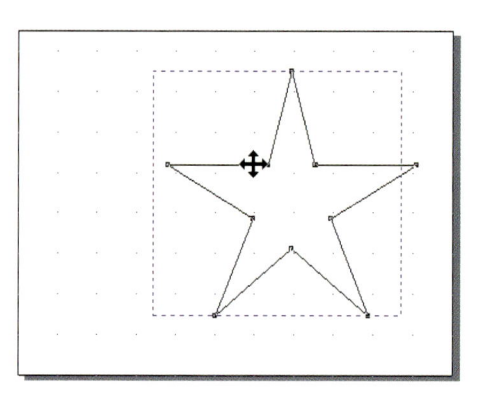

Figure 5.2
The marquee shows the new position of the object.

3. Repeat this procedure to move the object to the left side of the page. As you drag, watch the status line. It tells you the horizontal and vertical distance the object has moved.

4. Repeat the procedure again to move the object to the right, but hold down the Ctrl key. The Ctrl key *constrains* the action to exactly horizontal or vertical movements. In this case, it constrains the object to move in a straight line to the right. The status bar reflects this constraint by showing a Y axis change of 0.

Using the Move Command

You also can move objects using menus and dialog boxes.

1. With the object on the right side of the page and still selected, choose **M**ove from the **A**rrange menu. The Move dialog box appears, as shown in figure 5.3.

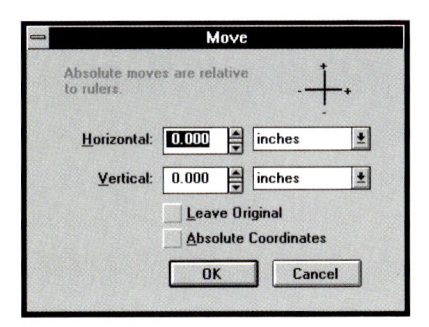

Figure 5.3
The Move dialog box.

The Move dialog box enables you to move an object a specified distance or to an exact location by specifying coordinates.

2. Enter **–4.00** inches for the horizontal move and **1.00** inch for the vertical move. Click on OK. The object moves 1 inch up and 4 inches to the left.

3. You can move an object to an exact location by specifying a set of coordinates. Choose the **M**ove command from the **A**rrange menu to access the Move dialog box, then select **A**bsolute Coordinates. A grid appears in the dialog box. This grid enables you to select which area of the object you want to place on the specified coordinates.

*The rulers currently are displayed on the screen. You can turn off the rulers to get a slightly larger work area on the screen. If you wish to use **A**bsolute Coordinates, however, the rulers must be displayed.*

Chapter 5: Moving, Duplicating, and Transforming Objects

4. Click on the lower right handle of the grid, then enter **11.00** for the horizontal value and **0.000** for the vertical value. These coordinates place the bottom right corner of the object in the bottom right corner of the page.

5. Click on OK. The object moves to the desired position (see fig. 5.4).

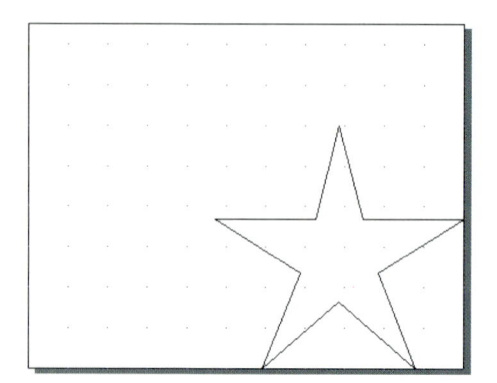

Figure 5.4

The object moves to the specified coordinates.

Moving Objects with the Keyboard

Using the keyboard to move an object is referred to as a *nudge*. It enables you to make fine adjustments to an object's position.

1. Select Preferences from the Special menu. When the Preferences dialog box appears, change the Nudge value to 0.050. Now, when you execute a nudge, the object will move 0.050 inches. Click on OK to save the change.

2. Using the Pick tool, select the object (if it is not already selected).

3. Press the up arrow while keeping an eye on the screen. The object moves up 0.05 inches. You can use all four arrow keys to move an object on the screen.

Stretching Objects with the Mouse

You can change the shape and size of an object by stretching it.

1. Select New from the File menu. If Draw asks if you want to save the current changes, choose No.

2. Select the Artistic Text tool. Click on the center of the page and type **OBJECT**. Click on the Pick tool to discontinue text mode, then select the object.

3. Open the Text dialog box (Ctrl+T) and enter the following values:

   Fonts: Timpani
   Alignment: Center

Stretching Objects with the Mouse   75

   Si<u>z</u>e: 100 Points
   S<u>t</u>yle: Normal

4. Click on OK (see fig. 5.5). The text string reflects the changes.

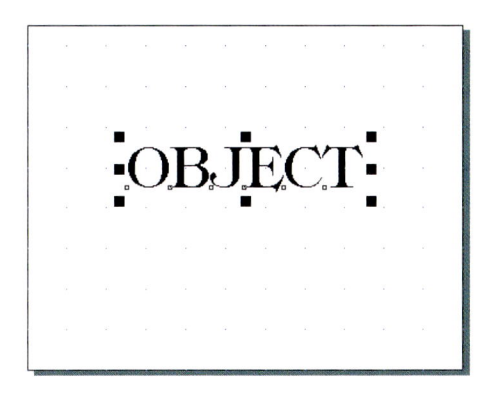

Figure 5.5
Artistic text string.

5. When an object is selected, it is surrounded by eight *control handles*. Place the cursor on the top center handle. The cursor changes to a crosshair, which can move the handle. Drag the handle up about 1 inch.

6. Place the cursor on the right center handle and drag it 2 inches to the left. The text is stretched vertically and squeezed horizontally (see fig. 5.6).

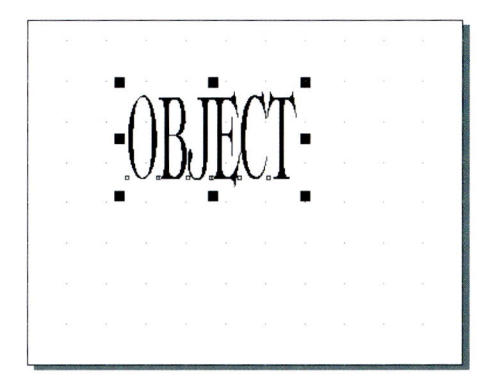

Figure 5.6
Text reflects the stretch changes.

When you stretch an object by dragging a control handle, the opposite handle of the object is anchored *(does not move), and the object stretches from the side the mouse is on. If you want the object to stretch from the center out, hold down the Shift key as you stretch.*

7. From the Effe<u>c</u>ts menu, choose <u>C</u>lear Transformations to return the object to its original shape.

Chapter 5: Moving, Duplicating, and Transforming Objects

8. Drag the top center handle up 1 inch again, but this time while holding down the Shift key. The object stretches from its center, 1 inch in each direction.

9. Choose Clear Transformations again (or Undo from the Edit menu) to return the object to its original state.

10. Drag the top center handle up slowly, but this time hold down Ctrl to constrain the stretch to 100-percent increments of the original size. The original text was 100 points, so the constrained text can be 200 points, 300 points, 400 points, and so on.

11. With Ctrl held down, bring the handle back down to its original position and release the mouse button. The object should appear unchanged.

12. Select any one of the corner handles. Press and hold Ctrl and Alt, then drag the handle away from the center of the object. When the text is at 200 points (refer to the status line), release the mouse button and the keys. The resulting text is larger by 100 percent (Ctrl), it has stretched from its center (Alt), and is in the same proportion as the original (corner handle). See figure 5.7.

Figure 5.7
Text is stretched but retains its original proportions.

When you stretch an object using one of the corner handles, you are scaling the object. Scaling means that you are changing the object's width and length at the same time and in the same proportion.

Stretching Objects Using the Stretch & Mirror Command

If you know the exact percentage you want to stretch or scale an object, you can use the Stretch & Mirror command.

1. From the Effects menu, select Stretch & Mirror to bring up its dialog box.

Mirroring an Object

2. Enter a value of 50% for Stretch **H**orizontally and **S**tretch Vertically to return the text object to its original size. Click on OK.

Mirroring an Object

You also can use **S**tretch & Mirror to create a mirror image of an object.

1. Select the object, then hold down Ctrl and drag the top center handle down across the text.

2. As you move the handle, a marquee appears around the object. Keep moving the cursor down until the marquee appears below the object. Release the mouse button. The object is mirrored, as shown in figure 5.8.

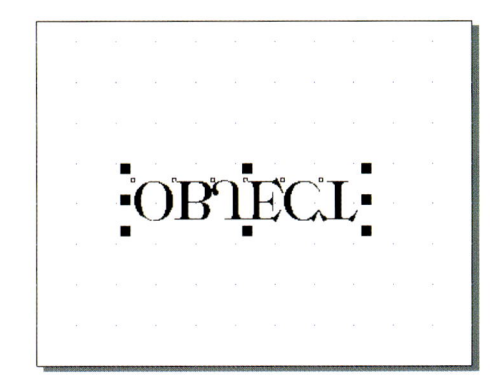

Figure 5.8
A mirror image of the object.

You can mirror an object using any of the four side handles. In the preceding example, Ctrl is used to retain the original size, but you can mirror an object to any size.

Mirroring an Object Using the Stretch & Mirror Command

If you know the percentage you want, you can mirror an object using menu and dialog box commands.

1. Select the object, then choose **S**tretch & Mirror from the Effe**c**ts menu.

2. The default values of 100% are shown. Leave them as they are, and click on the V**e**rtical Mirror button. The vertical value changes to –100%.

3. Click on OK. The text string changes back to its unmirrored state.

78 Chapter 5: Moving, Duplicating, and Transforming Objects

> *Like stretching, when you mirror an object with the mouse, the opposite control handle is anchored. When you mirror an object from the menu, it mirrors from the object's center point.*

Rotating Objects with the Mouse

The simplest way to rotate an object is by using the mouse button.

1. Using the Pick tool, select and move the object to the center of the page.

2. With the object still selected, click on the object again. The control handles are transformed into a set of double-sided arrows, and a circle appears in the center of the object (see fig. 5.9). This circle is called the *center of rotation*. The four corner arrows enable you to rotate the object, and the center of rotation is the point around which the object rotates.

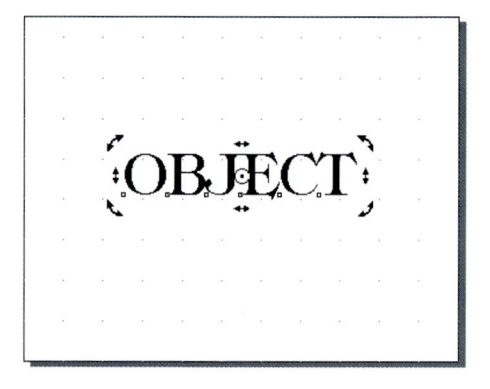

Figure 5.9
Text object in Rotate & Skew mode.

3. Drag the upper right corner arrow in a counterclockwise direction. A marquee appears that shows the new position of the object.

4. Without releasing the mouse button, press and hold down Ctrl.

5. Continue to rotate the object and refer to the status bar. Ctrl constrains the rotation to 15-degree increments.

> *In the Preferences dialog box (from the **S**pecial menu, choose Pr**e**ferences), Constrain Angle was set at 15 degrees.*

6. Rotate the text to an angle of 60 degrees and release the mouse button (see fig. 5.10).

7. The rotation point of an object need not be its center. To change the rotation point, begin by placing the cursor on the center of rotation (it changes to a crosshair).

8. Move the center point down so that it sits on the letter O's node.

Rotating Objects Using the Rotate & Skew Command 79

9. Drag the upper right arrow clockwise as you press Ctrl. Rotate the object –30 degrees (watch the status line). Now when you rotate the object, it no longer rotates on its center, but on the lower left corner where the center point was positioned (see fig. 5.11).

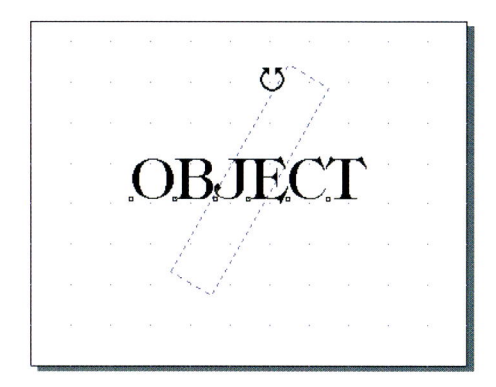

Figure 5.10
Marquee shows the object's new position.

Figure 5.11
Marquee shows the way the object will rotate.

Rotating Objects Using the Rotate & Skew Command

For precise rotation, use the **R**otate & Skew command.

1. With the object selected, choose **C**lear Transformations from the Effe**c**ts Menu. Move the text to the center of the page.

2. Select **R**otate & Skew from the **E**ffects menu.

3. In the Rotation Angle window, enter a value of –60 degrees. Click on OK (see fig. 5.12).

The Rotate & Skew dialog box contains a diagram that shows the direction an object rotates depending upon a positive or negative value. A positive (+) value rotates the object counterclockwise; a negative (–) value rotates clockwise.

NOTE

4. Save this file as ROTATE.

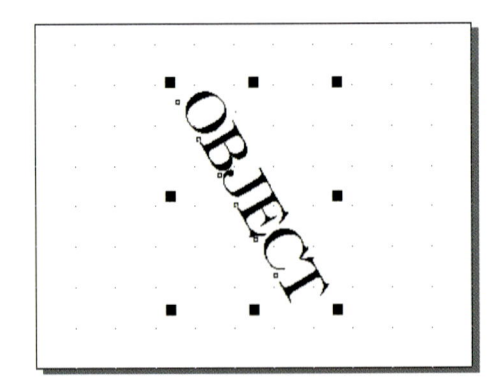

80   Chapter 5: Moving, Duplicating, and Transforming Objects

Figure 5.12
The object rotates 60 degrees counterclockwise.

Skewing Objects with the Mouse

Skewing an object simply means to slant it.

1. If ROTATE.CDR is not currently open, open the file now.
2. Select the object using the Pick tool, then choose **C**lear Transformations from the Eff**e**cts menu to return the text to its original state.
3. Click on the text again to convert the handles into arrows. In an earlier exercise, you used the corner arrows to rotate the object. Use the top, bottom, and side arrows to skew it.
4. Drag the top skew arrow to the right. A marquee shows the angle to which the object is slanted.
5. Press and hold Ctrl. Like previous commands, it constrains the angle to 15-degree intervals (watch the status bar).
6. Skew the text to –30 degrees and release the mouse button (see fig. 5.13).

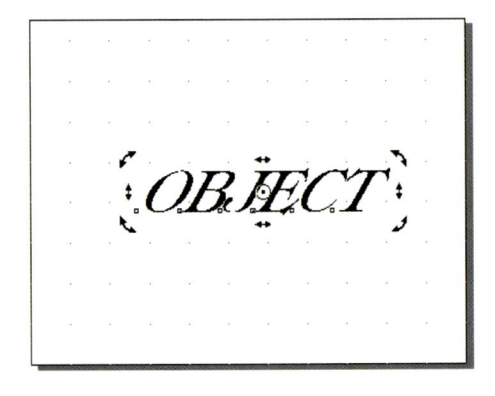

Figure 5.13
The skewed object.

Skewing Objects Using the Rotate & Skew Command

You can use the Rotate & Skew command to skew in exact increments.

1. With the text you just skewed as the selected object, select **R**otate & Skew from the Effe**c**ts menu.

2. Enter a value of 30 degrees for **H**orizontal Skew and –15 degrees for the **V**ertical Skew.

3. Click on OK. The object appears skewed as shown in figure 5.14.

   The 30-degree horizontal skew returns the text to an upright position, and the –15 degree vertical skew slants the text down.

4. Save file as SKEW.

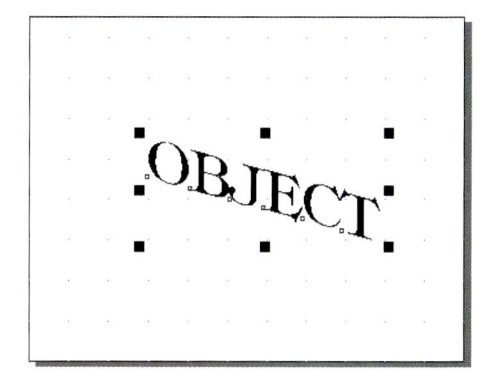

Figure 5.14
Text skewed using Rotate & Skew.

Duplicating Objects

You can make a duplicate copy of an object using several different methods. The method you choose might depend on personal preference or an effect you want to achieve.

In the following steps, you make copies of an object using the Duplicate command.

1. Choose **N**ew from the **F**ile menu.

2. Select the Rectangle tool and draw a 3-inch square (press Ctrl to constrain to a square) on the left side of the page.

3. Select Pr**e**ferences from the **S**pecial menu. For Place Duplicates and Clones, enter **0.200** inches for **H**orizontal and **–0.200** inches for **V**ertical. Click on OK.

   These larger values make things easier for this example.

Chapter 5: Moving, Duplicating, and Transforming Objects

4. Click on the Pick tool and select the square if it is not already selected. You can duplicate the object by choosing **D**uplicate from the **E**dit menu, but the shortcut key (Ctrl+D) is faster.

5. The object is duplicated and placed 0.200 inches down and to the right (see fig. 5.15).

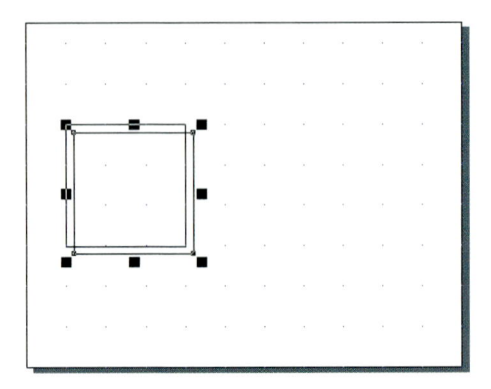

Figure 5.15

The square is duplicated and offset .200

6. The duplicate square becomes the currently selected object. Press Del to delete it.

*De**l**ete also is available from the **E**dit menu, but the keyboard shortcut (Del) is faster to use.*

7. Select the remaining square using the Pick tool. Press the + key on the numeric keypad. This makes a duplicate of an object and places it directly on top of the original.

Be sure to use the + key on the numeric keypad, not the one on the top row of the regular keyboard.

8. To prove the point, drag a marquee around the square with the Pick tool. The status bar now shows that two objects are selected: the original square and its duplicate.

9. Press Del; both squares are deleted.

10. Using the Rectangle tool, draw another square about 1 inch wide on the left side of the page.

11. Click on the Pick tool to select the square.

To jump to the Pick tool from one of the drawing tools, press the space bar. Press the space bar again to return to the drawing tool you were just using.

12. Press Ctrl and drag the square to the right until the marquee is about 1 inch from the original position.

Cloning Objects 83

13. Click the right mouse button without releasing the left mouse button.

> *On the left side of the status bar, the words* `Leave Original` *appear. By clicking the right mouse button, you tell the program that you want the original object to stay where it is—you want to move a copy of it. The right mouse button has the same effect when you stretch, skew, or rotate an object.*

14. Release the mouse button. A copy of the original moves to the new position.

15. You can automatically repeat this procedure and place additional copies to the right. Press Ctrl+R (or select **R**epeat from the **E**dit menu); a third square appears on the page. Press Ctrl+R two more times. You now have five squares (see fig. 5.16).

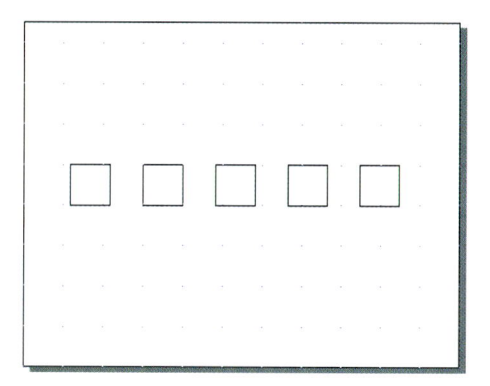

Figure 5.16
The original square and four duplicates.

Cloning Objects

When you duplicate an object, the resulting copies are independent objects that you can edit individually. When you *clone* an object, however, the changes you make to the original ("master") object automatically are applied to the clones.

1. Using the Pick tool, select all the squares on the page and delete them.

2. Select the Rectangle tool, then draw a 3-inch square on the left side of the page.

3. Press the space bar to switch to the Pick tool, and select the square.

4. From the **E**dit menu, choose Cl**o**ne.

> *The Clone command does not have a shortcut key.*

5. A cloned copy appears offset down and to the right, just as it did when you executed the **D**uplicate command.

84   Chapter 5: Moving, Duplicating, and Transforming Objects

6. Drag the clone to the right side of the page (see fig. 5.17).

7. Select the square on the left side of the page using the Pick tool. Drag the bottom right corner handle and scale the square larger by about 1 inch.

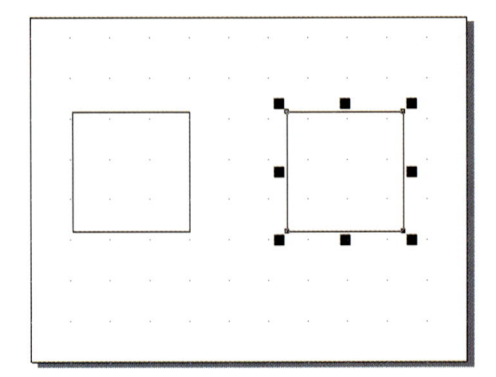

Figure 5.17

The original square and its clone.

8. Click on the object again to enter Rotate & Skew mode. Drag a corner arrow clockwise 45 degrees (use Ctrl to constrain the angle). See figure 5.18.

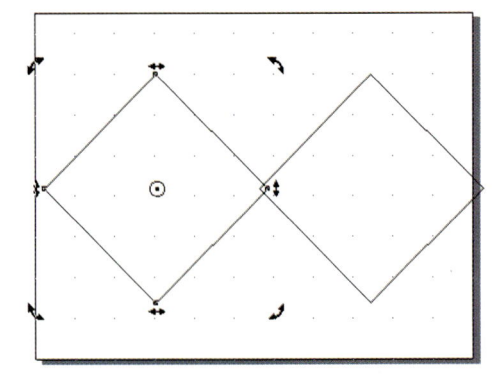

Figure 5.18

Changes to the original object affect the clone.

You can make a number of changes to a master that can be repeated in the clone, including line color, fill type and color, and many special effects. These effects are discussed in later chapters.

After you create a clone, you can duplicate that clone an infinite number of times. Changes made to the master object are applied to all the duplicate clones.

If you have a drawing with numerous clones of an object, you might forget which one is the master. To find out, place the cursor on an object and press the right mouse button. The Object Menu appears (see figure 5.19). If the object is a clone, the Select Master command appears on the menu. Use this command to find the master object.

Using Transformation Commands 85

Figure 5.19
The Object Menu.

Using Transformation Commands

Here's a simple example of the ways you can use some of the functions covered in this chapter. The task is to illustrate text so that it appears to be standing in late afternoon sun with the sun behind it.

1. Select New from the File menu.

2. Select the Artistic Text tool. Click on the center of the page and type **CorelDRAW! Now**. Select the Pick tool to discontinue text mode and select the text object.

3. Using the Text roll-up menu (select Text menu) or the Text dialog box (Ctrl+T), enter these attributes:

> Fonts: Avalon
> Alignment: Center
> Size: 70 points
> Style: Italic

Click on OK from the dialog box, or on Apply from the roll-up menu. (Close the roll-up menu if it was used.)

4. With the Pick tool, drag the top center handle down across the text. Hold down Ctrl to constrain the size to 100-percent increments.

5. Click the right mouse button to leave the original copy.

6. Move the handle down until the stretched text object is twice the size as the original.

The status bar will show movement on the y axis of –200%.

7. Release the mouse button. The text string is mirrored, and the new object is twice the height as the original (see fig. 5.20).

The illustration is not quite right. The late afternoon sun would cast a long shadow as shown, but at an angle.

8. Click on the mirrored object to enter Skew mode.

86   Chapter 5: Moving, Duplicating, and Transforming Objects

Figure 5.20

Text object is copied, stretched, and mirrored.

9. Click on the bottom center arrow, and Ctrl+drag the arrow to the right 45 degrees (the status bar will show the skew value). The final result is shown in figure 5.21.

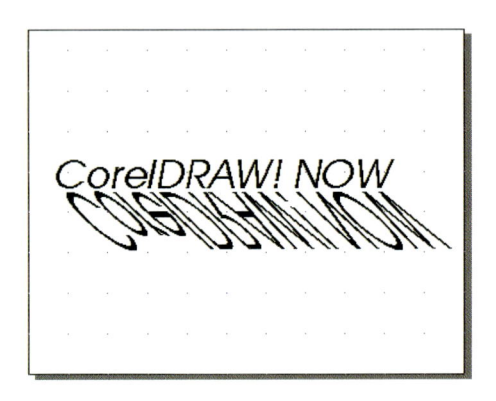

Figure 5.21

The shadow looks more realistic.

By skewing the shadow (the mirrored object), you get a much more realistic image. You return to this example later in the book to see how using color and special effects can help enhance an image.

10. Save the file as EXAMPLE1.

Chapter 6
Using Outlines and Fills

Every closed object within CorelDRAW!—including text strings—has an outline and a fill. Imagine the object as a container that you fill with a liquid. The container must be closed to hold the liquid.

The outline of an object is the border that defines its edges. You can edit the width and color of an outline as you did earlier with lines and curves.

The fill of an object is its interior, the space inside the outline. A fill can be transparent, a solid color, a gradated color, or a pattern of shapes or textures.

Setting Outline Width and Color

In Chapter 2, you learned to use the Pen tool and the Pen roll-up menu to create and edit lines and curves. The Pen tool and the Pen roll-up menu also are used to edit object outlines.

1. Select the Ellipse tool.
2. Place the cursor in the center of the screen, hold the Shift key, and draw an ellipse the approximate size and shape of the one in figure 6.1.
3. Click on the Pick tool to select the ellipse.
4. To edit the width and color of the ellipse's outline, click on the Pen tool to bring up its fly-out menu. You can use one of the preset widths and colors shown, or you can access the Outline Pen dialog box or the Pen roll-up menu.
5. Click on the Pen icon (see fig. 6.2) to access the Outline Pen dialog box, as shown in figure 6.3.

In this chapter you will learn to:

- Set outline width and color
- Use solid fills
- Use the color palettes
- Create fountain, bit-map, and pattern fills
- Use the Fill roll-up menu

Chapter 6: Using Outlines and Fills

Figure 6.1
Using the Ellipse tool to draw an ellipse.

Figure 6.2
The Outline Pen fly-out menu.

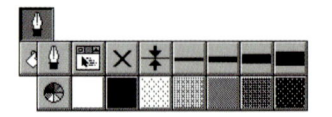

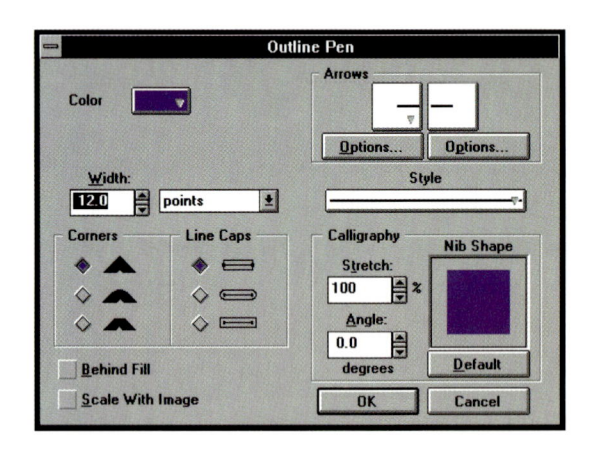

Figure 6.3
The Outline Pen dialog box.

6. To edit the outline color, click on the Color button to access the color palette. Then you can click on any color in the color palette to change the outline color. If the color you want is not displayed in the color palette, click on More to access the complete color palette. For now, click on blue.

7. Adjust the width value to 12 points. To do this, use the up arrow, or highlight the current value with the mouse, enter **12.0**, and change the unit of measurement to points.

8. All other settings can be left as the default for now.

9. Click on OK.

The status bar at the top of the screen shows the ellipse as the selected object. On the right side of the status bar, the outline value is shown as 12 points and illustrates the color is blue. The X in the center of the blue square indicates that the object has no fill.

Using the Calligraphic Outline Pen

The ellipse now has a 12-point uniform outline. CorelDRAW! enables you to draw outlines as if they were done with a calligraphic pen.

Calligraphic pen tips have different shapes, enabling you to vary the width of a line by changing the angle at which you hold the pen.

1. With the ellipse still selected, select the Outline Pen from the Pen tool fly-out menu. This will bring up the dialog box.
2. Go to the Calligraphy section of the dialog box.
3. Adjust the stretch value to 20%. The new nib shape (the pen point) is illustrated in the window.
4. Adjust the angle to –50 degrees. Again the change is shown in the window. Click on OK. As you can see from figure 6.4, the width of the outline varies in relation to the pen shape used.

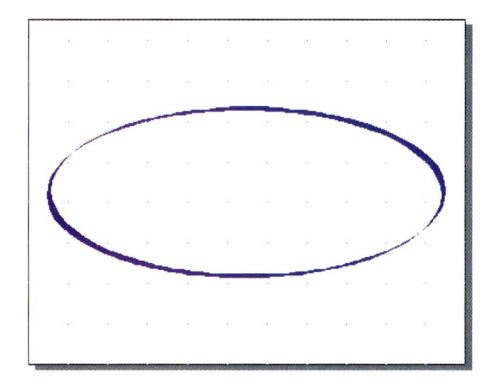

Figure 6.4
The outline width varies with a calligraphic nib shape.

5. Save the drawing as OUTLINE1.

Filling Objects with a Solid Color

1. Select **N**ew from the **F**ile menu.
2. Select the Rectangle tool, and draw a rectangle in the center of the page, approximately 6 by 9 inches.

*Here's a quick way to draw and position the rectangle. Place the cursor in the bottom left corner at 0,0. Drag the cursor up 6 inches and over 9 inches and release the mouse button to draw the rectangle. Select **A**lign from the **A**rrange menu. Click on the box for Align to Center of **P**age. Click on OK. The rectangle is now dead center.*

90 Chapter 6: Using Outlines and Fills

3. Press the space bar to access the Pick tool. The quickest way to fill an object is to use the color palette at the bottom of the screen.

4. Place the cursor on the red square and click. The rectangle now is filled with red. Notice that this is indicated on the right side of the status bar. Clicking on a color in the color palette will fill any selected object with that color.

You also can use the color palette to edit the color of an object's outline. With the object selected, click on the color palette with the secondary mouse button, and the outline changes to the selected color.

5. You also can edit an object's fill color with the Fill tool in the toolbox. Click on the Fill tool to bring up the fly-out menu, as shown in figure 6.5.

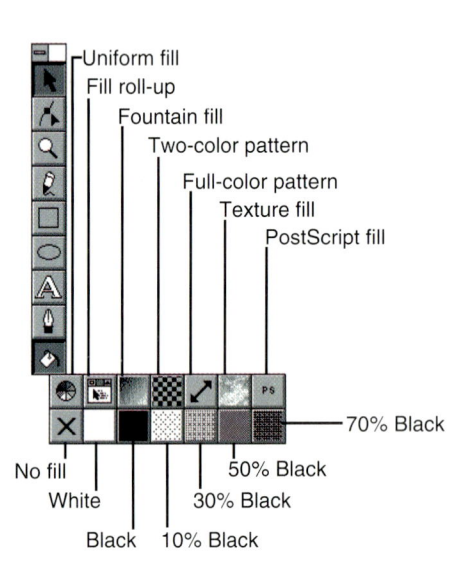

Figure 6.5
The Fill tool fly-out menu.

Uniform fill
Fill roll-up
Fountain fill
Two-color pattern
Full-color pattern
Texture fill
PostScript fill
70% Black
50% Black
30% Black
10% Black
Black
White
No fill

6. You can click on one of the preset colors to fill an object. Select Uniform fill to bring up its dialog box, as shown in figure 6.6.

7. Click on the drop-down menu of the Show window, and select Custom Palette. Click on the box for Show color names to check it. Click on the Custom Button and select Set as Default. From here on the dialog box will display the custom palette by name.

The palette in the Fill dialog box now matches the on-screen palette.

8. Click on Orange to change the color of the fill. The preview window displays the new fill color as well as the current one. Click on OK. The rectangle now is filled in orange.

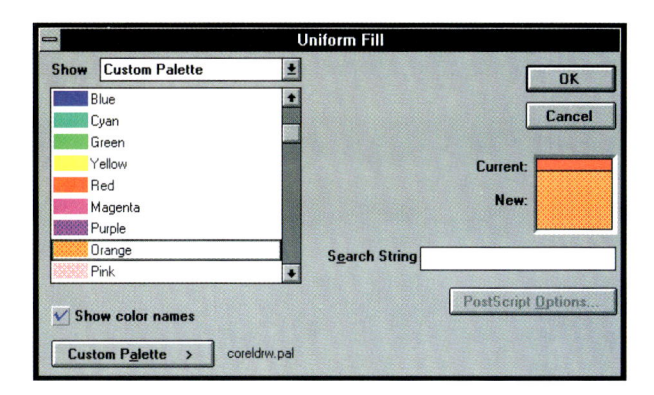

Working with Color Palettes

Figure 6.6
The Uniform Fill dialog box.

Working with Color Palettes

CorelDRAW! has many powerful color handling capabilities. It comes with a number of color palettes, including a TRUMATCH palette. When used along with the TRUMATCH color reference book, you can get a reasonably good idea of what the colors will look like when printed.

> *It is important to remember that often, on-screen color may not match perfectly with the final product. Whether you output to slides, color laser prints, four-color printing, and so on, some colors will not reproduce accurately. Your best bet is to test whenever possible.*

1. With the rectangle selected, bring up the Fill dialog box with the Fill tool.

2. The Custom Palette is displayed, and the current color is orange. From the Show list box, select CMYK Color Model (see fig. 6.7). This displays the current color in terms of percentages of cyan, magenta, yellow, and black. *CMYK* refers to the colors used in separations in four-color printing.

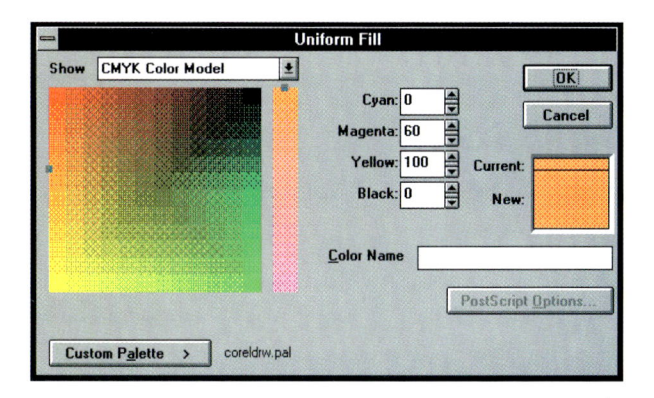

Figure 6.7
CMYK Color Model in the Show window.

92 Chapter 6: Using Outlines and Fills

3. From the Show list box, select the RGB Color Model, which displays the color in terms of red, green, and blue. This refers to the way your computer monitor displays color.

4. From the Show menu, select the HSB Color Model. This displays the color in terms of hue, saturation, and brightness. *Hue* refers to one of 360 possible color tints. *Saturation* adjusts the amount of color by adding gray and removing hue (or adding hue and removing gray) so that the color does not get lighter or darker. *Lightness* basically makes the color lighter or darker. This obviously is a very sophisticated color model, but you need not understand color theory to use it.

5. With the HSB model selected, the dialog box displays a color model. The color wheel represents hue and saturation, and the bar represents brightness. Each of these has a node attached.

6. Click on the node of the Brightness bar and drag it down about one-third of the way. The value in the brightness window has decreased and the color in the preview window is darker.

The CorelDRAW! palette contains about 100 named colors. By editing the nodes on the color model, you can visually select from an almost infinite amount of colors. The same visual adjustments are available for the CMYK and RGB color models.

7. Click on OK. The rectangle now is a darker shade of orange, and the status bar displays it as an *unnamed color*, meaning it is not one of the 100 named colors.

Adding Colors to the Palette

For this example, let's say you're creating artwork for the Acme Nuts & Bolts Company. They supplied you with a color swatch of their corporate color, and through some testing, you have found a value that matches it when printed. Now you want to save this color so you can use it for all the art you create for Acme.

1. Select **N**ew from the **F**ile menu. (If prompted, do not save changes.)

2. Using the Rectangle tool, draw a 2-inch square anywhere on the page. (Use the Ctrl key to constrain the square.)

3. Press the space bar to activate the Pick tool, and select the square.

4. Click on blue in the on-screen palette to fill the square with blue.

5. Select Uniform fill from the fill tool fly-out menu.

6. From the Show list box, select HSB model.

Adding Colors to the Palette

7. We will say that after some testing, the Acme color has the following values:

Hue: 244
Saturation: 85
Brightness: 90

8. Enter these values in the appropriate windows.

Reminder—instead of clicking the arrow keys, click and drag the mouse across the value to highlight it, then enter the value from the keyboard.

9. Place the cursor in the Color Name window and click. You now can enter a name for this new color. Type **Acme Blue**, and click on OK (see fig. 6.8).

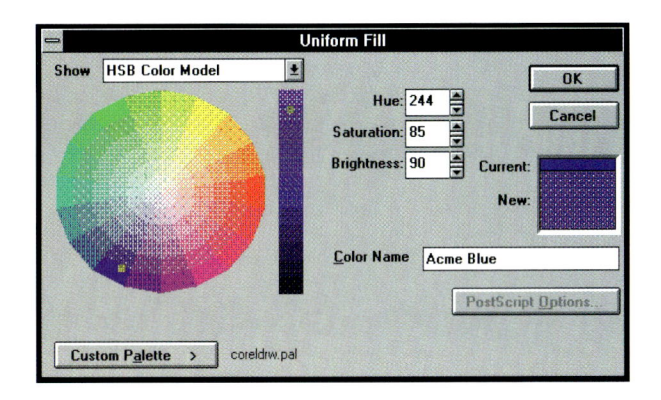

Figure 6.8
Settings in the Uniform Fill dialog box.

10. The square now is filled with Acme Blue, as shown in the status line.

11. Select the Uniform Fill dialog box from the Fill tool. From the Show menu, select Custom Palette. Acme Blue has been added to the palette list. Click on OK.

12. On either side of the on-screen palette are arrow keys. They enable you to scroll through the palette. (There isn't room on-screen to display 100 colors.) Click and hold the right arrow of the on-screen palette until it no longer scrolls. The last color is Acme Blue, the color you added to the palette. You can move it so that it will be easier to access.

Rearranging the Color Palette

If you find you work with certain colors often, you can rearrange how they appear in the color palette, giving you quicker access to those colors.

1. With the square selected, bring up the Uniform Fill dialog box.

2. From the Show list box, select Custom Palette.

Chapter 6: Using Outlines and Fills

3. Click on the Show color names box to uncheck it. The colors are displayed as a grid of squares.

4. Click and hold the mouse button on the Acme Blue square and drag it up. As you begin dragging, a black dot appears (see fig. 6.9).

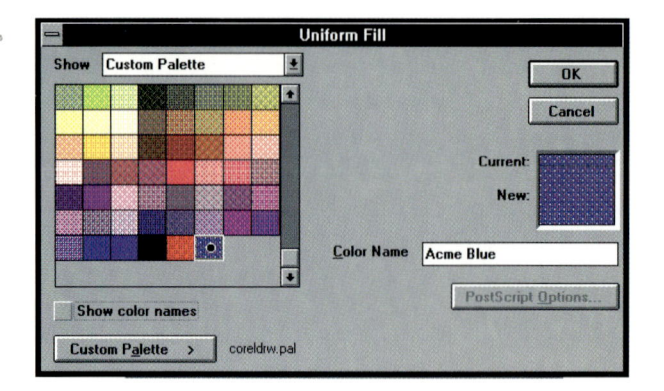

Figure 6.9
A black dot appears in the grid of squares.

5. Drag the black dot up just above the grid of colors, and they will scroll up. When they stop scrolling, the black square should be in the upper left corner.

6. Place the black dot in the black square and release the mouse button. The Acme Blue square is positioned there and all the colors shift down once. Click on OK.

7. Click and hold the left arrow of the on-screen color palette to return to the beginning. Whereas black was the first color in the palette, it now is Acme Blue.

Using Fountain Fills

With a fountain fill, two colors are selected and the program creates a smooth shading gradation between them. The gradation can go in a straight line (linear), from the center out (radial), or in a circle from one color to the other and back again (conical), as shown in figure 6.10.

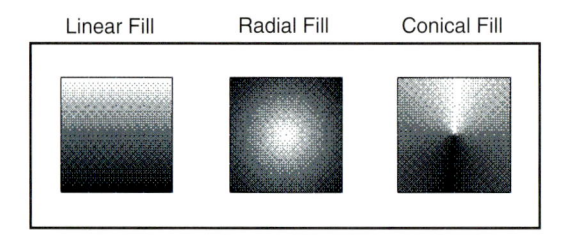

Figure 6.10
Linear fill, radial fill, and conical fill.

1. Select New from the File menu. Do not save changes if prompted.

Using Fountain Fills 95

2. With the Ellipse tool, draw a perfect circle in the center of the screen about 6 inches wide (use the Ctrl and Shift keys). Press the space bar to activate the Pick tool and select the circle.

3. Select Fountain Fill from the Fill tool fly-out menu. The Fountain Fill dialog box appears.

The shortcut key for Fountain Fill is F11. Use it.

4. The fountain fill defaults to a gradation from black to white. Click on OK to apply it to the circle (see fig. 6.11).

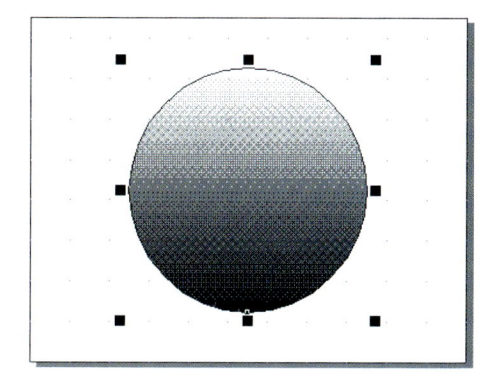

Figure 6.11
The circle now has a black-white fountain-fill.

With the current fill, the circle does not show any depth. You can correct that by editing the fill.

5. Press F11 for Fountain Fill.

6. Under Type, click on Radial. The fill is displayed in the preview box.

7. Under Center Offset, enter 20% for Vertical and Horizontal. This shifts the center of a radial fill. It enables you to make it appear as if light is hitting an object from a specific direction.

8. Under Options, increase Edge Pad to 15%. Edge Pad increases the amount of starting and ending color in the gradation.

A fountain fill actually fills the entire highlight box of an object, although it only is displayed within the object. Because the highlight box is sometimes larger than the object itself, the beginning and ending of the gradation can get cut off. You use Edge Pad to compensate for that.

9. Click on OK. The fountain fill makes the circle appear more spherical in shape.

10. Save as SPHERE1 (see fig. 6.12).

Chapter 6: Using Outlines and Fills

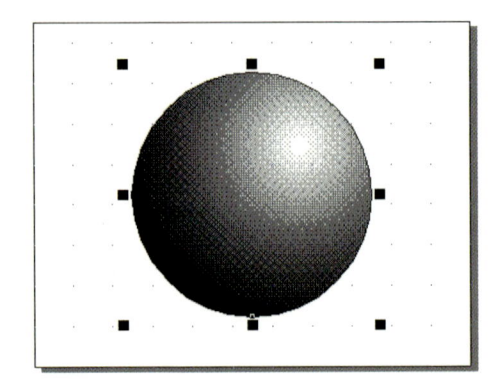

Figure 6.12
The circle appears more spherical.

Creating a Preset Fountain Fill

You created a custom color for Acme Nuts & Bolts. You can create a custom fountain fill as well.

1. Select New from the File menu.
2. Using the Rectangle tool, draw a 6-by-9-inch rectangle in the center of the page.
3. Press the space bar to select it.
4. Press F11 for the Fountain Fill dialog box.
5. Under Type, click on Linear.
6. Have the fill gradate from Black on the top to Acme Blue on the bottom.

When colors are picked in a linear fill, the From color is at the bottom and the To color is at the top.

7. Click on the From color button. Select Acme Blue.
8. Click on the To color button. Select Black.
9. To make it more intersting, you can angle the direction of the fill. In the Options section, change the angle from 90 degrees to 135 degrees. Click on OK; the fountain fill goes diagonally through the circle (see fig. 6.13).
10. At this point you will save the fill. With the object selected, press F11.
11. Click the cursor in the Presets window and type **Acme Blue**. Click on Save. The fill has been added to the preset fills that come included with the program.

Creating Custom Fountain Fills   97

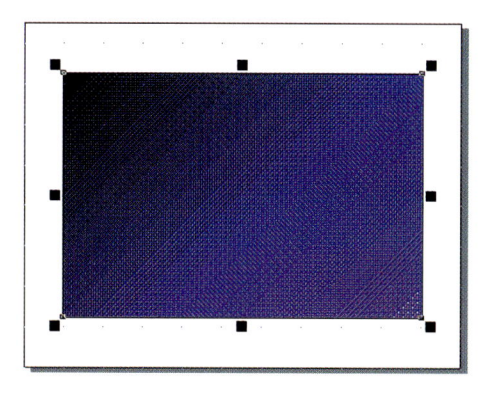

Figure 6.13
A diagonal fountain fill.

You might want to create a series of fountain fills based on a specific color (such as Acme Blue). You could have a radial, a linear on an angle, a straight linear, and so on. You would just name them accordingly. Then, when working on graphics for the Acme Co., you'd have quick access to a variety of fountain fills using their Acme Blue corporate color.

Creating Custom Fountain Fills

Generally you create fountain fills by picking the beginning and ending colors and letting the program choose the intermediate colors between them. You can create some interesting fills by making adjustments to those intermediate colors.

1. Select <u>N</u>ew from the <u>F</u>ile menu. If prompted, choose No to Save changes.

2. Using the Rectangle tool, draw a rectangle that covers the entire page (8 1/2 by 11 inches). Press the space bar to select the rectangle.

3. Press the F11 key to access the Fountain Fill dialog box. Click on the Options button. The Fountain Fill Options dialog box appears.

4. Click on the From button. Select Blue.

5. Click on the To button. Click on More. Scroll down the list until you see Sky Blue. Select it and click on OK. The preview box shows the fountain fill.

The intermediate colors are shades of blue that create a smooth blend between Blue and Sky Blue.

6. Click on Options again. Look at the color wheel displayed. A short, black line appears between the starting and ending colors of the fill, and the path of the line indicates the intermediate colors (see fig. 6.14).

98   Chapter 6: Using Outlines and Fills

Figure 6.14

Starting, ending, and intermediate colors are displayed in the color wheel.

7. In the Blend section, click on **R**ainbow. Now the black line has changed to a curve, and two directional arrow buttons appear.

8. Click on the counterclockwise arrow. The black path line now takes the indirect route around the wheel, passing through many different colors.

9. Click on OK in the Fountain Fill Color Options dialog box. From the Fountain Fill dialog box, click on OK.

10. As you can see in figure 6.15, the starting and ending colors of the fill are the same, but the intermediate colors are radically different.

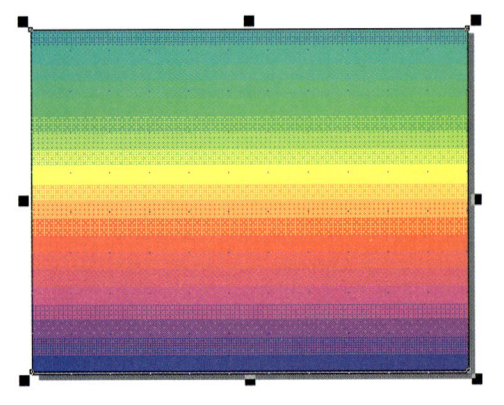

Figure 6.15

The rectangle has a rainbow fountain fill.

If you want specific control of the intermediate colors, use the **C**ustom Blend.

11. Press F11 to access the Fountain Fill dialog box. Click on the Options button. Click on **C**ustom Blend; the Fountain Fill Color Options dialog box displays the custom fill preview box (see fig. 6.16).

12. The Options dialog box now displays a horizontal preview window and a color palette below it.

13. On either end of the preview window is a black square. Click on the left square; an arrow marker appears. Click and drag the marker about one-third of the way right.

Creating Custom Fountain Fills 99

Figure 6.16
The custom fill preview box in the Fountain Fill Color Options dialog box.

As you move the marker to the right, the value in the position window increases. As you want to move the marker one-third of the way, the marker will be in the correct spot when the position value is 33%.

14. The marker indicates where along the fountain fill you want to add a color. You do so by clicking on the palette below. Click on red.

15. Click on the right square to bring up a marker arrow. Drag it one-third to the left (66% position).

16. In the palette below, click on yellow. Click on OK.

17. You now are back at the Fountain Fill dialog box. At this point you could edit the angle of the fill, or change it from linear to radial or conical. You also can save it as a preset fill. For now, click on OK (see fig. 6.17).

Figure 6.17
The rectangle has a custom fountain fill.

You now have a fill going from blue to red to yellow to sky blue.

To remove a color you've added in a custom blend, click on its marker arrow and press the Del key.

Chapter 6: Using Outlines and Fills

Using Bit-Map and Pattern Fills

CorelDRAW! comes with a set of two-color and full-color patterns that you can use to fill any object.

Two-Color Patterns

A two-color pattern fill is composed of repeating black and white bit-map images, to which you can add color.

1. Select New from the File menu. If prompted, choose No to Save changes.

2. Draw a perfect circle in the center of the page, about 8 inches in diameter. Press the space bar to select it.

A pattern can be used to fill an object of any shape. We will use a circle to illustrate that.

3. From the Fill tool fly-out, select the two-color fill (the checkerboard pattern).

4. Click on the preview window (it currently displays a pattern) to bring up the pattern selections shown in figure 6.18.

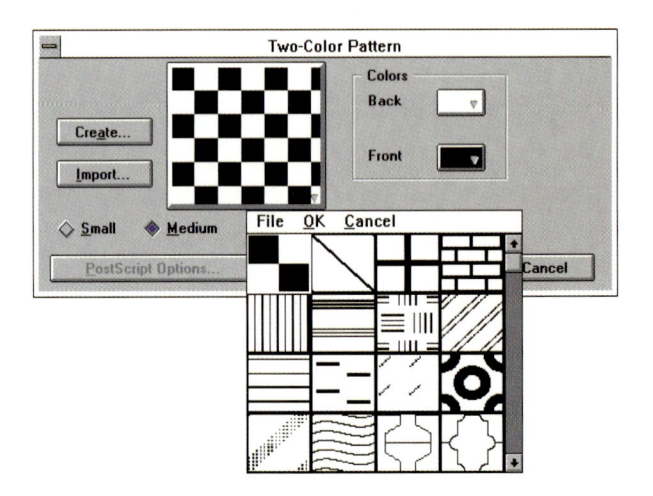

Figure 6.18
Pattern selections.

5. Double-click on the brick pattern. Click on OK.

6. The circle now is filled with a pattern of white bricks on a black background. To edit the pattern, select two-color pattern from the Fill tool.

7. Click on the Back color button, and click on more. Scroll down the list until you find Brick Red, then select it. Click on OK.

Using Bit-Map and Pattern Fills

8. Repeat this procedure for Front color and select Sand.

9. Click on the Tiling button to expand the dialog box.

A pattern fill is made up of tiles that are repeated over and over to create a pattern. A good example are floor tiles you might have in your kitchen. The tile might be 12 inches square with a geometric pattern. When the tiles are in place, they create a pattern over the floor.

Click on the Create button to view the selected tile. Notice that the tile is two bricks wide and four bricks high. To return, click on Cancel.

10. Under Tile Size, the default setting of medium is selected. As indicated, the height and width of a medium tile is 0.50 inches.

11. Click on Large. The values now are 1 inch for height and width. The resulting pattern will be two bricks wide and four bricks high for every square inch of the object.

The pattern size can be one of the three preset sizes, or you can enter whatever values you want. The height and width need not be the same. Equal values will make the tile a square, while unequal values will make it rectangular.

12. Click on OK (see fig. 6.19).

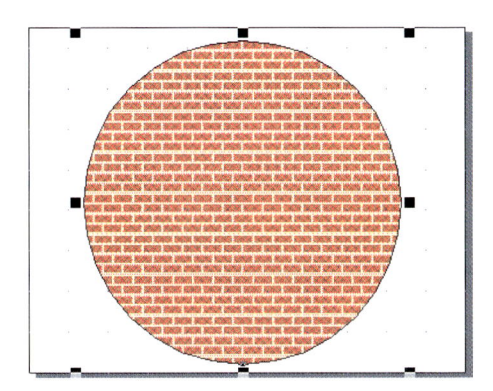

Figure 6.19
A brick pattern.

Creating a Pattern

You can use one of the supplied patterns for a fill, or you can create your own pattern.

1. Select two-color pattern from the Fill tool. Click on the Create button. The current tile is displayed.

Chapter 6: Using Outlines and Fills

2. Under Bitmap Size, click on 16 x 16. The current tile is cleared and the grid now is 16 by 16 boxes.

3. To create a pattern, click in a box to make it black, or click and drag the cursor to fill many boxes.

4. Fill all the boxes around the perimeter of the grid. Then fill the boxes to create two diagonal lines going from corner to corner (see fig. 6.20).

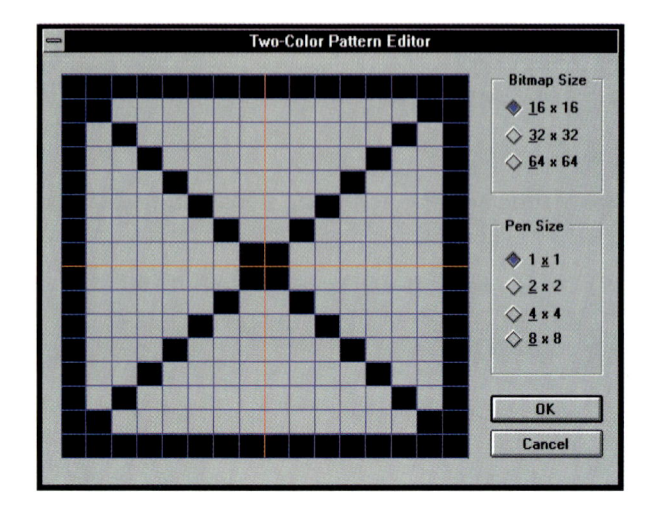

Figure 6.20
Settings in the Two-Color Pattern Editor dialog box.

If you color the wrong box, click on it using the secondary mouse button to erase it.

5. Click on OK when you're done creating the tile.

6. At this point you can edit the size of the tile you want or the color combination. Click on OK. The circle is filled with the new pattern using the same colors as the brick tile.

File and Row/Column Offset

Besides creating new pattern titles, you also can edit the way the patten tiles are aligned.

1. Select the circle with the Pick tool, and press the Del key to delete it.

2. Select the Rectangle tool and draw a 6-by-6-inch square. Press the space bar to select the square.

3. Select the two-color pattern from the Fill tool. Click on the preview window to bring up the tile selections.

4. Scroll down to the bottom of the tile selections. The last tile displayed should be the one you just created. Double-click on it.

5. For the colors, choose Blue for the Back, and Yellow for the Front. Select large for a 1-inch pattern. Click on OK (see fig. 6.21).

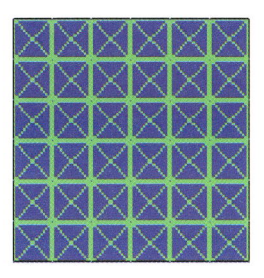

Figure 6.21
The beginning pattern.

6. Select two-color patterns from the Fill tool. Click on Tiling to expand the dialog box.

7. In the First Tile Offset section, click on the up arrow for the X value, and watch the preview window. The tile pattern shifts to the right. Click on the arrow until you reach 20%.

8. Click on the up arrow for the Y value until you reach 40%. Notice how the pattern in the preview window moves down. Click on OK (see fig. 6.22).

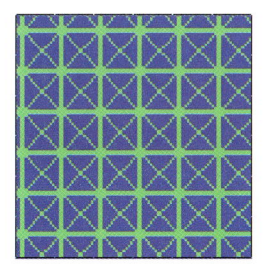

Figure 6.22
The tile pattern has shifted down and to the right.

The First Tile Offset allows you to shift the enter tile pattern, either vertically or horizontally. You might want to adjust the tile offset so that the fill pattern is not so symmetrical.

Row/Column Offset

You also can shift tiles either by row or columns.

1. Select the two-color pattern from the Fill tool. Click on Tiling to expand the dialog box.

2. In the Row/Column Offset section, select Row.

3. Click on the up arrow for % of Tile Side to change the value to 50%. Watch the preview box as you do so. Click on OK (see fig. 6.23).

104 Chapter 6: Using Outlines and Fills

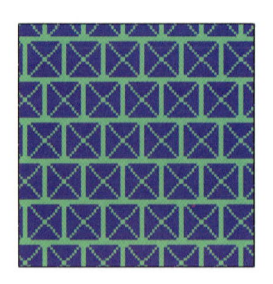

Figure 6.23
The rows of the pattern are offset by 50 percent.

> Rows refer to the lines of tiles that run horizontally, while columns are the tiles that run vertically.

Using a Full-Color Pattern

CorelDRAW! also supplies a set of full-color pattern fills comprised of repeating vector images.

1. Make sure that the square is the selected object, and choose full-color pattern (the double-sided arrow) from the Fill tool.

2. From the dialog box, click on the Lo**a**d button. A menu comes up with the available patterns listed by name. If you knew which pattern you wanted, you would just click on it. Click on the Cancel button.

3. Click on the preview window. A menu drops down showing you the pattern in full color.

4. Double-click on the tile of concentric red squares to select it.

5. Click on the Tiling buttons. The options available are the same as with the two-color fill, except you cannot edit the tile itself.

6. Click on Large, and click on OK (see fig. 6.24).

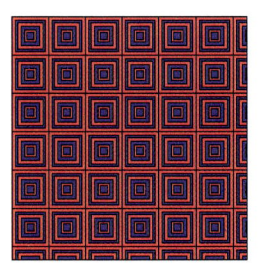

Figure 6.24
The full-color pattern fill.

Filling with Bit-Map Textures

Bit-map textures are fill patterns that resemble marble, quartz, water, sand, and many other natural and man-made substances. There are over 100 such textures included in CorelDRAW!, and each can be changed to almost an infinite number of variations.

Using Bit-Map and Pattern Fills 105

1. Select New from the File menu. Click No to Save changes if prompted.

2. A bit-map texture can be used to fill any object. For this example, select the Rectangle tool and draw a 3-by-6-inch rectangle in the center of the page. Press the space bar to select it.

3. From the Fill tool, select texture fills. The Texture Fill dialog box appears, as shown in figure 6.25.

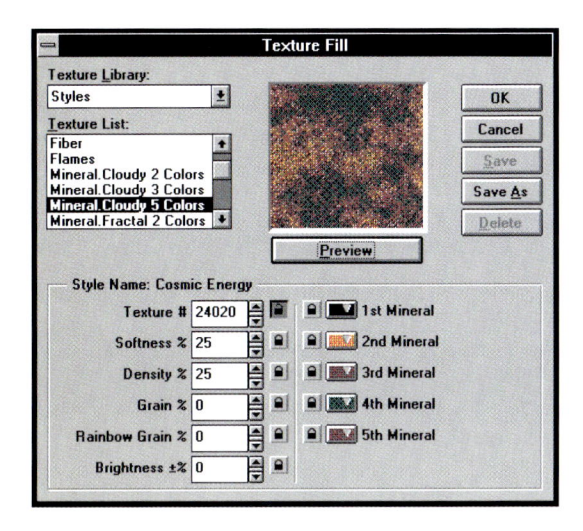

Figure 6.25

The Texture Fill dialog box.

4. From the Texture Library window, select Styles.

5. From the Texture List, select Mineral Cloudy 5 Colors.

6. The selected texture is displayed in the preview window.

Each texture has over 32,000 variations to choose from. Each variation has a number that is displayed in the Texture # window.

7. The bottom section of the dialog box lists a number of attributes that can be adjusted. Each has a small padlock icon next to it. Set all to the locked position except for Texture #. If one is not locked, click on the icon to lock it.

8. Click on the Preview button. The image in the window changes as well as the Texture #. Clicking on the Preview button will randomly pick variations of the unlocked attributes.

9. Click on all the padlock icons that are now locked, so that all are in the unlocked position.

10. Click on the Preview button. With the attributes unlocked, the program makes random selections for all the attributes of the texture. Click on Preview a number of times and watch the changes.

Chapter 6: Using Outlines and Fills

11. When you see a color pattern you like, click the locks on all the color buttons.

*You can click each color button and individually select the color for that portion of the texture. After you make a change, click on the **P**review button to view it.*

12. In the case of this texture, there are five colors that can be edited, as well as the Texture # and four attributes. The four attributes are:

    Softness. This affects the number and size of the shapes that make up the texture. A higher value yields fewer and larger shapes.

    Density. This affects the amount of chaos in the texture pattern. A higher value of density yields larger amount of chaos.

    Grain. This affects the intensity of the colors. A higher value increases the intensity.

    Rainbow Grain. This also affects the intensity of the colors, and shifts their values as well, creating a rainbow effect. A higher value yields a greater shift in color. This results in the rainbow effect.

Not all attributes are editable for all textures. When you choose one from the library, only those attributes that can be changed will be presented.

*The best way to understand what these changes mean is to see them on the screen. Lock all the functions first, then concentrate on one at a time. Change the color on one of the color buttons and press **P**review while you watch the window. For the attributes, enter extreme values (like 0, then 50, then 100), press the **P**review button, and watch what happens.*

13. If you arrive at a texture you really like, click on the Save **A**s button, type in a new name for it, and click on OK.

14. To apply the texture to the selected object, click on OK from the main dialog box (see fig. 6.26).

Figure 6.26
A texture fill.

Using PostScript Textures

A selection of PostScript textures are available for filling objects. These will not appear on-screen, but are indicated by a pattern of the letters PS.

1. Select the object you wish to fill with a PostScript texture.
2. From the Fill tool, select the PostScript icon (PS).
3. From the menu presented, click on the name of the texture you want.
4. You then adjust the various attributes that are presented.

Appendix C in the CorelDRAW! 4.0 manual lists all the available PostScript textures, as well as examples of various settings of the PostScript attributes.

Setting Defaults

CorelDRAW! enables you to preset the default outline and fill of objects before you draw them.

1. From the File menu, select New. If prompted, click on No to Save changes.
2. From the Outline Pen tool, select the pen tool. Because there are no objects in the drawing, no object is selected. Instead of the Pen tool dialog box, the box in figure 6.27 appears.

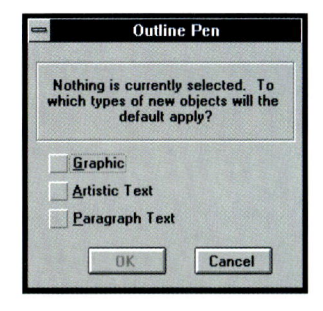

Figure 6.27
The Outline Pen dialog box.

3. Click on the Graphic box to check it. Click on OK.
4. The Outline Pen dialog box appears. Adjust the pen width to 8 points, leave all other settings the same, and click on OK.
5. From the Fill tool, select fountain fill. Again you are prompted to choose the type of object you want the fill to apply to. Click on the Graphic box and click on OK.
6. Click on the From button and select Blue. Select Radial Fill and click on OK.

108 Chapter 6: Using Outlines and Fills

7. Select the Ellipse tool and draw a circle about 3 inches in diameter to the left of center page.

8. Select the Rectangle tool and draw a 3-inch square to the right of center page (see fig. 6.28).

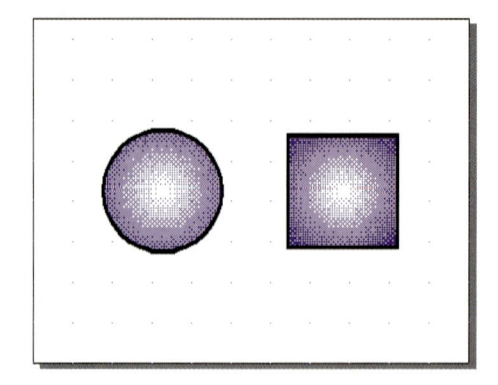

Figure 6.28
Both objects share the same outline and fill attributes.

Both objects have an 8-point outline and a radial fountain fill.

These settings will remain as defaults until you choose to change them.

You can change any attribute of the outline or fill and apply it as a default setting. Uniform fills, patterns, and textures can be used as well.

Using the Fill Roll-Up Menu

As with many of the CorelDRAW! commands, a roll-up menu is available. Selecting the roll-up icon in the Fill tool fly-out menu brings up the Fill roll-up menu, as shown in figure 6.29.

Figure 6.29
The Fill roll-up menu.

Fountain Fills

The Fill roll-up menu enables you to easily apply fountain fills to objects.

1. Choose New from the File menu.

Using the Fill Roll-Up Menu   109

2. Select the Ellipse tool and draw a 6-inch circle on the right side of the page.

The circle will be drawn with the radial fill you set as the default in the last section. You can leave it alone or reset the default to whatever you want. The standard is No Fill and a Hairline Outline. For now, click on the X to the left of the on-screen palette for No Fill in the ellipse.

3. From the Fill tool, click on the Fill roll-up icon.
4. In the Fill roll-up menu, click on the box for conical fill. The preview window shows you what it will look like.
5. The colors are the default black and white. Click on the black box to bring up the palette, and select Red. Click on the white box, and select Yellow.
6. Click on apply. The fountain fill is applied to the ellipse (see fig. 6.30).

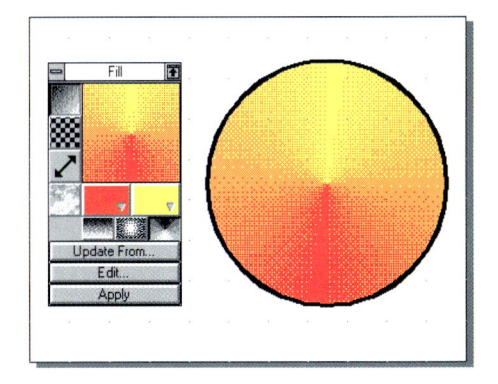

Figure 6.30
Fountain fill applied to the ellipse.

The Fill roll-up menu gives you quick access to basic tools for editing fountain fills. If more extensive control is needed, click on the Edit button to bring up the regular Fountain Fill dialog box.

Two-Color Patterns

Two-color patterns also are easy to access from the Fill roll-up menu.

1. With the circle still selected, click on two-color pattern in the roll-up menu.
2. Click on the preview window to bring up the patterns available.
3. Scroll down to the star pattern and double-click on it.

Chapter 6: Using Outlines and Fills

4. The fill pattern will be white stars on a blue field. Click on the white box and select Blue. Click on the black box and select White. The new pattern is displayed in the window.

5. Click on Apply (see fig. 6.31).

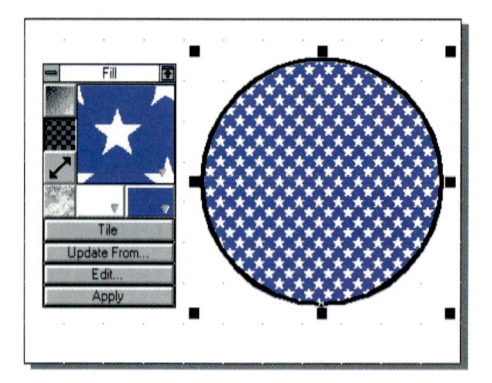

Figure 6.31
The circle now has a two-color Pattern fill.

As with the fountain fill, clicking on Edit will bring up the dialog box for two-color pattern. The Edit button will always bring up the dialog box for whatever type of fill is selected.

Full-Color Pattern

The full-color pattern option is available from the Fill roll-up menu as well.

1. Click on full-color pattern from the roll-up menu.

2. Click on the preview window to bring up the patterns available.

3. Scroll down to the Brick pattern and double-click on it. It appears in the preview window.

4. Click on Apply.

5. Click on the Edit button. From the dialog box, select Large Tile Size and click on OK.

6. Click on Apply, and the Brick pattern is applied to the circle (see fig. 6.32).

Bit-Map Texture Fills

You can select a bit-map texture fill directly fom the Fill roll-up menu.

1. From the roll-up menu, select texture fill.

2. Click on the drop-down menu for the libraries, and select Styles.

Using the Fill Roll-Up Menu 111

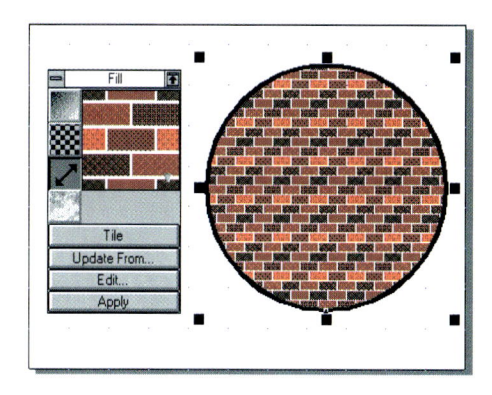

Figure 6.32
A full-color pattern Fill.

To choose a texture, you can click on the drop-down menu and select a texture by name. The roll-up menu enables you to display a selection of textures at once.

3. Click on the preview box to display the texture styles available, as shown in figure 6.33.

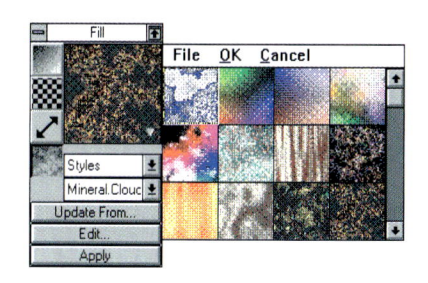

Figure 6.33
Available texture styles.

4. Choose one of the textures displayed by double-clicking on it, or scroll down to see what other textures are available in the library.
5. At this point you can click on the Edit button to bring up the dialog box and make any subtle changes you want to the texture.
6. When done with the changes, click on OK. From the roll-up menu, click on Apply (see fig. 6.34).

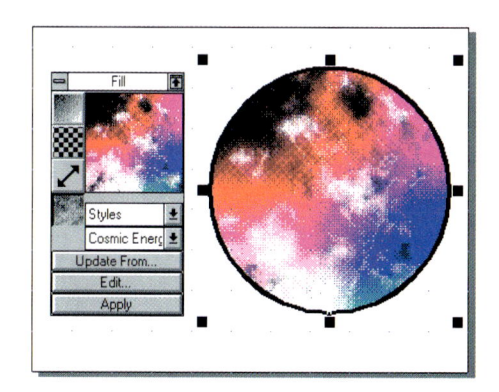

Figure 6.34
The selected texture fill is applied.

Chapter 6: Using Outlines and Fills

Copying Styles

Often you'll add an object to a drawing and would like it to have the same outline and fill characteristics as an object drawn earlier. CorelDRAW! enables you to quickly copy attributes from one object to another.

1. Select New from the File menu.

2. Select the Artistic text tool, and enter the following text in the top center of the page: **Master Text Style**. Click on the Pick tool to leave text mode and select the text string.

3. Press Ctrl+T to access the Text dialog box. Edit the text as follows:

   Typeface: SwitzerlandBlack
   Alignment: Center
   Size: 72 Points
   Style: Normal

   Click on OK.

4. With the text string selected, click on Yellow in the color palette to fill the text. Click on Blue with the secondary mouse button to make the outline blue.

5. Select the Pen tool, and click on the 2-point width icon (see fig. 6.35).

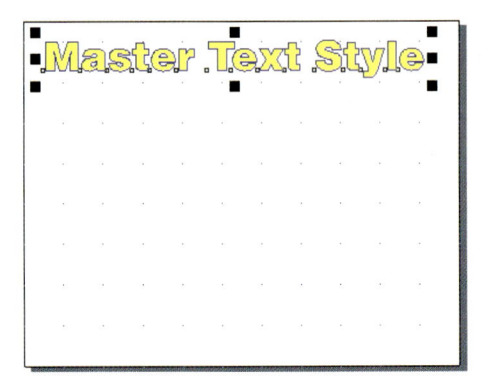

Figure 6.35
The master text string.

6. Using the Artistic text tool, add the following text at the bottom of the page: **Additional Text Added**.

7. You now can copy any and all attributes of the master text to the added text. With the added text selected, click on Copy Attributes From in the Edit menu. The Copy Attributes dialog box appears, as shown in figure 6.36.

8. Click on the boxes for Outline Pen, Outline Color, and Fill to check. Click on OK.

Copying Styles   113

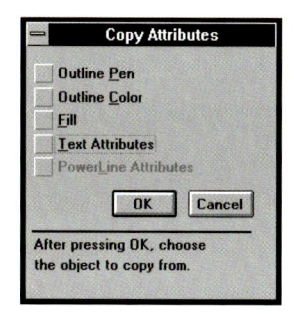

Figure 6.36
The Copy Attributes dialog box.

*In this instance the **T**ext Attributes are not copied. You want the new type to be of smaller size and weight, but the same color style. The Text Attributes setting will copy all attributes from the original, including any changes to character, word, or line spacing.*

9. The From arrow appears. Place it on the master text and click once. The outline and fill attributes are copied to the added text (see fig. 6.37).

Figure 6.37
The attributes of the master text are copied.

The attributes copied over to the new text correctly, but the text doesn't look quite right. That's because the 2-point outline width is too much, and the typeface is too small.

10. With the added text selected, click on the Pen tool and select Hairline width outline.

11. Press Ctrl+T for the Text dialog box. Change the typeface to Switzerland and the style to Bold. Click on OK (see fig. 6.38).

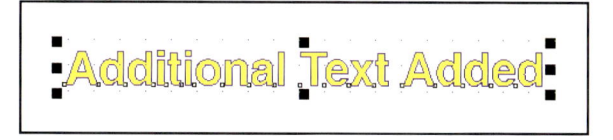

Figure 6.38
Editing the attributes of the text makes it cleaner-looking and easier to read.

Attributes can be copied between different types of objects (except text attributes). For instance, a texture fill in a rectangle can be copied to a text string. Attributes also can be copied to a group of selected objects from one original object.

114 Chapter 6: Using Outlines and Fills

Practical Uses

Now you can apply some of these features to the drawing you created in the last chapter.

1. From the File menu, select Open. Click on No to save changes if prompted.

2. Scroll down to EXAMPLE1 and double-click on it to open.

3. Click on the text string to select it. Fill it in Yellow from the on-screen palette.

4. Click on the skewed type and color it Deep Navy Blue.

5. Using the Rectangle tool, draw a 5-by-11-inch rectangle around the two text objects (see fig. 6.39).

Figure 6.39
Adding a rectangle to the text objects.

The rectangle may have a heavy outline and a radial fill if you did not reset the defaults. To reset, click on the Pick tool in an empty part of the screen so that no object is selected. From the Pen tool, click on Hairline width. With the Graphic box checked, click on OK. From the Fill tool, click on the X for No Fill. With the Graphic box checked, click on OK. Delete the rectangle and draw it again.

6. Press the space bar to select the rectangle. Use the arrow keys to nudge it if it is not centered around the text strings.

7. From the Fill tool, select fountain fill.

8. Select a linear fill. Change the From color to Deep Navy Blue. Change the To color to Blue. Adjust the angle to 120 degrees. Click on OK.

9. The rectangle is filled, but it covers the text. From the Arrange menu, click on Order. The Order fly-out menu appears. Click on To Back (see fig. 6.40).

Figure 6.40
The rectangle moves behind the text objects.

10. The rectangle moves behind the text objects. Using simple color and fountain fill changes makes the drawing look much more realistic.
11. Save the file as EXAMPLE2.

Chapter 7
Arranging and Aligning Objects

As your drawings become more complex, you will appreciate the powerful organization features in CorelDRAW!. They can help you align objects with exact precision, integrate a group of objects to act as one, or adjust the order in which they appear. To demonstrate these features, you will create a monthly calendar that you can easily change from month to month.

Aligning Objects

Before you start, you need to change the page layout from landscape to portrait.

1. Select Page Setup from the Layout menu.
2. Check the Portrait box and then click on OK.
3. For the title of the graphic, use your own name or the name of your company. For this example, use CorelDRAW! Now! Calendar. Use the Artistic Text tool to enter this type anywhere on the page. Click on the Pick tool when done.
4. Press Ctrl+T to edit the text as follows:

   Font: Switzerland
   Alignment: Center
   Size: 40 Point
   Style: Bold Italic

5. One way to align an object is by its relationship to the page. Select Align from the Arrange menu. The Align dialog box appears, as shown in figure 7.1.

In this chapter you will learn about these operations:

- Aligning objects
- Aligning objects to the grid
- Grouping objects
- Combining objects
- Creating window masks
- Welding objects
- Rearranging objects
- Working with layers

Chapter 7: Arranging and Aligning Objects

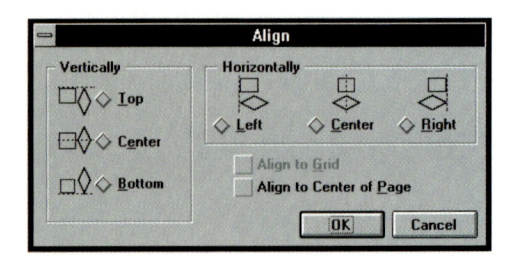

Figure 7.1
The Align dialog box.

TIP

The shortcut to Page Setup is to double-click anywhere along the page border.

NOTE

You will need to change the size of the text if it is longer than the width of the page.

6. Check the box for Align to Center of Page and click on OK.

7. Click on the text with the Pick tool, and with the Ctrl key pressed, move the text up until it is 1 inch from the top of the page (see fig. 7.2).

Figure 7.2
The calendar title.

8. Another way to align an object is by its relationship to the grid. Select Snap To from the Layout menu, and click on Grid from the fly-out menu. In Snap To mode, newly drawn objects (or current objects that are moved) align to the nearest vertical and horizontal grid lines.

NOTE

If you recall, during setup we set the grid at eight units per inch. While you cannot see it on the screen, there is a 1/8-inch grid pattern. You can alter the settings as often as needed, as you will see shortly.

Aligning to Guidelines 119

9. Use the Rectangle tool to draw a rectangle 1 1/2 inches high and 7 inches wide, anywhere on the page.

Notice that when you drew the rectangle, it jumped in size as you moved the cursor. Because Snap to Grid is activated, the rectangle jumped from grid point to grid point.

10. Press the space bar to select the rectangle. Click and drag it so that it is centered horizontally (3/4 inch from either edge of the page), with the bottom on the 7 1/2-inch line (see fig. 7.3).

Figure 7.3

The rectangle is centered and bottom-aligned on the 7 1/2 inch line.

Aligning to Guidelines

Another way you can align objects is by using guidelines. *Guidelines* are non-printing lines you can put in a drawing to help align objects.

1. Place the cursor on the ruler on the left side of the screen. Click and drag the cursor into the screen area, dragging a vertical guideline with it. Position the guideline 3/4 inch from the left side of the page. Repeat this process to place another guideline 3/4 inch from the right side of the page.

The guidelines should now be aligned with the sides of the rectangle you drew earlier.

For horizontal guidelines, click and drag from the top ruler. There is no limit to the number of guidelines you can use.

2. From the top ruler, drag down two horizontal guidelines, aligning one with the top of the rectangle and one with the bottom (see fig. 7.4).

Chapter 7: Arranging and Aligning Objects

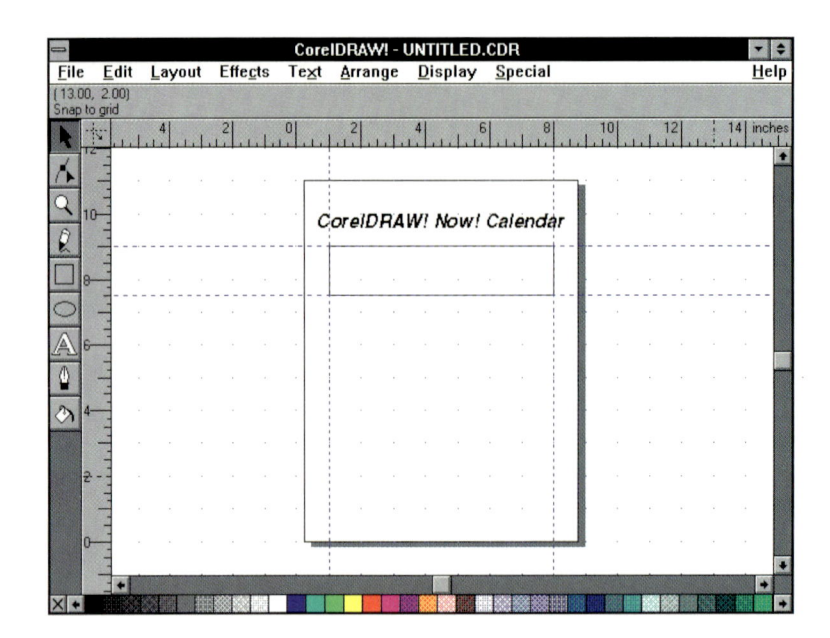

Figure 7.4
Vertical and horizontal guidelines help to align the object on the page.

*For more precise placement of guidelines, select G**u**idelines Setup from the **L**ayout menu, or drag a guideline to the approximate location and double-click on it with the Pick tool to bring up the Guidelines Setup dialog box. Enter the desired value in the Rule Position box, and click on Move.*

3. The rectangle will contain the current month and year. Instead of entering new type, copy the headline and edit it. Click on the title and drag it down while pressing the Ctrl key. Press the right mouse button to make a copy, and position it in the top center of the rectangle.

4. Press Ctrl+T to edit text. Change the type to read August 1993, and change the style to Bold. Click on OK.

5. Use the Pick tool to draw a highlight box around the rectangle to select it and the text it contains. The status bar displays two objects selected.

6. From the **A**rrange menu, select **A**lign (or press Ctrl+A). In the Vertical section, check the center box and click on OK.

7. The type now is centered in the rectangle, but the rectangle has moved out of position. You can fix that, but first lock the two objects together by grouping them.

Grouping Objects

Within a drawing you might have a group of objects that you want to keep together as one unit. You can do this by *grouping* them.

Grouping Objects   121

1. The rectangle and text should still be selected. If not, select them now.

2. From the Arrange menu, select Group. The text and rectangle are now grouped together. The status bar displays them as a group of two objects.

When objects are grouped, any editing changes you make are applied to all objects of the group. If you change the outline from hairline black to 2-point blue, for example, all outlines in the group will change.

When you want to select objects that are joined as a group, you need not use the highlight box technique. Just click on any object in the group with the Pick tool, and the entire group is selected.

3. With the Pick tool, move the rectangle down so that it again aligns with the guidelines.

The next elements you will add to the calendar are the days of the week.

1. To make the day easier to see, select the Zoom In tool and draw a highlight box, about 3 inches square, around the bottom left corner of the rectangle.

2. With the Rectangle tool, draw a rectangle 1 inch wide and 1/2 inch high, touching the bottom left corner of the rectangle containing the month and year.

3. Use the Artistic Text tool to type **Sunday** in this new rectangle. Click on the Pick tool when done.

4. From the Text menu, select Text Roll-Up. From the roll-up menu, select Switzerland Condensed, centered, normal, 15 point (see fig. 7.5). Click on the Apply button. Close the Text Roll-up.

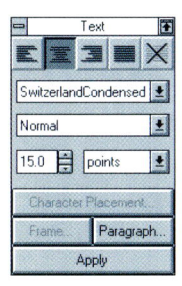

Figure 7.5

The Text roll-up menu, showing the specifications for the day text.

5. Use the Pick tool to select Sunday and the rectangle around it. From the Arrange menu, click on Align. Check Center in the Vertical section, and click on OK.

Chapter 7: Arranging and Aligning Objects

6. With both objects still selected, select **G**roup from the **A**rrange menu.

7. With the Pick tool, click and drag this object group to the right. Press the right mouse button to make a copy, and position the copy so that it touches the original directly to the right.

8. With the Zoom tool, click on the full page view.

9. The copy you made and moved is still selected. You can repeat the copy and move process five more times for the other days of the week, but there is a shortcut. Press Ctrl+R to repeat the last command. Do this four more times so that there is a box for each day of the week (see fig. 7.6).

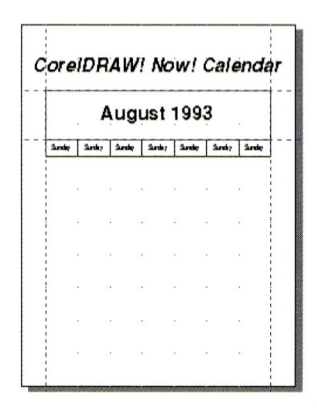

Figure 7.6
The calendar, showing seven Sundays.

Editing Objects within a Group

The next step to completing your calendar is to change all those Sundays to the correct days of the week.

1. With the Pick tool, click on the second Sunday in the row to select it. Press Ctrl+T to edit the text. Nothing happens! That's because the text is grouped with the rectangle. You can ungroup the group and then select the text, but that's a lot of extra work, so why group them in the first place?

   The solution is: CorelDRAW! lets you cheat, sort of.

2. Hold down the Ctrl key and click on the second Sunday in the row. The word is highlighted, but with round control marks instead of square. This is called *selecting a Child*, as noted in the status bar.

   Once a Child is selected, you can apply changes to it as you would any other object (stretching, skewing, rotating, and so on).

3. Press Ctrl+T and the Text dialog box appears. Change the text to Monday and click on OK.

4. Repeat this process with the five remaining text objects to add the proper days of the week (see fig. 7.7).

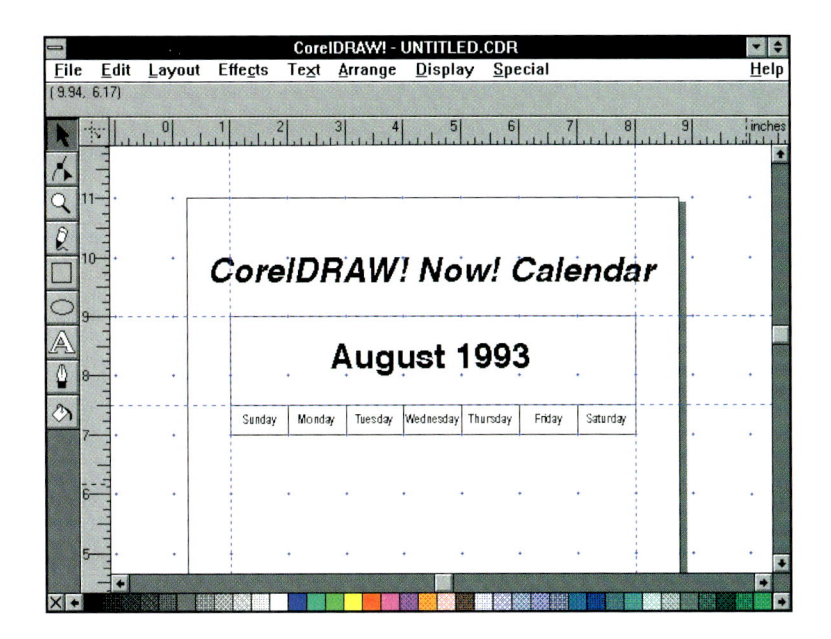

Figure 7.7
The calendar with the correct day names entered.

Changing Grid Origin

In the next step you will add the dates of the month as 1-inch squares. Note that in full page view, the grid appears in a 1-inch pattern, but does not align with the objects on the page. You could shift everything over to the right, but then it would print off-center. Instead, alter the grid origin.

1. The grid origin point (0,0 inches) currently is the bottom left corner of the page.
2. From the Layout menu, select Grid Setup.
3. In the Grid Origin section, change the horizontal value to 0.25. Click on OK. Now the grid points align with the graphic.

Now you can add the dates of the month.

1. Draw a 1-inch square with the Rectangle tool. Move it so it is directly below and touching the Sunday box.
2. With the Text tool, type **1** in the upper right corner of the square.
3. Edit the text (Ctrl+T) to Switzerland, right align, normal style, 18 points.
4. Select the square and the text object, and choose Group from the Arrange menu to group them.

Chapter 7: Arranging and Aligning Objects

Adjusting the Grid Size

Before you copy the boxes for the rest of the month, you need to change the grid pattern.

1. Select Grid Setup from the Layout menu.

2. In the Grid Frequency section, change the horizontal and vertical values to 1 per inch. Click on OK.

3. Select the square with the first date of the month with the Pick tool.

4. Move it to the right while pressing the right mouse button. Because you changed the grid to a 1-inch frequency, it jumps right into position when you move it.

5. As before, you can use Ctrl+R five times to copy the square for the rest of the week (see fig. 7.8).

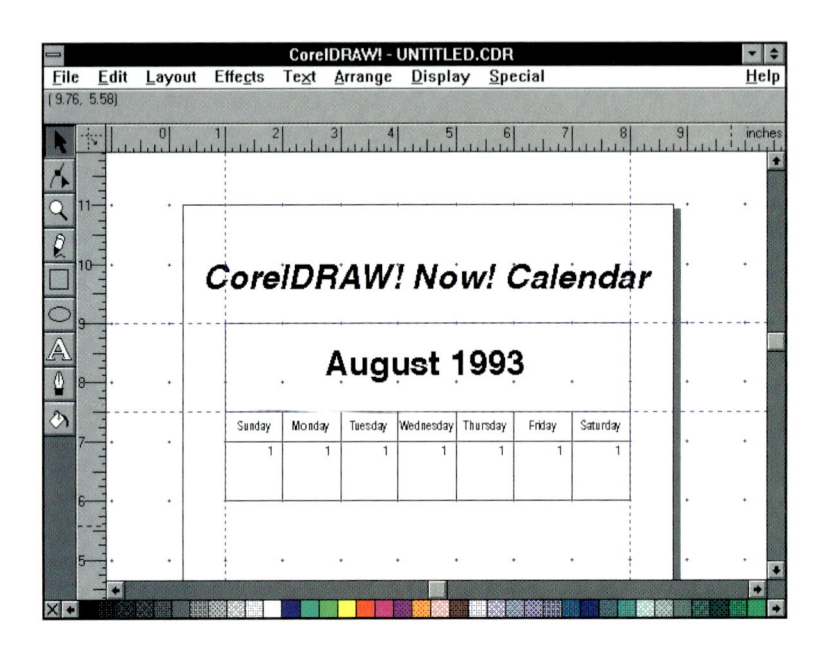

Figure 7.8
Seven date squares, all numbered 1.

6. With the Pick tool, draw a highlight box around the seven date squares. Be careful not to surround the days of the week, or they will be selected too.

To select an object with a highlight box, the box must completely surround the object.

If done correctly, the status box will display 7 objects selected.

7. Drag the selected group down 1 inch while pressing the right mouse button. Press Ctrl+R three times to repeat the command and create five rows of squares.

Changing the Order of Objects

8. Now you need to edit the 1 in each square so that the dates are correct. Press the Ctrl key and click on the number (remember, we grouped the number and the square, so you must press Ctrl to make it a Child). Press Ctrl+T and change it to the proper number. Repeat the process until you have 31 dates (see fig. 7.9).

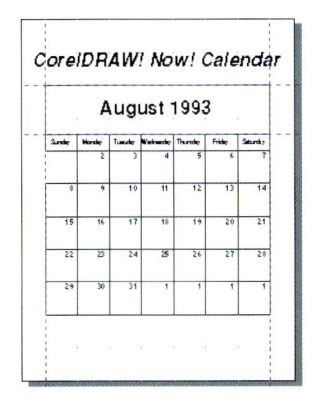

Figure 7.9
The calendar with correct dates.

Here's a shortcut: Select the number with the Ctrl key pressed, then click on the Text tool. A text cursor appears, allowing you to edit the text on-screen. Click on the Pick tool to leave Text Mode.

Now you have to remove the 1 from the four extra squares.

1. Click on the first 1 with the Pick tool to select it. From the Arrange menu, select Ungroup.
2. Click the mouse in an empty area of the screen to unselect the objects. Now, click on the number 1 you just ungrouped. It is selected as a single object.
3. Press the Del key to remove it.
4. Repeat this process with the remaining three squares.

Changing the Order of Objects

The next step in creating your calendar is to fill the Sunday boxes with a gray screen.

1. With the Pick tool, select one of the empty squares at the bottom of the page.
2. Click and drag it off the page while pressing the right mouse button.

An object moved off the page will not print, but will be saved with the file and thus be available for future use.

Chapter 7: Arranging and Aligning Objects

3. Click on 10% Black in the on-screen palette. You will use this gray square as a marker to indicate days you are closed for business.

4. Click and drag the gray square while pressing the right mouse button, and position it on the first day of the month.

5. From the Arrange menu, select Order. The Order fly-out menu appears (see fig. 7.10), enabling you to change the stacking order of objects.

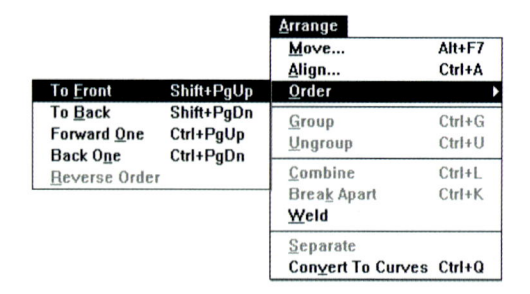

Figure 7.10

The Order fly-out menu.

6. Click on To Back. The gray square moves to the back of the stack, so now the date is visible in front of it (see fig. 7.11).

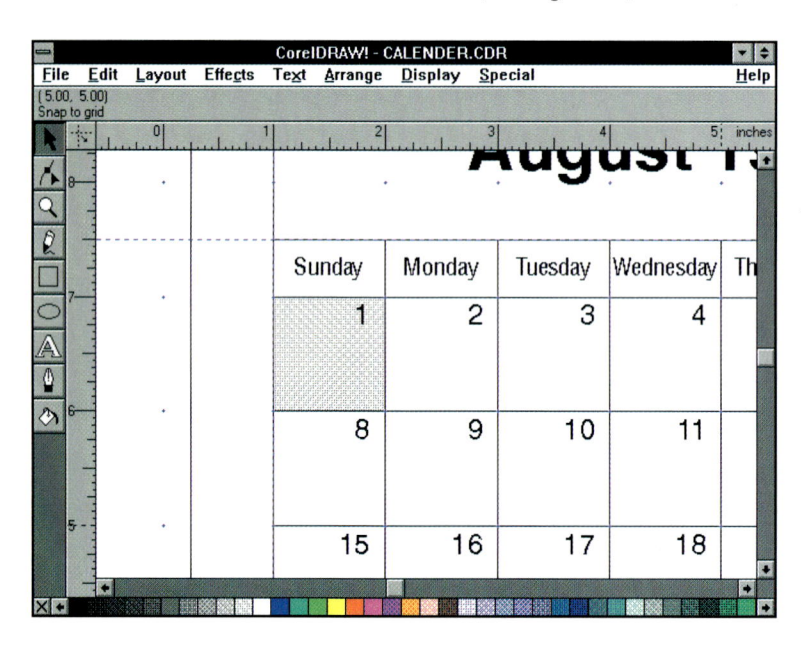

Figure 7.11

The date appears in front of the screen.

7. Click and drag the gray square down while holding the right mouse button, and position it on the date directly below. Press Ctrl+R three times so that all the Sundays are shaded.

8. Save the file (Ctrl+S) as CALENDAR.

What about next month? First, select the month and edit it. Then, use the Pick tool to shift the days around. This is a great example of changing the grid frequency to suit your needs. The days pop right into position, so it won't take but a minute to change the calendar each month.

Combining Objects

Combining objects is similar to grouping them. The difference is that when you combine objects, they become a single object. Text, ellipses, and rectangles are automatically converted to curves when combined. There are a few reasons you might want to combine objects in a drawing:

- To conserve memory
- To create a window mask
- To join two lines or curves together

Conserving Memory

As your graphics become more complex, you can have hundreds of objects in the file. This can eat up a lot of memory and slow down the redraw speed. If many objects share the same attributes (fill color, outline color, and width, for example), they can be combined.

1. Select New from the File menu (or use Ctrl+N).
2. Double-click on the page border to access Page Setup. Click on Landscape and then on OK.
3. From the Layout menu, select Grid Setup. Adjust the grid frequencies to 8 per inch. The Snap to Grid box should be checked. Click on OK.
4. Use the Rectangle tool to draw a rectangle 1/2 inch wide and 8 1/2 inches high, on the left edge of the page.
5. Press the space bar to select the rectangle.
6. Press the F11 key to access Fountain Fill. The default Linear fill, black to white, is fine for this example. Click on OK.
7. Click and drag the rectangle to the right while holding down the Ctrl key and the right mouse button. Position the copy 1/8 inch to the right and release the mouse button.
8. Press Ctrl+R to repeat this command. Keep pressing Ctrl+R until the rectangles fill the page (see fig. 7.12).
9. Save the file (Ctrl+S) as RECT1.

128 Chapter 7: Arranging and Aligning Objects

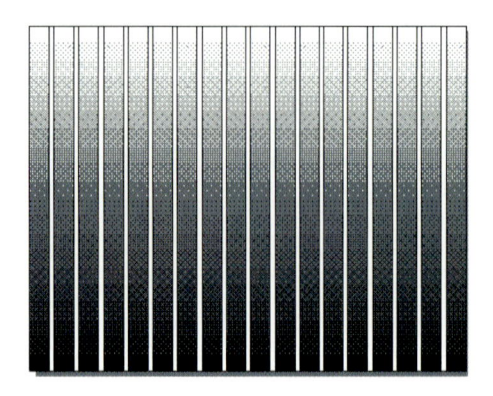

Figure 7.12
The rectangles fill the page.

10. Use the Pick tool to select all the rectangles by drawing a highlight box around them. The status bar shows 18 objects selected.

*From the **E**dit menu, click on Select **A**ll. As the name suggests, this selects all the objects in the drawing.*

11. From the **A**rrange menu, click on **C**ombine (or use the keyboard shortcut, Ctrl+L). Nothing changes visually, but the status bar shows 1 curve.

12. Save as RECT2.

13. Switch to the Windows File Manager and compare the size of the files. RECT1.CDR is 14,848 bytes, and RECT2.CDR is 12,246 bytes. This is a difference of about 18 percent.

Remember, you combined only 18 objects in a rather small file. If it were 180 objects in a 500,000-byte file, the memory savings could be considerable.

Combining Objects that Overlap

When two overlapping objects are combined, the overlap area becomes transparent. This has some interesting and practical applications.

1. RECT2 should currently be open. If it isn't, open it (Ctrl+O).

2. Use the Ellipse tool to draw a circle in the center of the page (hold down Ctrl+Shift), about 7 inches in diameter. Press the space bar to select it.

3. Hold down the Shift key and click on one of the rectangles (RECT2 had all the rectangles combined as one object). Both objects now are selected.

4. From the **A**rrange menu, click on **C**ombine (or use Ctrl+L). The part of the circle that overlapped the rectangle is now transparent, and

Combining Objects   129

the spaces between the rectangles have taken on the fountain fill (see fig. 7.13).

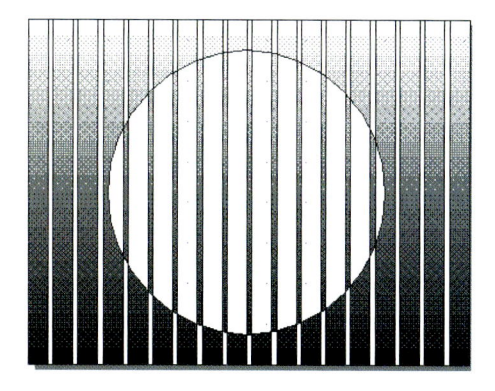

Figure 7.13
The circle is combined with the rectangles.

5. Save the file as RECT3.

Breaking Apart an Object

You can use the Break Apart command to return a combined object to a collection of single objects. You can break apart any object that is made up of subobjects.

1. Select New from the File menu (or press Ctrl+N).

2. Use the Text tool to type **8** in the center of the page. Click on the Pick tool to select the text.

3. From the Text menu, open the Text Roll-up and change the point size to 400. Click on Apply. Close the roll-up.

4. Click on Yellow in the on-screen palette to fill it. Click on Black with the right mouse button to outline it in black.

5. From the Arrange menu, select Convert to Curves (Ctrl+Q).

As the number 8, the text object carried specific shape attributes. Once converted to a curve, it becomes the result of three combined objects: the two ellipses and the outside shape of the number.

When an object is broken apart, the individual objects do not revert to their original forms (rectangle, ellipse, or text). They still are curves and retain the fill and outline of the combined object.

6. From the Arrange menu, select Break Apart.

7. The transparent sections have filled yellow and now are separate objects.

Chapter 7: Arranging and Aligning Objects

8. Click in the empty area of the screen to unselect the objects, or press the Esc. key. Now click in the center of one of the circles, hold the shift key, and click on the other. Click and drag them to the left about 3 inches (see fig. 7.14).

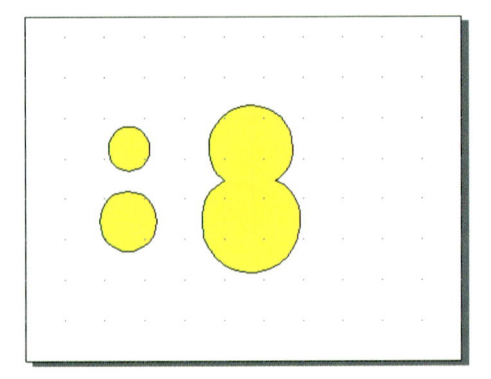

Figure 7.14
The result of breaking apart an object.

Creating Window Masks

If one object is entirely inside another, you can create a transparent window, called a *mask*. In this exercise, you will create one and combine it with the calendar graphic.

1. Select New from the File menu (Ctrl+N).
2. Double-click on the page border, and select Portrait. Click on OK.
3. Using the Text tool, type the words **GONE FISHING** on two lines in the center of the page. Click on the Pick tool when done.
4. Press Ctrl+T, and edit the text as follows: Switzerland Black, 100 points, center alignment. Click on the spacing button and change the line spacing value to 65%.
5. Select the Rectangle tool and draw a rectangle around the text, leaving about 1/4 inch of space around the text.
6. With the Pick tool, select both objects. From the Arrange menu, select Align. Check Centered for both vertical and horizontal and click on OK (see fig. 7.15).
7. With both objects selected, choose Combine from the Arrange menu (or use Ctrl+L).

When you select objects as a group (using a highlight box or the Select All command) to combine them, the program assigns the attributes (fill color, outline color, and so on) of the bottom object to the new object. If you select the objects one at a time and combine them, the resulting object takes its attributes from the last object selected.

8. Click on 50% Black in the on-screen palette.

Combining Objects   131

Figure 7.15
Gone Fishing is centered in the page.

9. Click on the object again to enter rotate/skew mode.
10. Hold down the Ctrl key and click and drag the upper right corner arrow counterclockwise to rotate it 30 degrees (see fig. 7.16).

Figure 7.16
Gone Fishing is combined as a mask, filled and rotated.

11. Save the file as FISHING.
12. With the object selected, select **C**opy from the **E**dit menu (to copy the object to the Windows Clipboard).
13. From the **F**ile menu, **O**pen CALENDAR.
14. Click on **P**aste in the **E**dit menu.
15. From the **L**ayout menu, select **S**nap To, and click on Grid to deactivate it. Select **S**nap To again, and click on Guidelines to deactivate.
16. Use the Pick tool to position the fishing banner over the calendar (see fig. 7.17).
17. Save the file as CALENDR2.

Chapter 7: Arranging and Aligning Objects

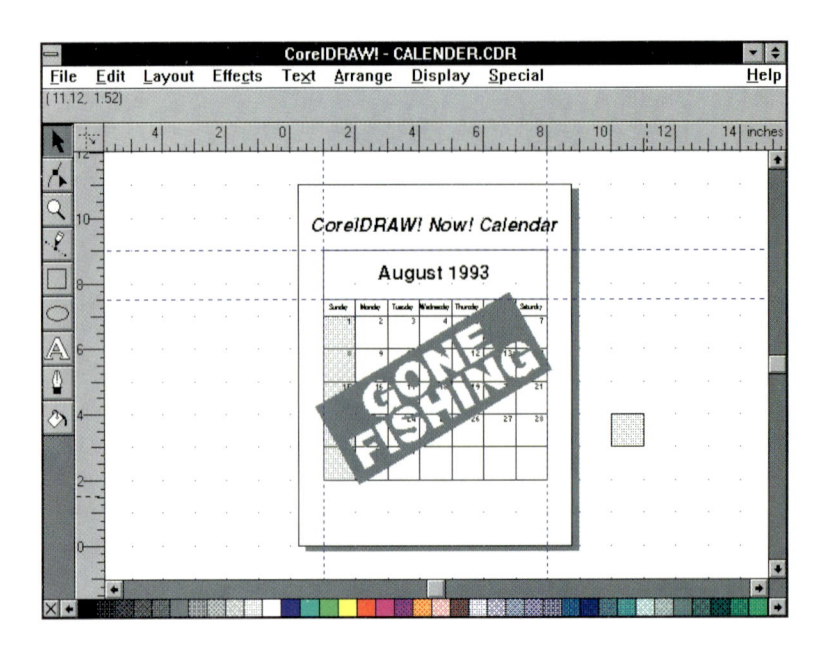

Figure 7.17
The calendar with the window mask.

Welding Objects

The Weld command is similar to Combine. The difference is that when you join objects that overlap with the Weld command, the objects join together at the points where they intersect. The following example will demonstrate.

1. Choose **N**ew from the **F**ile menu (Ctrl+N).

2. Draw a 2-by-7-inch rectangle in the top half of the page. Fill it Blue.

3. With the Text tool, type the word **OVERLAP** on the rectangle. Click with the Pick tool to select the text.

4. Using the upper corner control points, stretch the text so that it is the same length as the rectangle. Position it so that it overlaps the top half of the rectangle (see fig. 7.18).

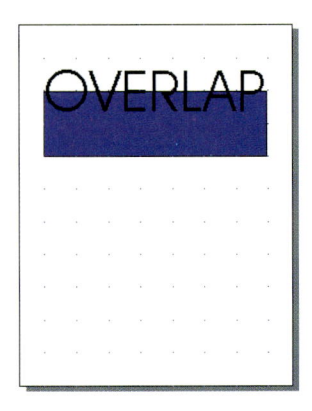

Figure 7.18
Overlapping the text on the rectangle.

Working with Layers   133

5. Select both objects, click and drag them down while pressing the right mouse button, and place the copy in the bottom half of the page.

6. Select the text and rectangle on the top of the page, and choose **C**ombine in the **A**rrange menu (Ctrl+L). The overlapping areas now are transparent in the new object.

7. Select the text and rectangle at the bottom of the page, and choose **W**eld from the **A**rrange menu. The objects have joined together at their intersection points.

*From the **D**isplay menu, select **E**dit Wireframe. This view better demonstrates how the Weld command joins objects together. To return to full-color view, just click on **E**dit Wireframe again (or use the keyboard shortcut, Shift+F9).*

8. Save the file as WELD.

Working with Layers

The layering feature of CorelDRAW! enables you to place objects on specific layers within a drawing. In previous exercises, when you checked the status bar to see that an object was selected, it was listed as being on Layer 1. You can create as many layers as you want, adding flexibility when creating complex drawings.

You control layers with a roll-up menu. From the **L**ayout menu, click on **L**ayers Roll-Up. The Layers roll-up menu appears (see fig. 7.19).

Figure 7.19
The Layers roll-up menu.

The roll-up displays the current layers in the order in which they appear. These layers include the following:

Grid layer. The screen grid resides on its own layer. You can use the Layers roll-up menu to make the grid invisible on-screen or to make it visible when printed.

Guides. When you add guidelines to a drawing, they appear on the Guide layer. The Layers roll-up menu enables you to temporarily remove the guidelines without losing their position. You also can add shapes (like ellipses) to the Guides layer.

Chapter 7: Arranging and Aligning Objects

> **Desktop.** This is also known as the *Master layer*. As you will learn in the next chapter, CorelDRAW! enables you to create documents of multiple pages. The Layers feature enables you to establish a Master layer, a layer of objects that will automatically appear on every page of the document.

> **Layer 1.** This always is the initial drawing layer when you open a new file. All objects automatically are added to this layer.

Displaying Layers

1. From the File menu, select Open (Ctrl+O) and double-click on CALENDR2.

2. In the Layers roll-up, double-click on Grid. The Layer Options dialog box appears (see fig. 7.20).

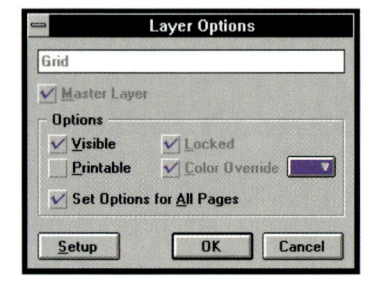

Figure 7.20
The Layer Options dialog box.

The dialog box lists the name of the layer, and available options for this layer are in black.

3. Uncheck the Visible box and click on OK. The grid no longer is visible on the screen, but the Snap to Grid function still works if acti-vated. Double-click on grid again, check Visible, and then click on OK.

> *If you want the grid to appear as a different color, click on the color button (currently default Blue) in the Layer Options dialog box and choose another color from the palette.*

Adding Layers

1. Click on the fly-out arrow of the Layers roll-up and select New.

2. The new layer is named Layer2, and is currently highlighted. Type **Fishing**, and it will replace Layer2. Click on OK. The Fishing layer is added to the list.

> *If you want to change the name of a layer, click on the name to highlight it, choose Edit from the fly-out menu, and type in a new name.*

Moving Objects between Layers

1. Use the Pick tool to select the Gone Fishing rectangle.
2. From the Layers fly-out menu, select Move To.
3. Place the Move To arrow on Fishing in the roll-up, and click.
4. While the image seems unchanged, the status bar shows that the object has moved from Layer1 to Fishing.

The Copy To command works the same as the Move To command, but it leaves the object on its original layer and places an additional copy on the new layer.

Adding Objects to Layers

When a new file is started, all objects are drawn on Layer1, the active layer by default (highlighted in the Layers roll-up menu). When you add new objects to a drawing, they appear on the active (highlighted) layer.

1. From the Layers roll-up menu, click on Fishing.
2. Using the Artistic Text tool, enter the following text at the bottom center of the page: **See you when we return!**. Click on the Pick tool and select the text.
3. Using Edit Te**x**t (Ctrl+T) or the Text **R**oll-up, edit the text as follows: Switzerland, 42 point, align center, Bold-Italic (see fig. 7.21).

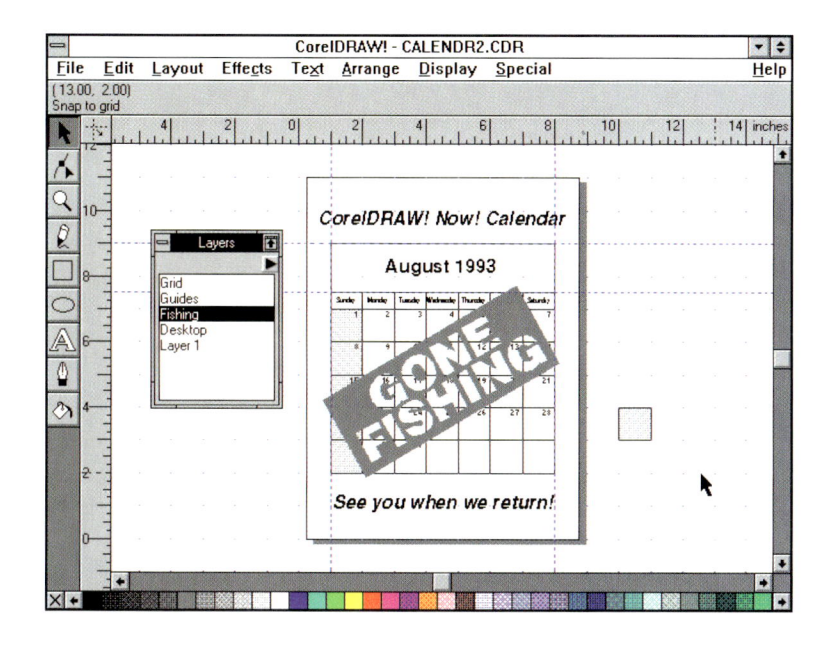

Figure 7.21

The object is added to the layer.

Chapter 7: Arranging and Aligning Objects

Reordering Layers

You can easily change the order in which layers are displayed.

1. In the Layers roll-up menu, click and hold down the mouse on Layer1 and drag the cursor up to Desktop. Release the mouse button (see fig. 7.22).

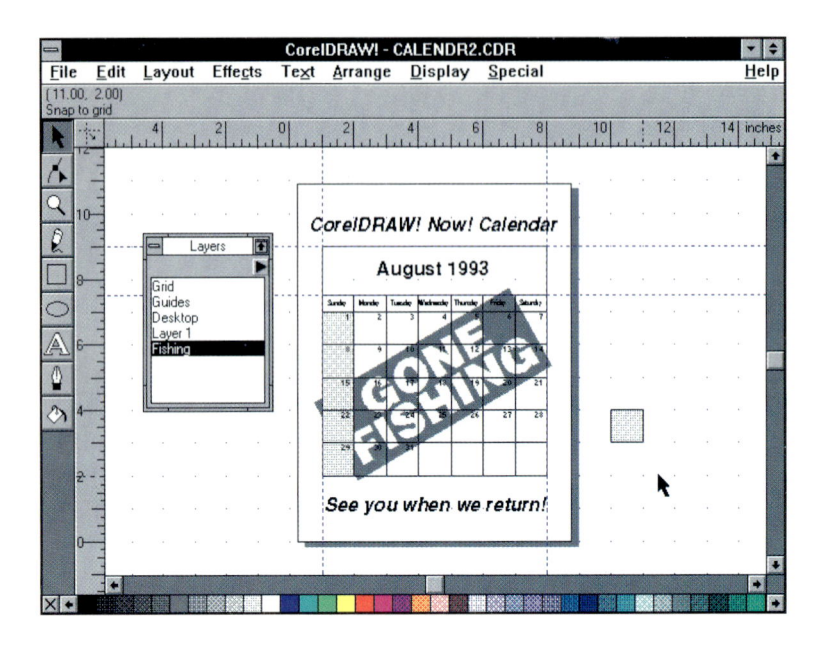

Figure 7.22
Gone Fishing now appears below the Sunday boxes.

The layer you move will be placed below the layer on which you position the cursor.

2. Repeat this procedure with the Fishing layer so that it again is on top of the calendar.

Just as you made the Grid layer invisible, the same can be done for all layers. If you want to edit the objects of the calendar, making the Fishing layer invisible gives you easier access to the calendar.

Distinguishing between Layers

In the calendar graphic, it is easy to keep track of what is on each layer. In more complex drawings, in which you might have several objects on each of several layers, you can get confused as to what is where.

Working with Layers

1. From the Layers roll-up menu, double-click on the Fishing layer.
2. Check the **C**olor Override box. Click on the Color button and select Red from the palette. Click on OK.
3. All objects on this layer (in this case, there is only one) will be displayed in Wireframe mode, outlined in Red.

*If you have objects on five different layers, you can make each layer a different color. When you edit objects on a particular layer, just uncheck the **C**olor Override for that level and they will appear in full color. When you check **C**olor Override again, it remembers the color you chose before and displays it as a wireframe in that color.*

Using the MultiLayer Option

1. Click on the fly-out arrow in the Layers roll-up. The MultiLayer option has a check mark indicating it is active. Click on MultiLayer to deactivate it.
2. Click on Fishing in the roll-up menu to highlight it. Using the Pick tool, select the August 1993 text string.
3. You cannot seem to select the text string.

*If the MultiLayer function is not activated, you can select objects only from the layer highlighted in the **L**ayers roll-up menu.*

4. Click on MultiLayer again to activate it.

Locking a Layer

Follow these steps to lock a layer:

1. Double-click on Fishing in the Layers roll-up menu.
2. Check the **L**ocked box. Click on OK.
3. Now you cannot select any objects on the Fishing layer.

If you have five layers of objects in a drawing and deactivate MultiLayer, you constantly have to highlight layers in the roll-up menu to edit them. By activating MultiLayer and locking a particular layer, you protect that layer from accidental editing and give yourself quick access to objects on all other layers.

Printing Layers

1. Double-click on Fishing in the Layers roll-up menu.

2. Uncheck the Printable box. Click on OK.

The image on-screen remains unchanged, but if you printed this file now, the objects on the Fishing layer would not print.

Making layers nonprintable can greatly increase print speed. You might have a large bit-mapped image on one layer, for instance, but only want to see how an object from another layer will look when printed. Making the bit-mapped layer nonprinting greatly increases print speed and might make it easier to inspect the object in question.

3. Double-click on Fishing again, and check the Printable box.

4. Click on Save from the File menu.

Chapter 8
Working with Graphic Styles

*Y*ou rarely, if ever, have as much time to complete a project as you would like. The powerful desktop publishing features of CorelDRAW! help you make the best of the time you do have. And in addition to saving you time, they help you keep a consistent look throughout your document.

Adding Pages to a Document

CorelDRAW! enables you to create documents of up to 999 pages, enough to satisfy most, if not all, of your needs.

1. From the File menu, Open CALENDR2.
2. From the Layout menu, select Insert Page. The Insert Page dialog box appears.
3. The Number of Pages value should be 1, and the After box should be checked. Click on OK (see fig. 8.1).

There are several things worth noting on the screen:

- Look at the left side of the bottom scroll bar. This status bar appears whenever there is more then one page in a document. It shows that you are on the second page of a two-page document. Clicking on the black arrow will take us to the previous page. Clicking on the + sign will bring up the Insert Page dialog box.

FEATURES COVERED

This chapter demonstrates the following:

- Adding and deleting pages within documents
- Creating master layers
- Working with paragraph text
- Using templates and styles

Chapter 8: Working with Graphic Styles

TIP *The keyboard shortcut for opening a file is Ctrl+O.*

TIP *If you are on the first or last page of your drawing, pressing PgUp or PgDn brings up the Insert Page dialog box.*

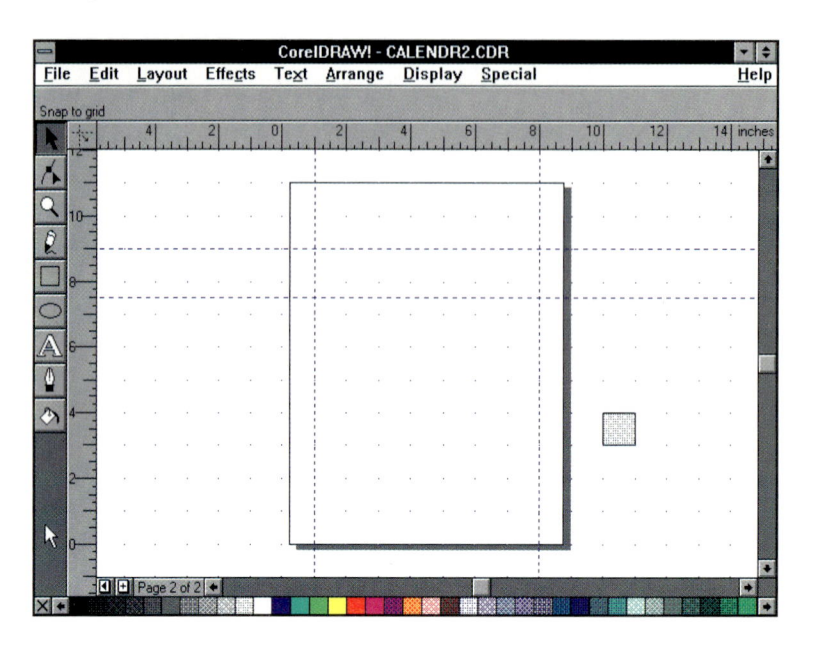

Figure 8.1
The new page is inserted.

- The guidelines are visible. Bring up the **L**ayers Roll-Up from the **L**ayout menu (or use the keyboard shortcut, Ctrl+F3) and double-click on Guides.

- The Master Layer box is checked, meaning that this layer appears on every page. To hide the guidelines on this page, uncheck the boxes for Visible and Set Options for All Pages. Click on OK. The guidelines now are invisible.

- Click on the arrow to go to the previous page. The guidelines are visible on this page.

NOTE *The arrow on the page status bar now points to the right. Clicking on it takes you to the next page. When there are three or more pages, both the left and right arrows will appear.*

- Click on the arrow to return to page 2.

- The square that was outside the page area is carried over to page 2. Select it with the Pick tool. The status bar shows it on the Desktop layer.

Adding Pages to a Document   141

Click and drag it to the middle of the page. The status bar now shows it on the Fishing layer.

Any object that is outside the page area is automatically moved to the Desktop layer when you move to a different page. Objects on the Desktop layer are displayed regardless of which page is current. When you move the object into the page area, it is placed on the nearest layer that is visible and not locked. You can use the Desktop layer much the same as you would the Windows Clipboard.

Copying Objects between Pages

Use the following steps to copy objects between pages.

1. Click on the previous page arrow to return to page 1.
2. From the Layers roll-up menu (Ctrl+F3), click on the fly-out arrow and unselect MultiLayer.
3. Click on Layer1 on the roll-up to make it the active layer.
4. Choose Select All from the Edit menu.

With MultiLayer unselected, the Select All command will select only those objects on the active layer.

5. From the Edit menu, click on Copy to copy the objects to the Windows Clipboard.
6. Click on the next page arrow.
7. From the Edit menu, choose Paste. The calendar now can be edited for the next month.
8. Click on the month text to select it (it is grouped with the rectangle, so hold down the Ctrl key while you click on it).
9. Press Ctrl+T to enter Edit Text mode and change the month to September. Click on OK.
10. Use the Pick tool to drag days 5–7 off the page. Now move days 1–4 over so that they range from Wednesday to Saturday (August 1993 ended on Tuesday).
11. Continue to move days off the page and replace them so that they are in the proper order.

Chapter 8: Working with Graphic Styles

12. There is no 31st day in September, so place it off the page. Click and drag one of the empty squares while pressing the right mouse button, and place it where the 31st would have been.

13. There is a gray square in the upper left where there is no date. Click and drag it off the page (see fig. 8.2).

14. From the File menu, click on Save.

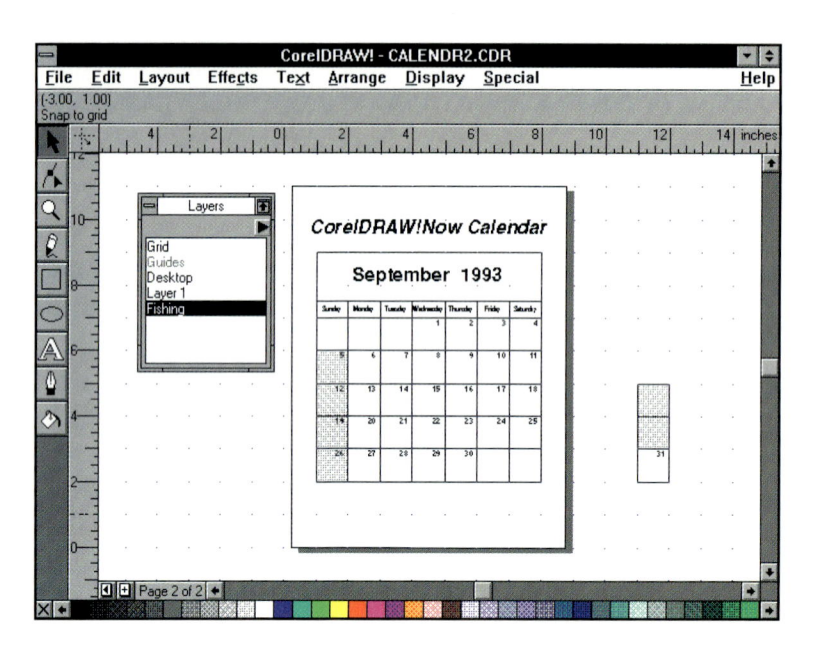

Figure 8.2
The completed September calendar.

Creating a Master Layer

Multipage documents often contain certain information on every page (such as a company logo). When you place this information on a master layer, it automatically appears on every page. You even can have multiple master layers if needed.

1. With CALENDR2 as the open file, click on the arrow to move to page 1.

2. Click on the fly-out menu of the Layers roll-up (Ctrl+F3) and select New.

3. For the name of the layer, type **Copyrite**. Check the box next to Master Layer. Click on OK.

4. We will place a copyright line 1/4 inch from the bottom of the page. From the Layout menu, select Snap To and click on Grid to deactivate it.

Deleting Pages   143

The grid was set at 1 unit per inch, so we could not place the text at a 1/4-inch interval.

5. Select the Artistic Text tool. Place the cursor 1/4 inch from the bottom of the page, centered horizontally, and click. Enter the following text: © **1993 CorelDRAW! Now**!. Click on the Pick tool when done.

The copyright symbol (©) is a special character. To type it, hold down the Alt key and type **0169**.

6. Using the Text roll-up (Ctrl+F2) or the Edit Text dialog box (Ctrl+T), edit the text as follows: Switzerland, Italic, 18 points, center alignment.

7. The status bar shows that the text is on the Copyrite layer. Because we marked Copyrite as a master layer, it should appear on all pages. Click on the next page arrow to go to page 2. The copyright line is there.

8. From the page status bar, click on the + sign. In the Insert Page dialog box, enter **3** for Insert Pages. Click on OK to add three pages after page 2. This will give us room for October, November, and December.

9. Click on the next page arrow, and the copyright appears at the bottom of each page.

Hiding a Master Layer

You can hide the Master Layer on a particular page.

1. Using the arrow keys in the page status bar, move to page 3.
2. From the Layers roll-up menu (Ctrl+F3), double-click on Copyrite.
3. Uncheck the Set Options for All Pages box.
4. Uncheck the Visible box. Click on OK.
5. The copyright line no longer is displayed on page 3. Use the arrows to look at the other pages. They all display the copyright line.

Deleting Pages

1. From the Layout menu, select Delete Page. To delete one page, enter the page number in the Delete Page dialog box and click on OK. Go ahead and delete the last three pages.

Chapter 8: Working with Graphic Styles

*Using **D**elete Page also deletes the contents of that page!*

2. Click on the box for Thru Page. Scroll up to 5 in the bottom box, and to 3 in the top box. Click on OK.

3. The page status bar shows that the document has two pages.

4. From the **F**ile menu, choose **S**ave.

Working with Paragraph Text

In an earlier chapter you used the Paragraph Text tool to add text to a drawing. Now you will take a closer look at Paragraph text and some of its editing commands.

Using Multiple Text Frames

1. From the **D**isplay menu, select **E**dit Wireframe.

When you use the Paragraph Text tool, the paragraph frame is displayed only when the text is the selected object. The Edit Wireframe command shows the paragraph frame as visible at all times, making the demonstration easier.

2. From the Te**x**t menu, select Text **R**oll-Up.

3. Select the Paragraph Text tool from the toolbox.

4. Click on the center of the page. A page-size paragraph text frame appears (see fig. 8.3).

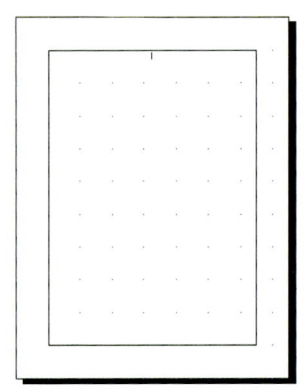

Figure 8.3
A page-size paragraph text frame.

Clicking the Paragraph Text cursor anywhere on the page draws the text frame centered on the page. Clicking outside the page draws the same size text frame with the upper left corner of the frame positioned where the mouse was clicked.

Working with Paragraph Text

5. Enter the following text (including line breaks):

   ```
   First line of text
   Second line of text
   Third line of text
   Fourth line of text
   Fifth line of text
   Sixth line of text
   Seventh line of text
   Eighth line of text
   ```

6. Use the Pick tool to select the text.

7. From the Text roll-up menu, edit the text as follows: Align left, Switzerland, Style—Normal, 36 point. Click on Apply when done (see fig. 8.4).

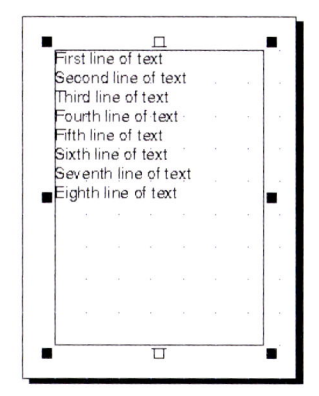

Figure 8.4
The edited text is easier to see.

8. The text frame currently is 9 inches high. Click and drag the bottom center control handle up until the frame is 3 inches high.

Notice that the top and bottom center control handles are hollow. These handles enable you to flow text between two paragraph objects.

9. From the File menu, click on Import. The file type should be CorelDRAW!, *.CDR; the directory should be the one in which the previous files you created are located.

10. Scroll down the list of files and double-click on SPHERE1.

11. Click and drag the sphere object down so that it is centered between the text and the bottom of the page.

12. You still need to show the last three lines of the text object, but there is no room on the page. From the Layout menu, select Insert Page and insert one page after the current one.

13. Click on the previous page arrow to return to page 1. Using the Pick tool, select the text object.

Chapter 8: Working with Graphic Styles

> **TIP**
>
> *In Full-color display mode, you can click anywhere within the text frame area to select it. In Wireframe mode, you must click on the frame line to select the text.*

14. With the Pick tool still active, click on the bottom center control handle. The cursor changes to a paragraph icon with a small arrow pointing out. This cursor is used to draw the text frame in which the text will flow.

15. Move the cursor down to the page status bar (it reverts to a normal pointer). Click on the next page arrow.

16. Bring the cursor up into the page area and draw a marquee box 3 inches high and 6 inches wide (see fig. 8.5).

> **NOTE**
>
> *The frame is drawn at the point of the arrow.*

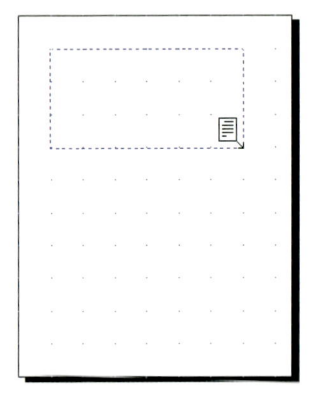

Figure 8.5

Draw a marquee box to position the paragraph text frame.

17. When the mouse button is released, the new paragraph frame is drawn. The text from the original paragraph text frame continues in the paragraph text frame on page 2 (see fig. 8.6).

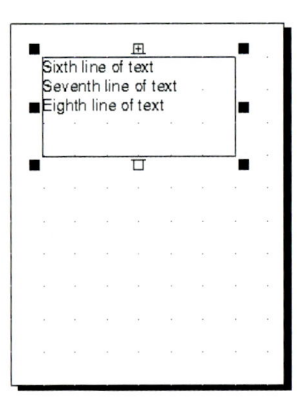

Figure 8.6

The text continues into the paragraph frame on the second page.

Working with Paragraph Text

18. Click on the previous page arrow to return to page 1. Select the sphere object and delete it. Select the text frame and stretch the bottom down to its original size, 9 inches high. All the text appears in the frame.

19. Click on the next page arrow; the text frame is empty. CorelDRAW! automatically updates the text frames as needed.

Formatting Paragraph Text

This section demonstrates how to format tabs, indents, and bullets.

Tabs

You can use tabs to align separate elements of text.

1. With the paragraph text frame selected, click on Paragraph from the Text roll-up menu (Ctrl+F2). The Paragraph dialog box appears, as shown in figure 8.7.

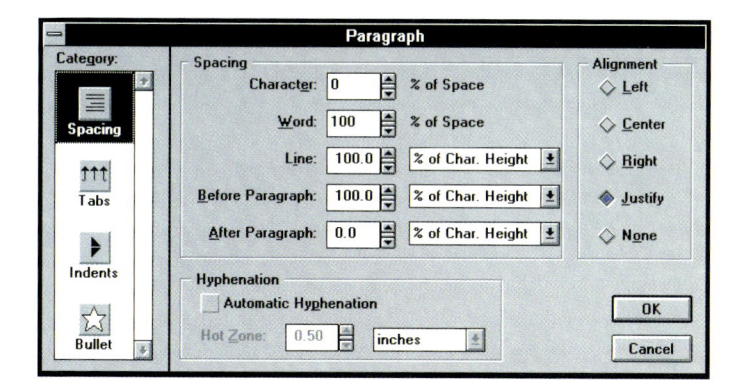

Figure 8.7
The Paragraph dialog box.

2. Click on the Tabs icon. The default setting is one tab every 1/2 inch. Click on Apply Tabs Every to set them. Small arrows appear beneath the ruler to indicate the tab positions, and a window lists the tabs by numerical value. To make these tabs active, click on OK, and then click on Apply in the Text roll-up menu.

Remember, you always must click on Apply in the Text roll-up menu if you want any of these changes to take effect.

3. To change the intervals, click on Clear All, change the value, and click on Apply Tabs Every again.

4. To place tabs individually, click the cursor just below the ruler where you want a tab marker. An arrow appears. You can drag the arrow marker along the ruler to reposition it.

Indents

You can use Indents to indent text in a paragraph.

1. Using the Paragraph Text tool, click the cursor just after the last word in the frame. Add the following text to the line: **is the last line of text in the frame**.

2. Click on the Pick tool to select the text frame, click on Paragraph from the Text roll-up menu to bring up the Paragraph dialog box, and choose the Indents icon.

3. Change the value for Indent First Line to 1 inch and click on OK. Click on Apply in the Text roll-up menu. A 1-inch indent is added to all the lines in the frame (see fig. 8.8).

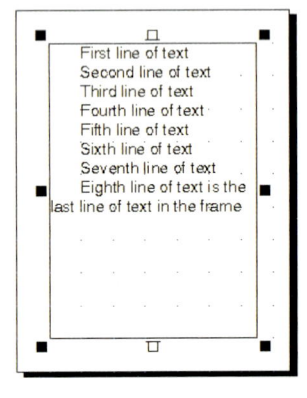

Figure 8.8

A 1-inch indent is added to each paragraph in the text.

Each time you press the Enter key to begin a new line, the program recognizes that text as a new paragraph. It currently sees eight paragraphs, and has indented each one. The last paragraph takes up two lines. As indicated, only the first line of the paragraph is indented 1 inch.

4. Access the Indents icon again, and change the value for Rest of Lines to .5 inches.

Look just below the ruler and you will see two small triangles. The upper triangle indicates the indent for the first line of the paragraph, and the lower one indicates the indent for the rest of the paragraph. By holding down the Shift key, you can drag each to a new position with the mouse. Drag one of them without pressing the Shift key, and both markers will move together.

5. Move the upper marker to 1 1/2 inches and the lower marker to 3/4 inch. Click on OK, then on Apply. The last two lines are indented as shown in figure 8.9.

Working with Paragraph Text

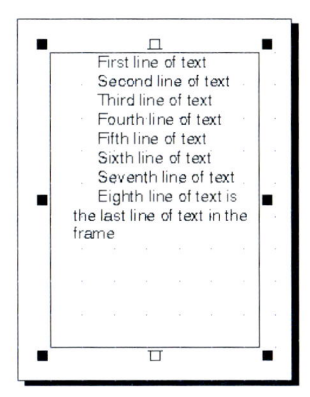

Figure 8.9
All paragraphs are indented 1 inch, and all other lines are indented 1/2 inch.

Bullets

You can use a variety of bullets within CorelDRAW! to enhance your text.

1. With the text frame selected, click on Paragraph from the Text roll-up menu to bring up the Paragraph dialog box. Select the Bullet icon.

   The entire CorelDRAW! symbols library is available for use as bullets.

2. Check the Bullet On box. Scroll down the list and click on Stars1.

3. In the Symbol # window, enter **40**. Change the Bullet Size to 36 points, and the Bullet Indent to 72 points.

4. Click on OK and click on Apply from the Text roll-up. A star-shaped bullet is added to the beginning of each new line, as shown in figure 8.10.

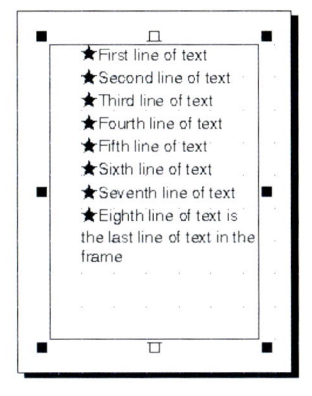

Figure 8.10
Bullets are added to the text.

In the examples for tabs, indents, and bullets, the formats are applied to the entire paragraph frame. Each one can be applied to portions of the text frame as well.

Chapter 8: Working with Graphic Styles

5. With the paragraph text selected, click on the Paragraph Text tool.

6. Position the bottom of the cursor to the left of the fourth line of text and drag it to the right to highlight the line (see fig. 8.11).

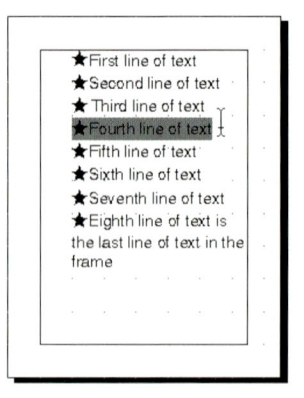

Figure 8.11

The fourth line of text is highlighted.

7. Select Paragraph from the Text roll-up menu. In the Paragraph dialog box, click on the Bullet icon.

8. Enter **39** for the Symbol #.

9. Select Paragraph again from the roll-up. Click on Indents.

10. Change the value for Indent First line to 2 inches. Click on OK.

11. Click on Apply. The format changes are made only to the fourth line (see fig. 8.12).

12. Save the file as PARATEXT.

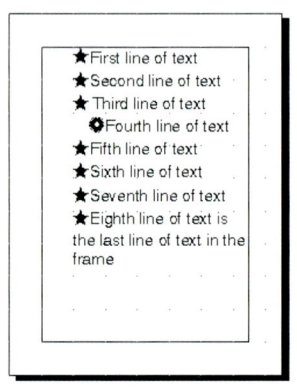

Figure 8.12

Format changes are made to the fourth line.

Formatting Columns

Through CorelDRAW!'s Text roll-up menu, you can separate text into columns.

1. Choose New from the File menu.

Working with Paragraph Text 151

2. From the Text roll-up menu, enter the following text attributes: Align left, Switzerland, Normal, 42 points. Click on Apply. When prompted for the type of text for applying the attributes, check Paragraph and click on OK.

3. Select the Paragraph Text tool, and click it on the page to create a text frame. Enter the text as shown in figure 8.13. Do not press the Enter key at the ends of lines; let the type wrap around by itself.

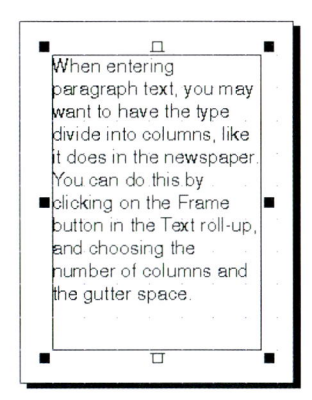

Figure 8.13

Enter the text as shown here.

4. Click on the Pick tool to select the text.

5. Click on Frame from the Text roll-up.

6. You can set up to eight columns with the Frame command. Set the number of columns to 2.

7. The Gutter Width is the space between each column. Set it to .5 inches. Click on OK. Click on Apply in the Text roll up.

8. The text has been formatted into two columns, as shown in figure 8.14.

9. Save the file as COLUMNS.

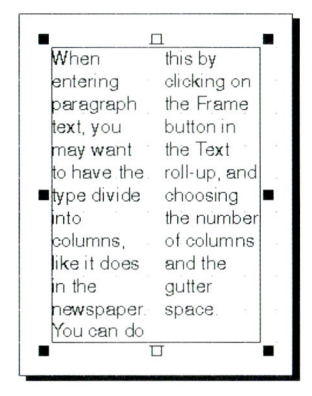

Figure 8.14

Text in two-column format.

Chapter 8: Working with Graphic Styles

Using Templates and Styles

Formatting changes take time, but they are important because they give documents a consistent look. The Styles feature enables you to predefine various formats and attributes and apply them quickly. Styles can be saved in groups called *templates* so that you can access them whenever you need to. CorelDRAW! also supplies a number of professionally designed templates that you can use as is, or edit as needed.

Creating a Template

Let's say you have spent the last three days designing a self-promotional flyer. You plan to create another one each month, and want the look to be consistent for all of them. You can create a template called Flyer, which would contain the styles for all the objects used to create the flyer. These styles then could be quickly applied when creating the new flyers.

1. Create a template called CORELNOW, which will contain styles from the files you have created so far. First, select St**y**le Roll-Up (Ctrl+F5) from the **L**ayout menu. The Styles roll-up menu appears as shown in figure 8.15.

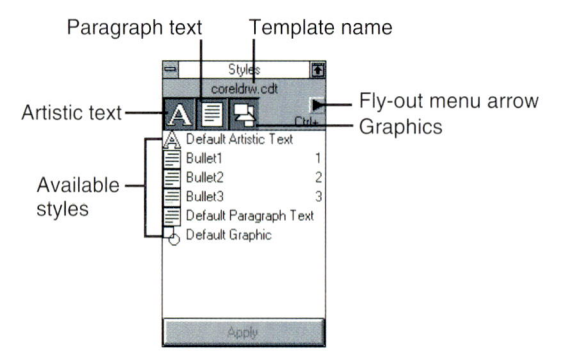

Figure 8.15
The Styles roll-up menu.

2. Click on the fly-out arrow and select Save Template. Type **CORELNOW** and click on OK.

You have just made a copy of the template and renamed it so that the original template is not edited by mistake.

3. From the **F**ile menu, click on **O**pen (or use the keyboard shortcut, Ctrl+O) and select EXAMPLE2.

4. Place the cursor on the rectangle. Click and hold down the right mouse button until the Object Menu appears.

5. Select Save as Style; the Save Style As dialog box appears. In the **N**ame window, type **Background**. Check the **F**ill and **O**utline boxes, and click on OK (see fig. 8.16).

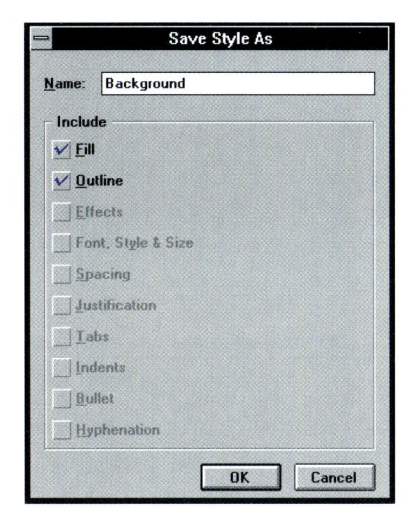

Using Templates and Styles

Figure 8.16
*The Save Style As dialog box, with Background entered in the **N**ame window and **F**ill and **O**utline checked.*

Background now appears on the list of available styles in the roll-up.

6. Open the file SPHERE1. When prompted to Save Changes? to EXAMPLE2, click on No. When prompted to Save Changes to the Template?, click on Yes.

7. When the new file opens, the template changes to the one used in creating the drawing (in this case, the default template). Click on the fly-out menu arrow in the Styles roll-up and select Load Styles. Choose CORELNOW by double-clicking on it.

8. Click and hold the right mouse button on the ellipse to bring up the Object Menu. Select Save as Style.

9. Type **sphere** in the name window and click on OK. Sphere is added to the style list.

10. Open the file COLUMNS. Click on No to Save Changes in the Drawing? and Yes to Save Changes in the Template?.

11. Load the CORELNOW template in the Style roll-up menu (Ctrl+F5).

12. Click and hold the cursor on the text frame, and select Save as Style from the Object Menu. There are several more style options that can be saved, as shown in the Save Style As dialog box in figure 8.17.

In this example you save all the style attributes available from a particular object. In some cases you will want to save just one or two attributes, or you might create several styles containing different combinations of attributes.

13. Name this style COLUMNS, and click on OK.

14. From the Styles roll-up fly-out, select Save Template. Click on OK to save as CORELNOW. Click on Yes to replace the existing file.

Chapter 8: Working with Graphic Styles

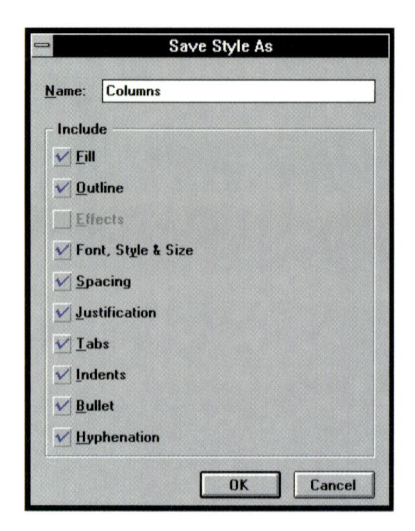

Figure 8.17
Saving styles in the Save Style As dialog box.

If you find you use a lot of fountain fills, the Styles roll-up menu can come in handy. You can create a template containing a selection of fill types (radial, linear, and so on) in different colors, for example. Use names for the styles like Blue Diagonal, Green Sphere, and Red/Yellow Radial.

Using Supplied Templates

You can use the New From Template command to open a supplied template.

1. From the File menu, select New From Template. Scroll down and choose Spec.
2. The template loads in the Styles roll-up menu and the document appears.

This template is chosen because it contains almost 70 styles. When you click on an object in the drawing, the corresponding style is highlighted in the Styles roll-up menu. You might want to zoom in on the document to get a better look. This one really illustrates how much you can do with styles.

3. The template now becomes one big piece of clip art. You can edit it with your own text, or change the graphics if you like. You then can save it as a CorelDRAW! file.
4. If you want to build the document from scratch, use the Load Styles command from the Styles roll-up menu to bring up the template.

Applying Styles

With CorelDRAW!, you can apply various styles that speed up your work and improve the quality of your text.

1. From the Styles roll-up menu, select Load Styles and choose CORELNOW.

2. Double-click on the page border, and select Landscape for the page orientation.

3. Using the Rectangle tool, draw a rectangle slightly larger than the page.

4. Select the Artistic Text tool and add this text to the top center of the page: **CorelDRAW! Styles**. Click on the Pick tool to select the text.

5. Using the Text roll-up, edit the text as follows: center align, Switzerland Bold, 52 points. Click on Apply.

6. With the Text tool, add the following line of text in the center of the page: **Reduce layout time**. Using the Text roll-up, edit as follows: left align, Switzerland Normal, 42 point. Click on Apply. Adjust its position if necessary so that it is centered horizontally.

7. Click and drag the text down 1 inch by holding the Ctrl key and pressing the right mouse button.

8. Press Ctrl+R to repeat this command.

9. Select the second line of text. Click on the Text tool and edit the line of text on screen to read **Consistent look**.

10. Click on the Pick tool and select the third line of text. Click on the Text tool and change text to **Professional templates** (see fig. 8.18).

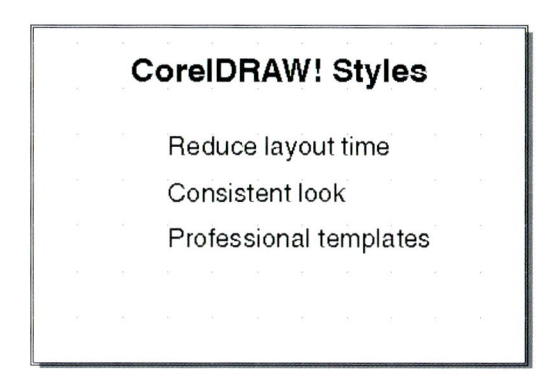

Figure 8.18
Text entered on the page.

11. Click and hold the Text tool to bring up the fly-out menu, and select the Symbols icon.

12. Click on the drop-down menu, then scroll down to Common Bullets and select it.

Chapter 8: Working with Graphic Styles

13. Change the size value at the bottom of the roll-up to 0.70.

14. Click and drag the first symbol (#31) to position it to the left of the word Reduce.

15. Click and drag the symbol by holding the Ctrl key and pressing the right mouse button. Position it next to Consistent.

16. Repeat this process to place a symbol next to Professional (see fig. 8.19).

Figure 8.19

Bullets appear next to the lines.

> **CorelDRAW! Styles**
>
> ○ Reduce layout time
> ○ Consistent look
> ○ Professional templates

17. Using the Pick tool, select one line of text, then hold down the Shift key and click on each of the other three text objects to select them.

18. Click on Yellow in the on-screen palette to fill all the text yellow.

19. With the Pick tool, draw a marquee box around the three symbols to select them. From the available styles list in the Styles roll-up, choose Sphere. Click on Apply.

> *If the Sphere style is not displayed, click on the graphics button above the list. Using these buttons enables you to display part of the list by category (artistic text, paragraph text, and graphic objects). This can make access easier when the style list is very long.*

20. From the **S**pecial menu, select Pr**e**ferences (or use the keyboard shortcut, Ctrl+J). Under Place Duplicates and Clones, change the Horizontal value to –0.10 and the Vertical value to –0.10. Click on OK.

21. Using the Pick tool, draw a marquee box around the four text objects and the three bullets.

22. Press Ctrl+D to duplicate. Click on Black in the on-screen palette to fill the objects black.

23. Hold the Ctrl key down and press the PgDn key.

Using Templates and Styles   157

Ctrl+PgDn is the keyboard shortcut for Send Back One. The rectangle was drawn first, so it will be the bottom object. If we used the Send to Back command, the objects would be behind the rectangle. With the rectangle filled, the objects would not be visible.

24. Click on the rectangle with the Pick tool, select Background from the Styles roll-up menu, and click on Apply (see fig. 8.20).

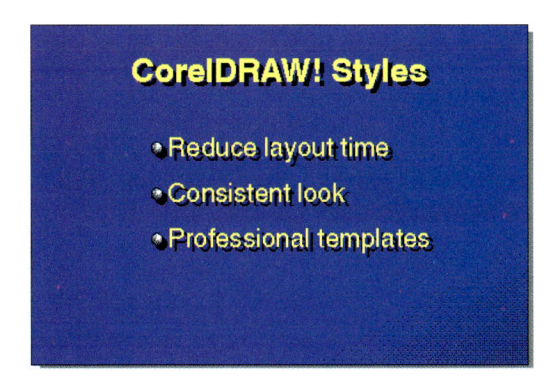

Figure 8.20
The finished page with the styles applied.

This drawing now can be saved as a template. It has styles for Headline and Body Text (including text attributes and fill), Bullet Fill, and Background Fill. There might be additional styles for Sub-Bullets, Sub-Text, and Text Notes.

25. Save the file as STYLES.

Chapter 9
Special Effects

*N*ow we come to the most dangerous part of the program: the special effects commands. "Dangerous" because you can get stuck for hours playing with these commands. Used individually or in concert, Draw's special effects tools can help you create dazzling graphics with relative ease.

Using the Envelope Effect

The Envelope function enables you to stretch and shape objects or groups of objects as if they were made of rubber. In this exercise, you use envelopes to create a waving checkered flag.

1. Double-click on the page border to open the Page Setup dialog box, then select Landscape. Click on OK.

2. From the Layout menu, select Grid Setup. Set the grid frequency to 1 unit per inch (Vertical and Horizontal) and make sure the box for Snap to Grid is checked. Click on OK.

3. Using the Rectangle tool, draw a 1-inch square. Position it 1 1/2 inches down and 1 inch in from the upper left corner of the page. Fill it in black.

4. Drag the square 2 inches to the right as you press the right mouse button.

5. Press Ctrl+R three times to repeat this command and create a row of five boxes, 1 inch apart (see fig. 9.1).

6. Click, drag, and copy the first square again, and position it between the first two squares. Change its fill to white.

7. Copy the white square so that one is positioned between each black square.

8. Select the entire row of squares. Copy and position them 1 inch down and 1 inch to the right of the originals.

FEATURES COVERED

The six special effects tools include the following:

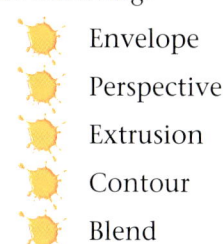

- Envelope
- Perspective
- Extrusion
- Contour
- Blend
- PowerLine

160   Chapter 9: Special Effects

Figure 9.1
A row of five boxes.

9. One black square now sticks out on the right of the second row. Fill it in white, then drag it left so that it occupies the first position in the row.

10. Select all the squares. Copy and position them 2 inches down on the page. Press Ctrl+R to repeat the command. You now should have a pattern of 54 black and white squares (see fig. 9.2).

Figure 9.2
The full pattern of squares.

11. Select all the squares. From the **A**rrange menu, choose **G**roup.

To apply the Envelope effect to a set of objects, you must group them first. You can ungroup them after you apply the envelope.

12. From the Effe**c**ts menu, select **E**nvelope Roll-Up. The Envelope roll-up menu appears, as shown in figure 9.3.

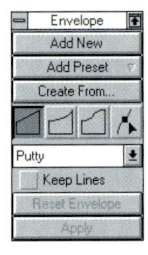

Figure 9.3
The Envelope roll-up menu.

Using the Envelope Effect

Across the center of the menu are buttons for the four envelope modes: Single Line, Single Arc, Two Curves, and Unconstrained. To best understand the differences between them, see figure 9.4.

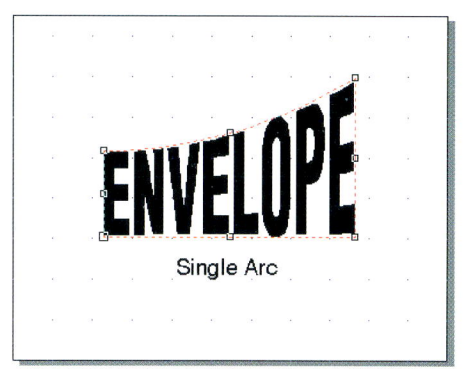

Figure 9.4
The four envelope modes.

To edit the first three envelope types, select one handle at a time and move it to change the shape of the object. The Unconstrained mode is far more versatile: click and drag anywhere along the envelope bounding box to change the shape of the object. Groups of handles can be marquee-selected and moved simultaneously. You also can access the controls of the Node Edit roll-up menu, which enables you to add or subtract control nodes; make nodes cusped, smooth, or symmetrical; and so on.

13. From the Envelope roll-up, click on the Unconstrained button, then select Add New.

14. Place the cursor on the top edge of the envelope between the center and right handles. Click and drag down about 3/4 inches. Place the cursor on the bottom edge of the envelope between the center and right handles. Click and drag down about 3/4 inches.

15. Click on Apply (see fig. 9.5).

Chapter 9: Special Effects

Figure 9.5
Unconstrained envelope is applied to pattern.

Although the envelope changes as you edit it, the object itself does not change until you click on the Apply button. You can make as many adjustments as you want, then apply them all at once. If you select Reset Envelope from the roll-up menu, you can cancel any changes you made to the envelope since you created it (or since the last Apply command was made).

The flag has a wave to it, but it looks a little stiff, not very natural.

16. Click and drag the bottom center node 1/2 inch to the right. Drag the center node on the right side to the left 1/2 inch. Click on Apply. Now the wave of the flag looks more realistic (see fig. 9.6).

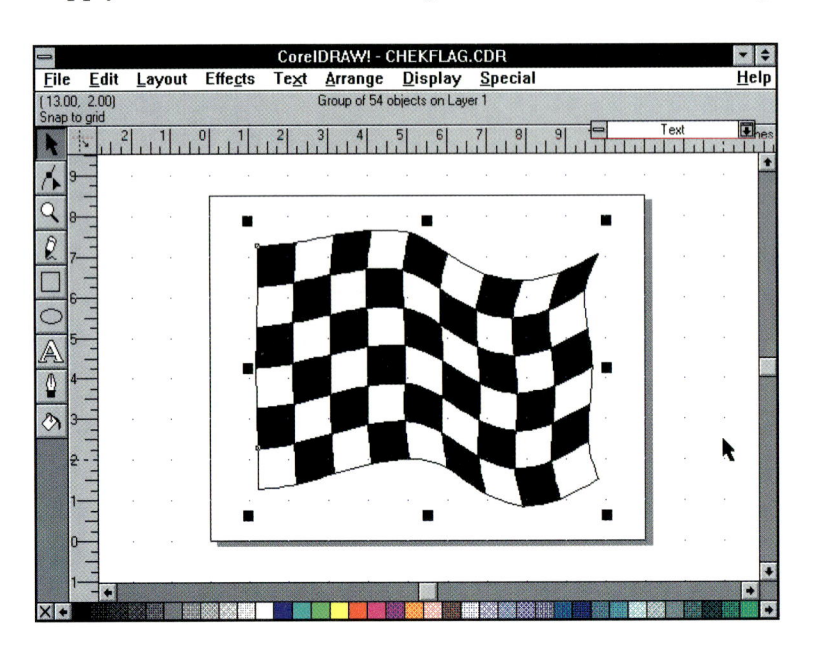

Figure 9.6
Now the pattern resembles a real flag.

Click on any node, and its control handles appear. Change the angle and length of the handles and see how it affects the shape of the envelope.

Using the Envelope Effect

17. Shape the flag as you see fit, then click on the Pick tool to select the flag.

18. From the Effects menu, select **S**tretch & Mirror. Enter 50% for vertical and horizontal stretch, and click on OK.

19. Save the drawing as CHEKFLAG.

Adding a Preset Envelope

As an alternative to manually editing the shape of an object's envelope, you can apply a preset envelope shape.

1. Select the flag with the Pick tool. (If CHEKFLAG is not the current file, open it now.)

2. From the Effects menu, select **C**lear Transformations. The flag returns to its original size and shape.

3. From the Envelope roll-up menu, click on Add Preset. A menu drops down, displaying 9 of the almost 40 preset envelope shapes available (see fig. 9.7).

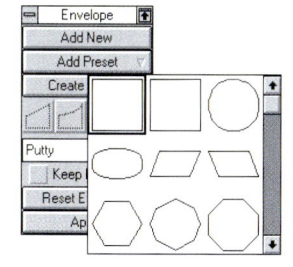

Figure 9.7
Preset envelope selections.

4. Click on the ellipse shape to select it (second row, left side), then click on Apply. The checkered pattern fills the ellipse (see fig. 9.8).

Figure 9.8
Preset ellipse envelope applied to pattern.

Chapter 9: Special Effects

5. From the Envelope roll-up, click on the drop-down list (which currently displays Putty). This list includes the mapping options for the Envelope command:

   - **Original.** The mode used in CorelDRAW! 3.0. You need to use this mode when you import objects that were created and shaped in version 3.0.

   - **Putty.** The default setting for Envelope. The distortions created are not as exaggerated as with Original.

   - **Horizontal.** You use this to maintain the horizontal integrity of the object. For example, parallel lines that run horizontally remain as such, and do not curve.

   - **Vertical.** This mode works the same as horizontal but applies to vertical lines of an object.

   From the menu, select Horizontal.

6. Click on Apply. Notice that the horizontal edges of the boxes do not curve now.

7. Select the Keep Lines option. Click on Apply (see fig. 9.9).

Figure 9.9
Horizontal mapping option applied.

> *Normally, straight lines are converted to curves to conform with the shape of the envelope. The Keep Lines option, however, maintains straight lines when you apply the envelope.*

Copying an Envelope Shape

In addition to the preset envelope selections, you can create a shape and use it as an envelope.

1. Select Clear Transformations from the Effects menu.

2. Select Stretch & Mirror from the Effects menu. Enter 75% for the vertical and horizontal values and click on OK.

Using the Envelope Effect 165

3. Move the flag to the top portion of the page so that you have room to draw below it.

4. Select the Freehand Pencil tool and draw a shape similar to the one shown in figure 9.10.

Figure 9.10
Freehand shape to be used as an envelope.

The ending point of the freehand line must meet the starting point so that the line is a closed path.

5. In the Envelope roll-up, select Putty as the mapping option and de-select the box for Keep Lines.

6. Select the checkerboard pattern using the Pick tool, then click on Create From in the Envelope roll-up.

7. Place the point of the From arrow anywhere on the new shape and click. An envelope shape appears on the pattern.

8. Click on Apply. The envelope has been copied and applied (see fig. 9.11).

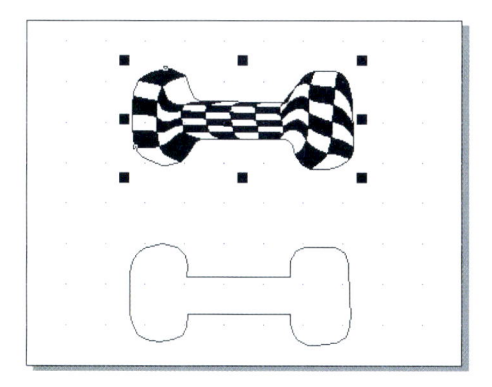

Figure 9.11
The freehand shape is applied as an envelope.

Chapter 9: Special Effects

Enveloping Paragraph Text

You can use the Envelope commands on paragraph text as well.

1. Draw a 4-by-4-inch paragraph box using the Paragraph Text tool. Enter the text in 24 point, as shown in figure 9.12. Select the Pick tool when you are finished. The paragraph object should be selected.

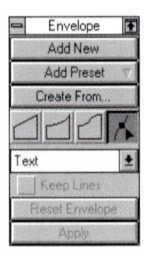

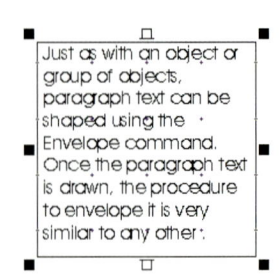

Figure 9.12
The paragraph text object.

When paragraph text is selected, the Envelope roll-up menu's Mapping option automatically changes to Text.

2. You can select Add New, Add Preset, or Create From just as you do with any other object. Select the slanted rectangle from the preset menu and click on Apply (see fig. 9.13).

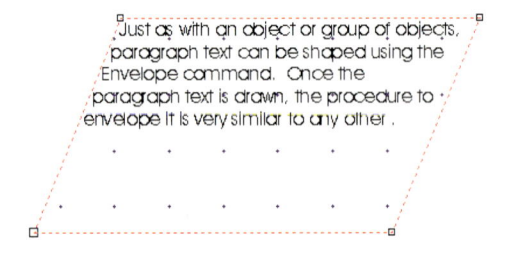

Figure 9.13
The envelope is applied to the text object.

The text conforms to the shape of the envelope and fills it from left to right. Make the text box the same height as it was before.

3. Click on the Pick tool to select the text, then drag one of the side control handles to shrink the box—in this case, 40% (see fig. 9.14).

Figure 9.14
The paragraph text in finished form.

Editing Perspective

All attribute commands (indent, tab, bullet, and so on) can be applied to the text after being reshaped. The text can be edited on-screen with the Paragraph Text tool or through the Text Edit dialog box.

4. Save the file as ENVTEXT.

Editing Perspective

The Perspective command enables you to create a perspective view of an object or a group of objects.

1. From the File menu, Open CHEKFLAG.

2. Select the flag with the Pick tool, and choose Clear Transformations from the Effects menu. Move the checkerboard pattern to the center of the page.

3. Select Add Perspective from the Effects menu. To edit the perspective, place the cursor on the upper left handle and with the Ctrl key pressed, drag it down about 2 inches. This creates a *one-point perspective*, meaning that the object seems to recede in one direction (see fig. 9.15).

Figure 9.15
One-point perspective.

As you might have guessed, holding down the Ctrl key constrains the movement to vertical or horizontal.

4. Place the cursor on the same handle and drag it 2 inches to the right. This creates a *two-point perspective*—the object seems to recede in two directions.

5. Select the Pick tool and click on the pattern to enter Rotate/Skew mode. Drag one of the corner handles clockwise while holding down the Ctrl key, and rotate it 30 degrees. You now have a perspective view of our flag lying on the ground (see fig. 9.16).

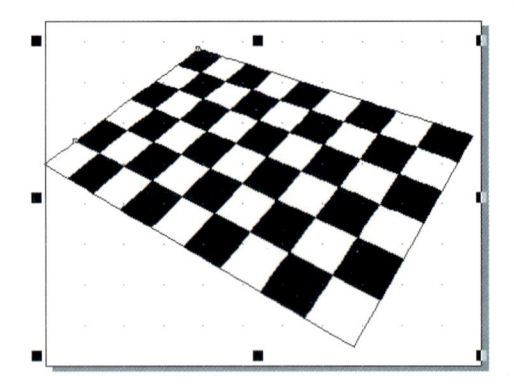

Figure 9.16

Two-point perspective.

6. Choose Clear Transformations from the Effects menu. Select the pattern with the Pick tool and choose Add Perspective from the Effects menu.

7. Drag the upper left handle 3 inches to the right, but this time holding down the Ctrl and Shift keys together (see fig. 9.17).

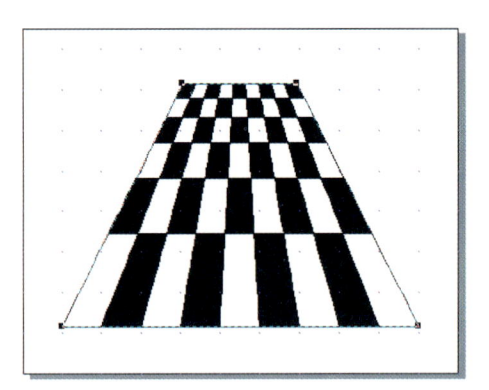

Figure 9.17

One-point perspective using Ctrl+Shift.

Hold down Ctrl+Shift to move the opposite handle an equal and opposite distance as the handle being dragged.

8. Click on the Zoom tool and select the Zoom Out (– sign) icon. In this view you will see a small X above the page area; this is the vanishing point of the perspective. You can edit the perspective by moving the vanishing point.

9. Click and drag the vanishing point 4 inches to the right. The object's perspective responds to this move.

Aligning Vanishing Points

You might want to draw two or more objects and edit the perspective of each so that they share the same vanishing point. You can accomplish this task by aligning their vanishing points.

Editing Perspective

1. Click the cursor on the upper ruler to drag down a guideline, and position it on the vanishing point. Repeat this from the left ruler.
2. Using the Rectangle tool, draw a rectangle in the open area on the left side of the page.
3. Select **A**dd Perspective from the Effe**c**ts menu. Hold down Shift+Ctrl and drag the upper left handle to the right until you can see its vanishing point.
4. Drag the vanishing point to where the two guidelines intersect (see fig. 9.18).

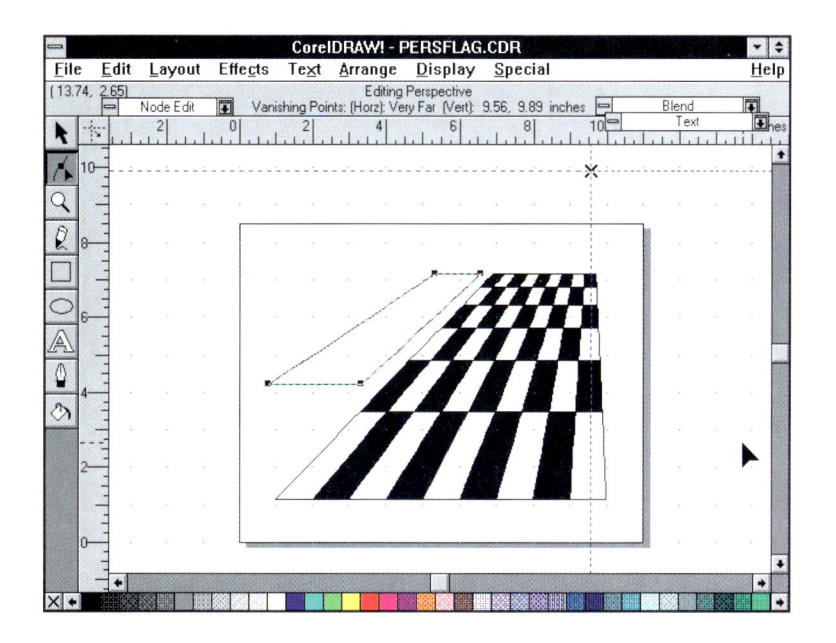

Figure 9.18
The rectangle and the box pattern group appear to vanish to the same point.

To remove the perspective change to an object, choose Clear Perspective from the Effe**c**ts menu. To edit an existing perspective, select the object and click on the Node Edit tool.

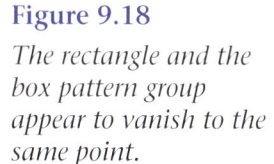

Copying Effects

You can copy the perspective (or envelope) from one object to another.

1. Select the rectangle on the left side of the page and choose **C**lear Transformations from the Effe**c**ts menu. Move the rectangle over if it now overlaps with the checkerboard pattern.
2. From the Effe**c**ts menu, click on Copy Effect **F**rom, and choose Copy **P**erspective From.
3. Place the From arrow anywhere on the checkerboard pattern and click. The rectangle now has the same perspective (see fig. 9.19).

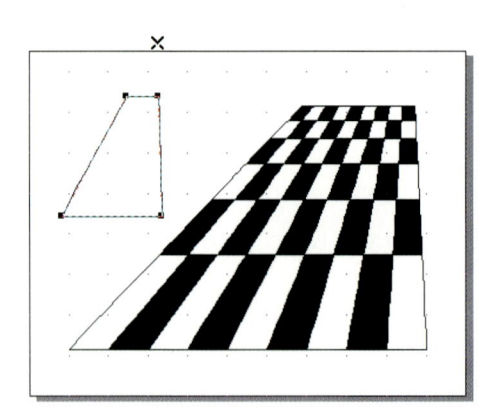

Figure 9.19
Two objects drawn in the same perspective.

> *When you copy the perspective of an object, it does not share the same vanishing point as the original.*

Creating an Extrusion

The Extrude command enables you to apply three-dimensional effects to an object.

1. Select New from the File menu.

2. Using the Artistic text tool, type **CorelDRAW!NOW** in the center of the page. Edit the text as follows: SwitzerlandBlack, Center Align, 80 Points.

3. Click on the Pick tool to select the text. Fill it Yellow, outline Black.

4. From the Effects menu, select Extrude Roll-Up. The Extrude roll-up menu appears, as shown in figure 9.20.

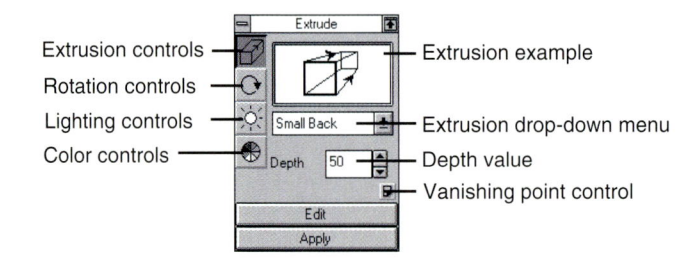

Figure 9.20
The Extrude roll-up menu.

5. From the drop-down menu, select Small Back. Change the Depth value to 50.

> *Big and Small extrusions refer to perspective extrusions, wherein the object approaches or recedes from a vanishing point. In a Parallel extrusion, the lines of the extrusion remain parallel to one another. Back and Front refer to the placement of the extrusion in relation to the original object.*

Creating an Extrusion   171

6. Drag the vanishing point to the upper right corner of the page and click on Apply (see fig. 9.21).

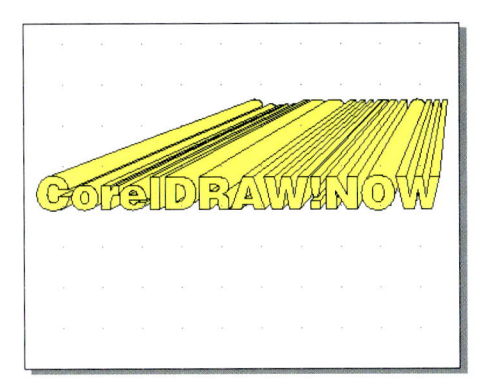

Figure 9.21
Text string with a small back extrusion.

Extruding by Specific Value

In the previous example, you set the extrusion manually. You can create extrusions with greater precision by entering specific values.

1. Click on the button for Vanishing Point Control. The position of the vanishing point is displayed as Measured From Page Origin. From the lower left corner of the page (the page origin), the vanishing point is 11 inches horizontal and 8.5 inches vertical.

2. Click on object center. The vanishing point now is denoted by its distance from the center of the original object. Enter **0.00** for horizontal and **3.00** inches for vertical and click on Apply. The extrusion goes up 3 inches and is centered (see fig. 9.22).

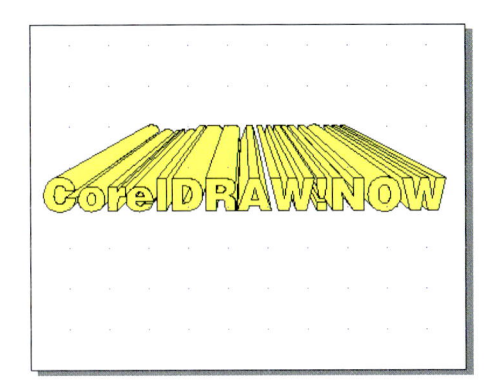

Figure 9.22
A horizontal value of 0.00 yields a centered, symmetrical extrusion.

There is no Copy Extrusion Effect command available. To do so, record the extrusion values as measured from object center and apply them with the same extrusion type when extruding another object.

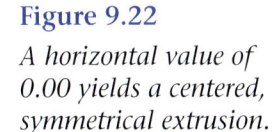

Chapter 9: Special Effects

Controlling Color

The Extrude roll-up menu offers special color options that can be used only with extrusions.

1. Click on the Color Controls button in the roll-up. Use Object Fill currently is highlighted. To change the fill, select Solid Fill, click on the Color button, and choose a new color. Select Blue. Click on Apply (see fig. 9.23).

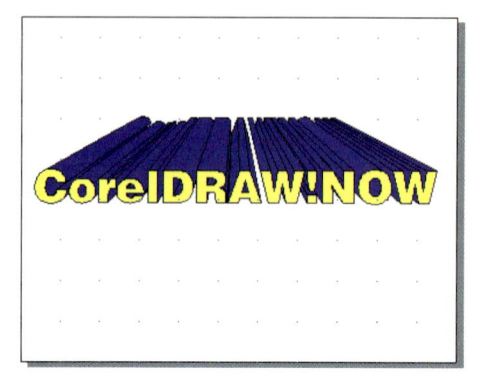

Figure 9.23
Extrusion is filled with a solid color.

2. For a fountain fill of the extrusion, select Shade. Choose Red for the From color and Yellow for the To color. Click on Apply (see fig. 9.24).

Figure 9.24
Extrusion with a fountain fill.

Rotating an Extrusion

The Extrusion roll-up menu also offers special rotation controls.

1. Click on the Rotation Control button in the roll-up menu; the Extrude Rotator appears. This enables you to rotate the extrusion visually.

2. Place the cursor on the arrow pointing out right from center. Click on it twice while watching the screen. The wireframe moves to the right to indicate the new position of the extrusion.

3. Place the cursor on the down arrow and click twice.

4. Place the cursor on the arrow pointing clockwise around the circle and click five times. Click on Apply (see fig. 9.25).

Figure 9.25
Rotated extrusion.

The Rotator tool will work only on perspective extrusions and cannot rotate parallel extrusions.

5. Click on the X in the center of the Rotator tool to remove the rotation applied. Click on Apply.

6. Save the file as CORELNOW.

Dynamic Linking

When an object is extruded, the object and the extrusion are connected by a *dynamic link*.

1. Using the Pick tool, click in an empty area of the page to unselect any objects. Now click on the extrusion. The status bar displays the objects as `Extrusion Group`.

2. Click in an open area of the page again, and then click on the text. The status bar displays the text as `Control Text`.

The text and the extrude group are dynamically linked objects. Simply stated, dynamically linked objects means that changes made in one object will be reflected in the other. In this case, the text is the control object. The extrude group will respond to changes we make to it.

3. With the control text selected, press Ctrl+T to access the Edit Te**x**t command.

4. Change the style from Normal to Italic and click on OK. The extrusion has shifted along with the text (see fig. 9.26).

174   Chapter 9: Special Effects

Figure 9.26

Type is now italic; extrusion adjusts automatically.

You can change the spelling of the text, the type size, the typeface, and so on. The extrude group is linked to the text and will change accordingly.

Separating Objects

Think of dynamic linking as a special kind of grouping. To ungroup linked objects, use the Separate command.

1. Select the Pick tool and click anywhere on the extrusion group.

2. From the **A**rrange menu, choose **S**eparate.

3. The Control text reverts to standard Artistic text, and the extrude group is a group of assorted objects.

Separating the extrude group from the control object enables you to edit the objects independently. Remember, though, there is no command to relink the objects.

4. Select the extrude group with the Pick tool. Press F11 for fountain fill.

5. Select Red for the From color and Yellow for the To color. Click on the Options button and select **R**ainbow. Click on OK, then click on OK again (see fig. 9.27).

Figure 9.27

Extrude group with rainbow fountain fill.

Creating an Extrusion   175

Controlling Lighting

CorelDRAW! also enables you to add special lighting effects to your extruded objects.

1. From the File menu, Open CORELNOW. When Draw prompts you to save changes, choose No.

2. Select the extrude group. From the Extrude roll-up menu, click on the color control button. Select Solid Fill, then click on the color button and choose Yellow. Click on Apply. The text and extrude group both are filled in yellow.

3. Click on the Lighting Control button, then click on the light switch icon. The light in turned On and a sphere appears in the wireframe grid (see fig. 9.28).

The X on the wireframe indicates the direction from which the light source is coming. Click on any one of the 16 intersect points on the wireframe; the sphere illustrates the selected lighting angle.

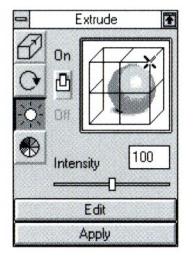

Figure 9.28
Lighting control model in the Extrude roll-up.

4. Click on the front upper left corner of the wireframe. The X jumps to that position and the sphere shows the light coming from that direction. Click on Apply (see fig. 9.29).

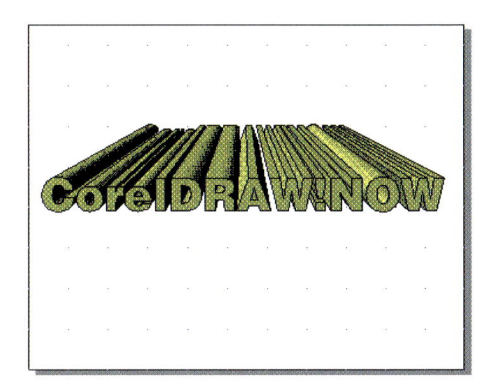

Figure 9.29
Object with upper left light source.

Chapter 9: Special Effects

5. Click on the front upper right corner of the wireframe. Change the Intensity value from 100 (default value) to 90. Click on Apply. As you can see in figure 9.30, the highlights and shading in the extrude group have changed, and everything is darker overall.

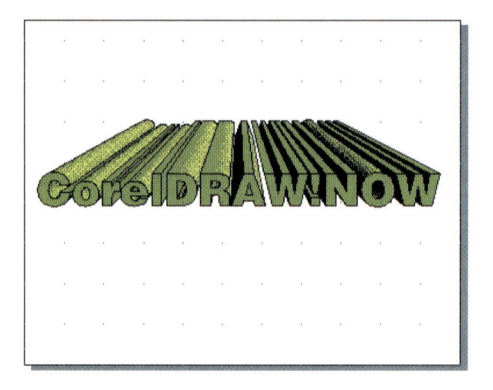

Figure 9.30

The shading on the extrusion responds to the changes.

TIP *The Intensity value changes the brightness of the light source. The values range from 0 (Black) to 200 (White).*

Using the Contour Command

When applied to an object, the Contour effect creates a concentric shape (or series of shapes) that appears inside or outside the original object.

1. From the File menu, Open CORELNOW. When Draw prompts you to save changes, choose No.

2. Using the Ellipse tool, draw a 6-inch circle in the center of the page. Click on the Pick tool to select the circle, and fill it White.

3. From the Effects menu, select Contour Roll-Up. Select To Center for the Contour type. For the offset value, enter 0.25 inches. Click on Apply. The resulting Contour effect is shown in figure 9.31. Not all that impressive, is it? Let's see how to make it interesting.

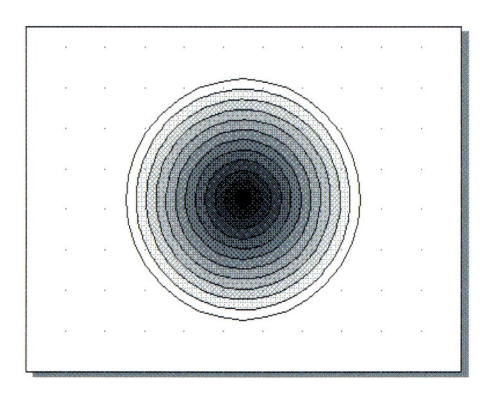

Figure 9.31

Circle with the To Center contour effect.

Using the Contour Command 177

The To Center option creates a series of steps to the absolute center of the object. The offset value is the width of each step. The Fill button in the roll-up shows the final color, and the Contour command will create in-between color steps if it is a different color from the original object.

4. Select the objects on the screen and delete them.
5. Using the Artistic text tool, enter the following text in the center of the screen: **Contour**. Edit the text as follows: Typeface: Dawn Castle, 220 point, Center Align, Bold.

If Dawn Castle is not available on your system, choose a typeface that is round-looking.

6. Check the status bar to see that the text outline is None. If it has an outline, click the X on the left of the palette with the right mouse button to remove it.
7. From the Contour roll-up menu, choose Inside as the contour type. Set the Offset to 0.015 inches and the Steps to 13. Click on the Fill color button and choose White.
8. Click on Apply. Depending on the speed of your computer, it might take a while for this command to complete. The new effect is shown in figure 9.32.

Figure 9.32
Contour can add a 3-D chrome look.

This effect looks really nice if you have a bold, script-like typeface.

9. Save the file as CONTOUR1.
10. Select **N**ew from the **F**ile menu.
11. Enter the following text in the center of the page: **TERMINATOR2**. Edit the text as follows: Typeface: Scott, 115 point, Center Align (see fig. 9.33).

178   Chapter 9: Special Effects

Figure 9.33
The "Terminator 2" logo.

If you don't have this typeface, try to find one with a high-tech look.

12. With the text selected, click on Outside for the contour type. (This effect works equally as well with Inside chosen.)

13. For the Steps value, enter 1. For the offset, enter 0.030 inches. Click on the Fill color button and select Blue. Click on OK.

14. Draw a marquee around the text with the Pick tool to select it.

15. From the Arrange menu, choose Separate.

The Contour command links the original object with the objects it creates, just like the Extrude command. You must separate them so that they can be edited.

16. Click in an empty area of the screen to unselect the objects. Now click in any black area of the text to select it.

17. Press F11 to open the Uniform Fill dialog box. Select Linear fill type. Set the From color to Black and the To color to White. Click on OK.

18. Click on the Blue outline to select it.

You might want to zoom in on the object to make it easier to select. The status bar shows a `Group of 1 Objects` *when it is selected.*

19. Press F11 for fountain fill again. Set the From color to White and the To color to Black. Click on OK. The white side of the outline gets lost against the white background (see fig. 9.34).

20. Using the Rectangle tool, draw a rectangle around the text.

21. Select the Bitmap icon from the Fill tool.

22. From the Texture Library menu, choose Samples. From the Texture List, choose Solar Flares. Click on OK.

Using the Blend Command

23. Press Shift+PgDn to send the rectangle to the back (see fig. 9.35).

24. Save the image as CONTOUR2. This is a really nice effect for type, and as you have seen, it doesn't take much time.

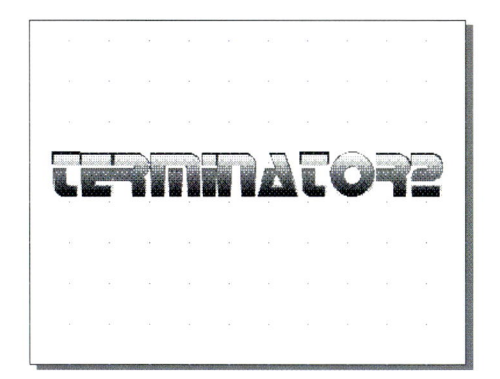

Figure 9.34
A simple way to create chrome type.

Figure 9.35
The finished logo.

Using the Blend Command

The Blend command enables you to blend to objects with a set of intermediate objects. It is very much like the morphing effects you see in the latest sci-fi movies, but on a more elementary level.

Creating a Simple Blend

One of the basic uses of the Blend command is to change one object into another.

1. Select New from the File menu.

2. With the Rectangle tool, draw a 1-inch square in the bottom left corner of the page. Fill it Blue.

3. With the ellipse tool, draw an ellipse 1 1/2 inches wide and 1 inch high in the upper right corner of the page. Fill it Yellow.

4. Marquee-select both objects.

5. From the Effects menu, select Blend Roll-Up. The Blend roll-up menu appears, as shown in figure 9.36.

6. Change the value for steps (the window just below the Steps menu) to 15.

Chapter 9: Special Effects

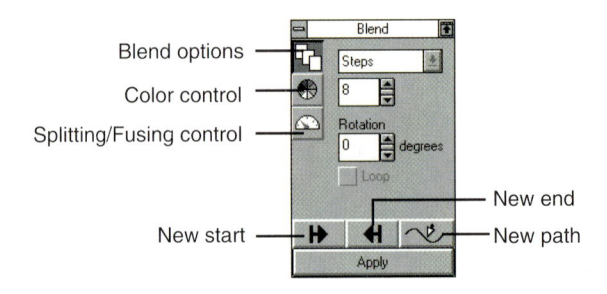

Figure 9.36
The Blend roll-up menu.

This value represents the number of intermediate steps created between the two objects.

7. Click on Apply. The objects blend together as shown in figure 9.37

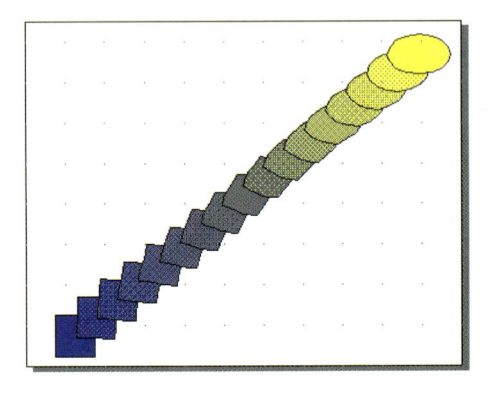

Figure 9.37
A simple blend.

The program creates 15 steps in which the shape of the square evolves into the shape of the ellipse. It also chooses intermediate colors from blue to yellow.

8. Select the Pick tool and click in an empty area to unselect the objects. Click on the square to select it. Notice that the status bar displays it as a Control rectangle.

When blending objects, the two original objects are both control objects. As with extrusions and contours, edits made to control objects are reflected in the blend group.

9. Fill the square Red. The blend group colors now adjust to blend from red to yellow.

10. Select the ellipse. Press Ctrl+PgDn to send the ellipse to the back. The blend group order changes to reflect this command.

11. Click and drag the ellipse down to the right bottom corner of the page. The blend group follows the ellipse.

Using the Blend Command   181

12. Click in the middle of the objects to select the blend group. In the roll-up menu, enter 180 degrees in the Rotation window. Click on Apply (see fig. 9.38).

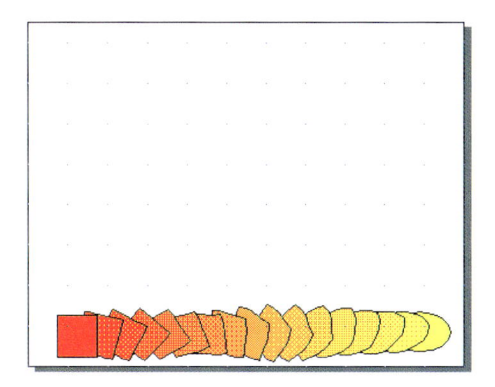

Figure 9.38
The blending objects rotate as they change.

Blending Objects along a Path

You can preset the path that the blended objects follow.

1. Select the Freehand Pencil and draw a line as shown in figure 9.39.

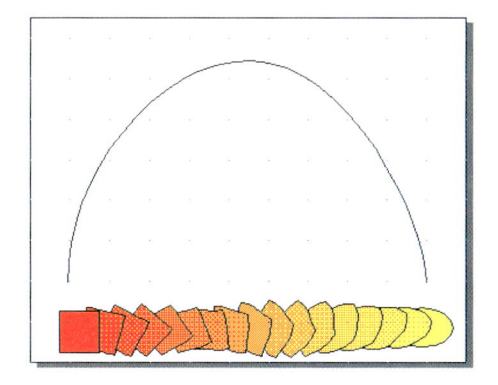

Figure 9.39
New path for the blended objects

2. With the Pick tool, click on the blend group to select it. From the roll-up menu, select the New Path icon and click on New Path.

3. The cursor appears as an arrow. Place the arrow on the line and click. Now click on Apply. As figure 9.40 illustrates, the objects follow the new path.

If you think you might want to edit the blend group later, but you do not want the line to be visible, click on the × in the lower left corner of the screen using the right mouse button.

The path line now is linked to the blend group. To remove it, you must use the Separate command first; then the line is an ordinary curve and can be deleted. At this point the blend group is just a group of objects, and will no longer be affected by the two control objects.

182   Chapter 9: Special Effects

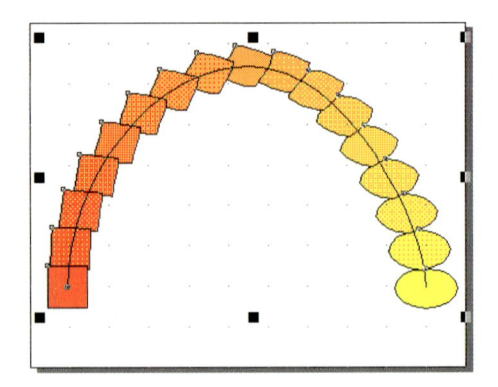

Figure 9.40

The blend group follows the line as its path.

Splitting a Blend Group

The Split command enables you to convert one of the intermediate objects of a blend group into a control object. Before you begin this exercise, select Undo from the Edit menu (or press Ctrl+Z) to cancel the last action you made.

1. Select the path line and delete it.
2. Click on the blend group with the Pick tool to select it.
3. From the Blend roll-up menu, choose the Splitting/Fusing icon. Click on the Split button.
4. Move the cursor to the page area; it changes to an arrow. Place the arrow on one of the objects in the center of the blend group and click on it. That object now is selected and displayed as a Control curve.
5. Click and drag the new control object up to the top of the page. Fill it with blue, as shown in figure 9.41.

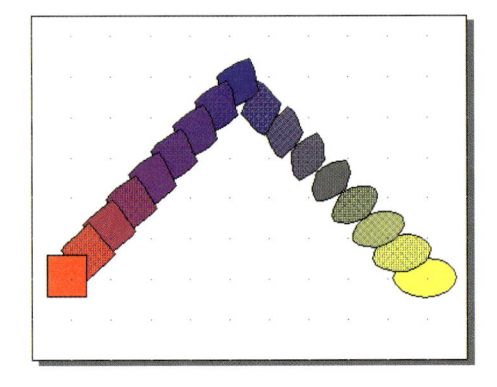

Figure 9.41

The blend group is split by a new control point.

Fusing a Blend Group

The Fuse command enables you to recombine a blend group that has been split.

Using the Blend Command

1. Using the Pick tool with Ctrl held down, click on one of the intermediate objects.
2. With the Split/Fuse command chosen, one of the Fuse options will be highlighted (Fuse Start or Fuse End). Click on whichever is available, and the blend will return to its original state.

Controlling Color

The Blend roll-up menu has its own set of special color controls.

1. With the blend group selected, click on the Color control icon in the roll-up.
2. Click on the box next to rainbow to check it. The color wheel shows a line taking the short route between the starting and ending colors.
3. Below the rainbow box are the rotation options. Click on the one not presently selected. The line on the color wheel now takes the long route around. Click on Apply (see fig. 9.42).

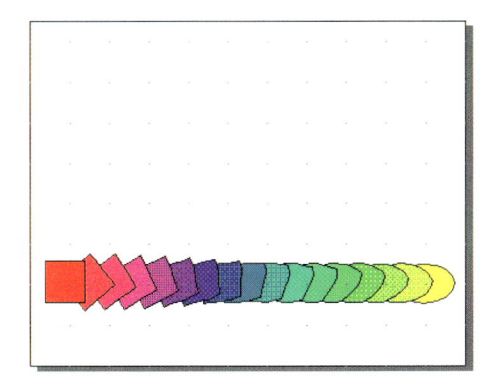

Figure 9.42
The blend now has a rainbow effect.

4. Save the file as BLEND.

Creating Multiple Objects

You can use the Blend command to make duplicate copies of an object.

1. Select New from the File menu.
2. With the Rectangle tool, draw a rectangle 2 inches wide by 3 inches high on the right side of the page. Fill it White.
3. With the Node Edit tool, drag one of the corners of the rectangle to round them.
4. Click and hold the Text tool down to access the fly-out menu, and click on the symbol icon.
5. Click on the drop-down menu for symbols and scroll down and select Dixieland. Enter **168** for the symbol and **.70** for the symbol size.

Chapter 9: Special Effects

6. Click and drag the highlighted symbol to the center of the rectangle. Fill it Black.

7. Select both objects with the Pick tool. Select **A**lign from the **A**rrange menu, and click on **C**enter for both horizontal and vertical. Click on OK. Your drawing should resemble figure 9.43.

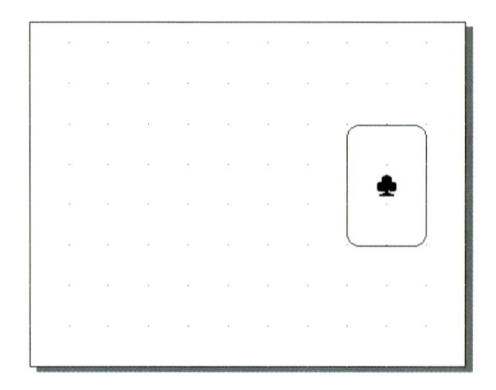

Figure 9.43
The clubs symbol is centered exactly.

8. With the Artistic text tool, type **A** in the upper left corner of the rectangle. Edit it as Casablanca, Bold, Center, 30 point.

9. Click and drag it to the bottom right corner of the rectangle while pressing the right mouse button.

10. Click on the A again to enter rotate/skew mode. Click and drag one of the corner arrows to rotate the letter 180 degrees.

Remember to hold down the Ctrl key when rotating the letter. This will rotate it in 15-degree intervals and make it easy to get it exactly 180 degrees.

11. Move it as necessary to position it comfortably in this corner (see fig. 9.44).

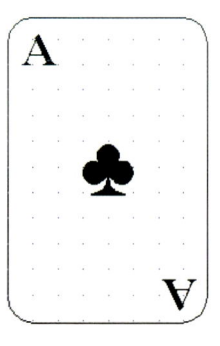

Figure 9.44
The Ace of Clubs.

12. **Select just the rectangle and click and drag it to the left of the page while holding down the Ctrl key and pressing the right mouse button.**

Using the Blend Command 185

13. Click the left rectangle again, and rotate it 15 degrees counterclockwise.

14. Marquee-select the right rectangle with its contents and rotate them 15 degrees clockwise.

15. Now select only the two rectangles. (Click on one, then hold down the Shift key and click on the other.)

16. Select the Blend Options icon from the roll-up menu. Enter **50** for the number of steps. Enter **-30** degrees for the rotation value and click on the Loop box to check it. Click on OK. The results are shown in figure 9.45.

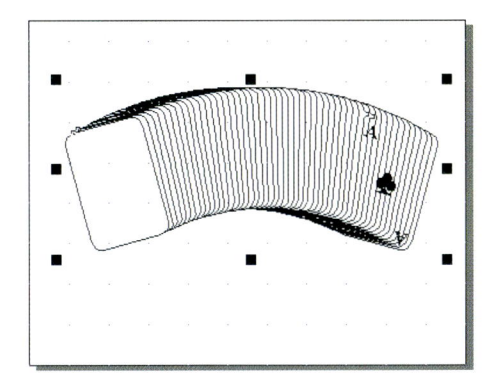

Figure 9.45
Shapes blend but image is not quite right.

17. From the <u>A</u>rrange menu, select <u>O</u>rder. Click on <u>R</u>everse Order (see fig. 9.46).

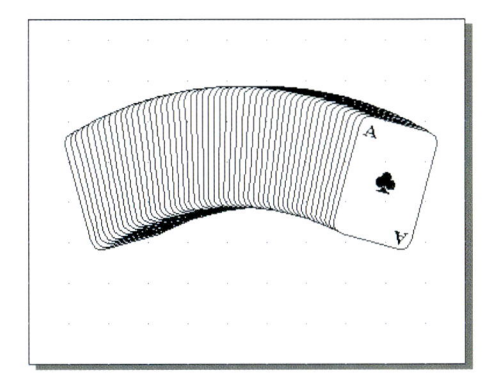

Figure 9.46
Now it looks like a fanned deck of cards.

18. Save the file as ACES.

Creating Airbrush Effects

Earlier you filled a circle with a radial fountain fill to add a highlight and give it some dimension. The blend command enables you add an airbrush-like highlight to any object.

Chapter 9: Special Effects

1. Open a new file.

2. Select the Symbols roll-up menu from the Text tool's fly-out menu, and scroll down to select Food. Enter **34** for the symbol number and set the size to 6.00. Drag the highlighted symbol to the center of the page (see fig. 9.47).

Figure 9.47
An apple symbol.

3. Click on the Pick tool to select the symbol. Choose Brea**k** Apart from the **A**rrange menu (or press Ctrl+K).

4. Click on the page to unselect the objects. Select the object in the apple as shown in figure 9.48.

Figure 9.48
One element of the apple art is selected.

5. Click and drag one of the corner control handles, and scale the object down to about 90% (watch the status bar) while holding down the Shift key and pressing the right mouse button.

6. Select the Node Edit (Shape) tool. The object is displayed with four nodes. By moving the two right side nodes and adjusting the control handles, move the right side of the object closer to right edge of the original object, as shown in figure 9.49.

Using the Blend Command

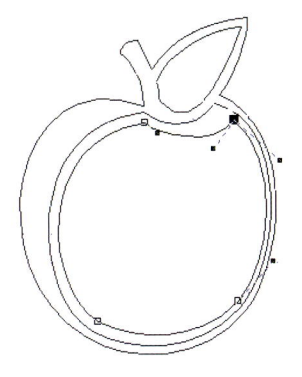

Figure 9.49
Edit the nodes to shape the object.

Move the two nodes first. The shape will extend out over the original. Now use the control handles to bring the edge back to within the original shape.

7. Move the left two nodes one at a time to the right until each is about 1/3 of an inch from the node to its right (see fig. 9.50).

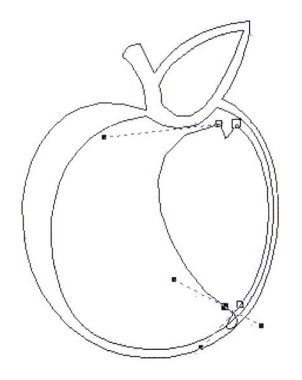

Figure 9.50
Moving the nodes using the Shape tool.

8. Click on the object in the center of its left side and drag it to the right until it is 1/2 inch from the opposite side.

9. Zoom in on the top portion of the object. Drag the center of the top of the object up, then click on the nodes and control handles and smooth out the shape. See the close-up in figure 9.51.

If you are having trouble getting the hang of this, don't be concerned. After you work in Node Edit mode for a while, you will become more attuned and intuitive with it. Just do the best you can for now.

10. Select the Pick tool and fill the object Orange.
11. Select the original object and fill it Red.

Chapter 9: Special Effects

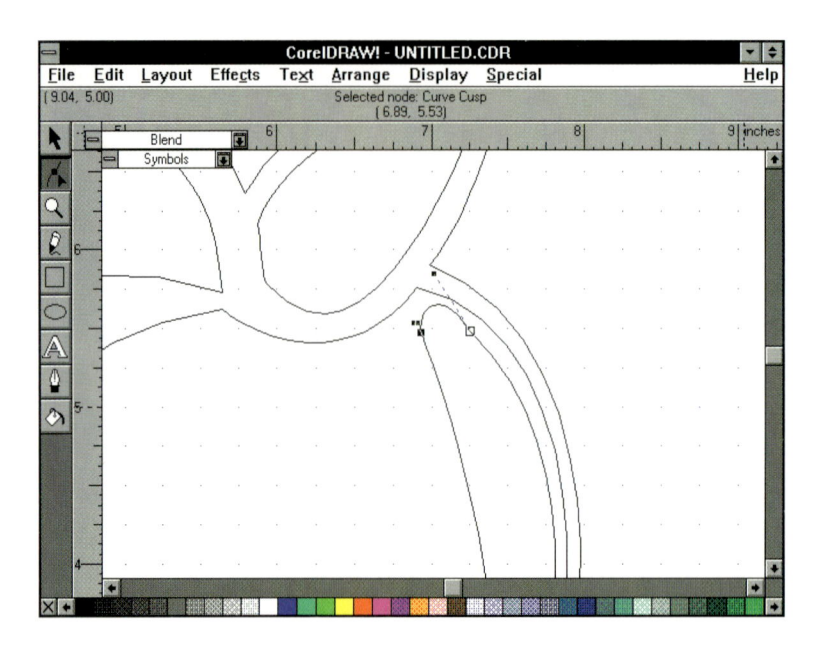

Figure 9.51
Fine-tuning the object's shape.

12. Select both objects (use the Shift key) and click on the X in the bottom of the screen with the right mouse button to set the outlines to none.

13. In the Blend roll-up menu, set steps to 20 and rotation to 0 and click on Apply.

14. Select the small leaf object on top of the apple. Select **S**tretch & Mirror from the Effe**c**ts menu. Set both values to 85% and check **L**eave original. Click on OK.

15. Fill the larger leaf Red and the smaller leaf Green. Select both and set their outlines to none.

16. In the Blend roll-up menu, set the steps to 10 and click on OK.

17. Select the outermost shape of the apple and apply a red fill. Press Ctrl+PgDn to place it behind the other objects. Set its outline to none (see fig. 9.52).

To create a shadow instead of a highlight, follow the same process, but make the inner object a darker color.

18. Save the file as APPLE.

Working with PowerLines

The PowerLine tools enable you to draw as if you are using traditional artists' tools. If you draw a circle with a paintbrush, for instance, the thickness of the line varies as to the angle of the brush, the pressure applied to

Working with PowerLines   189

the surface, and the amount of paint on the bristles. By using PowerLines, you can mimic this look. If you use a pressure-sensitive digitizing tablet instead of a mouse, the program responds to it. If you are an experienced illustrator, you probably can find many uses for these tools.

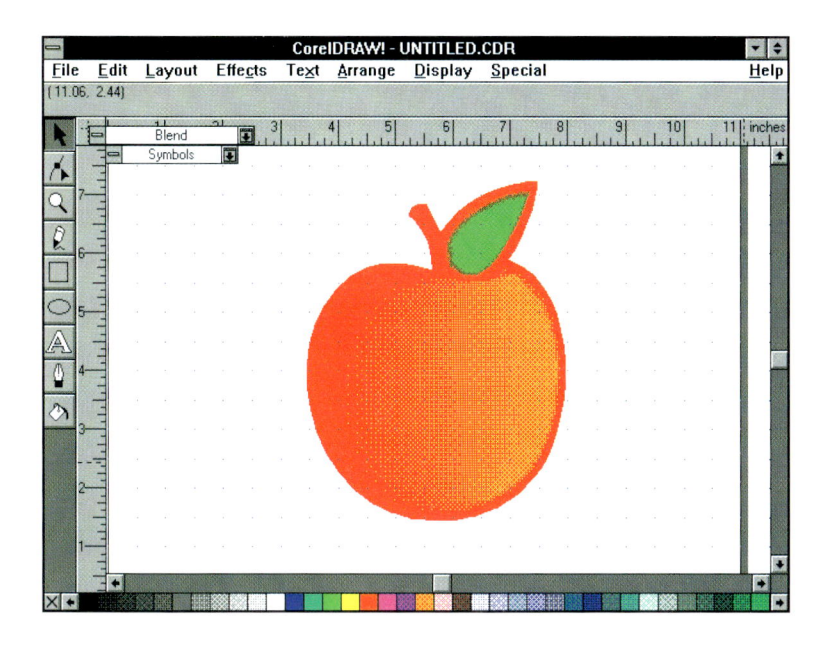

Figure 9.52
The finished apple.

Applying PowerLines

Up to now, all lines and curves have had uniform thicknesses. PowerLines enable you to vary the thickness of a line or curve.

1. Using the Freehand Pen tool, draw a curvy vertical line about 7 inches long in the left portion of the page.

2. Click and drag it to the right and create three copies of it, as in figure 9.53.

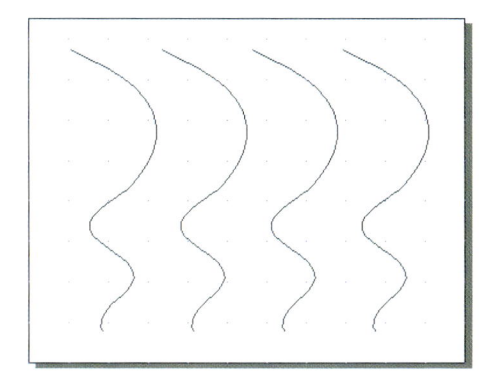

Figure 9.53
Four freehand curves.

Chapter 9: Special Effects

3. From the Effects menu, select **P**owerLine Roll-Up. The PowerLine roll-up menu appears, as shown in figure 9.54.

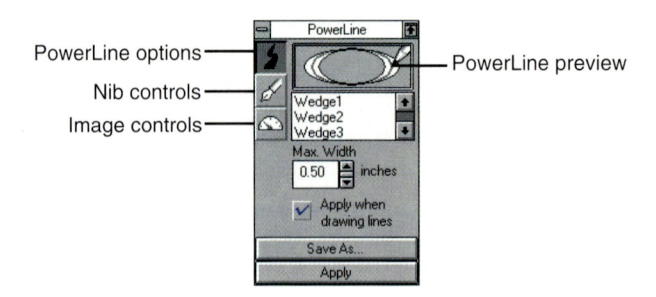

Figure 9.54
The PowerLine roll-up menu.

4. Select the first line from the left. Click on Wedge1 from the roll-up and click on Apply.

5. Select the second line from the left. Scroll down and select Woodcut2. Click on Apply.

6. Click on the third line and select Trumpet4 from the roll-up. Click on Apply.

7. Select the last line and apply Bullet3 to it. Click on Apply.

8. Select all of the lines. Fill them red and set the outlines for none. The various strokes are shown in figure 9.55.

Figure 9.55
An assortment of brushstrokes.

The brush width defaults to a maximum width of 0.50 inches. You just change the value to change the width of the brush. If you click on Apply when drawing lines, it will do just that: convert the line to the selected PowerLine as you finish drawing a line.

9. Save the file as PLINES.

Adjusting Nib Shape

PowerLine also enables you to edit the shape and angle of the brush (the *nib shape*).

1. Select the Nib Control icon from the roll-up menu.

2. Place the cursor over the Nib shape; it changes to a crosshair. Hold down the mouse button and move the crosshair around. The nib's shape and angle change as shown in figure 9.56.

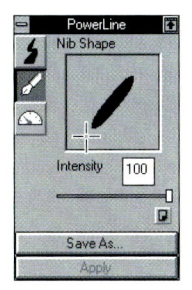

Figure 9.56
Editing the nib shape.

3. To change the Intensity, use the slide or enter a value from 1 to 100.

Intensity represents the change in width of the line as a percentage. If the maximum width has been set for 1 inch and the intensity is set at 50 (meaning 50 percent), for example, then the minimum width is 50 percent of the maximum, or 1/2 inch.

4. For precise adjustments, click on the page icon to reveal the numerical values for Angle, Nib Ratio, and Intensity.

Adjusting Image Controls

Click on the icon for Image Controls from the roll-up menu. The options are as follows:

Speed. This controls the width of a line at the points where it changes direction. If you were moving a brush quickly, the line probably would be wider at sharp turning points than if you were moving it slowly. The speed control simulates that effect.

Spread. This works in concert with the Speed control, acting as a smoothness control. When the Speed value is greater than zero, the Spread control is active. The higher the value, the smoother the line looks.

Ink Flow. This simulates the amount of ink left in your pen, 100 meaning full and 0 meaning almost empty. When set at a lower ink level, the pen will appear to dry up when the line becomes thin.

Scale With Image. When this box is checked, the PowerLine will stay in proportion when scaled larger or smaller. If a PowerLine with a max width of 1/2 inch is drawn, for example, and the line is scaled down by 50 percent, the resulting line has a max width of 1/4 inch. If Scale With Image was not selected, the resulting line would retain the max width of 1/2 inch.

Saving Custom PowerLines

As soon as you make any adjustments to a PowerLine style, it becomes a custom style.

1. Make whatever adjustments you want to a particular style.

2. Select Save As from the PowerLine roll-up menu. Enter a name for the new style and click on OK. The style is saved for future use.

The PowerLine feature is a truly advanced one. If you plan to use it, be prepared for a good deal of trial-and-error experimentation. Once mastered, you will see it was time well spent.

Chapter 10
Managing Files

CorelDRAW! offers a number of file management options including CorelMOSAIC!, a visual file manager. These options will help you keep track of your work, and enable you to easily work with files from multiple applications.

Sorting Files

By default, CorelDRAW! lists files saved in alphabetical order. However, you have the option of displaying files by date, from newest to oldest.

1. Click on **O**pen from the **F**ile menu.
2. In the Open Drawing dialog box, select **O**ptions.
3. Click on the **S**ort by menu and select Date. The files listed are no longer in alphabetical order, but start with the most recent file saved.
4. Click on the **S**ort by menu and select Name. The files are again listed in alphabetical order.

FEATURES COVERED

This chapter covers the following:

- Sorting files
- Keywords and notes
- Importing and exporting files
- Object linking and embedding
- CorelMOSAIC!

Chapter 10: Managing Files

Sorting by date can come in handy when you have multiple versions of artwork and want to see the most recent version. In general, however, it is best to sort files by name. You'll find it easier to keep track of your work.

Using Keywords and Notes

CorelDRAW! enables you to attach keywords and notes to files. *Keywords* enable you to group files by subject, client, and so on. *Notes* enable you to attach comments to a file.

1. Click on Open from the File menu.
2. Select Options from the dialog box.
3. From the list of files, click on chekflag.cdr to highlight it.

Do not double-click on the file name. You do not want to open the file—just highlight it.

4. Click in the Keywords box, and a text cursor will appear. Enter the text **SFX** (for special effects).
5. Click in the Notes box, and a text cursor appears. Enter the text **This file demonstrates the envelope effect.** (See fig. 10.1.)

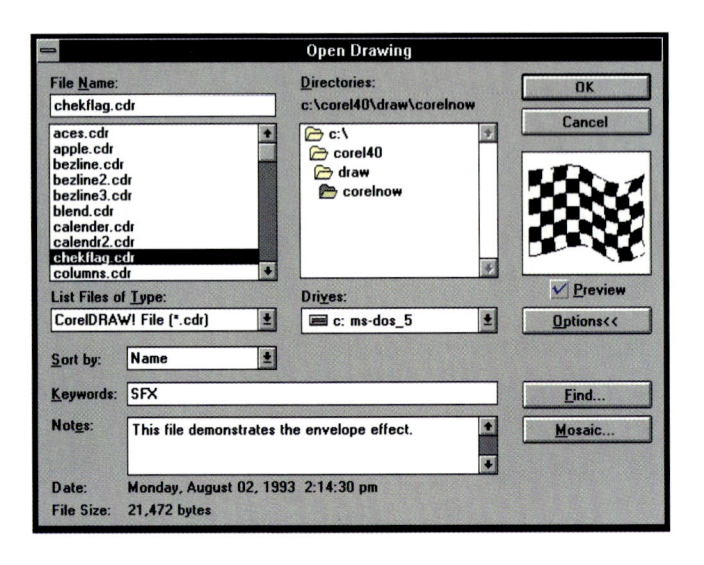

Figure 10.1
Entering text in the Keywords and Notes boxes.

6. Scroll down the file list and click on contour2.cdr. You are prompted to save changes to Keywords and Notes. Choose Yes to save changes.
7. With contour2.cdr highlighted, enter **SFX** in the Keywords box.
8. In the Notes box, enter the following: **This file represents the Contour effect.**

Importing and Exporting Files   195

9. Select any other file from the list and choose Yes to save changes to Keywords and Notes.

The Notes box might contain the date the file was started, the person working on it, the person the art is for, and so on.

10. Select the Find button in the Open dialog box. In the Keywords box, enter **SFX**. Select Search.

11. As seen in figure 10.2, only those files with the keyword SFX are displayed.

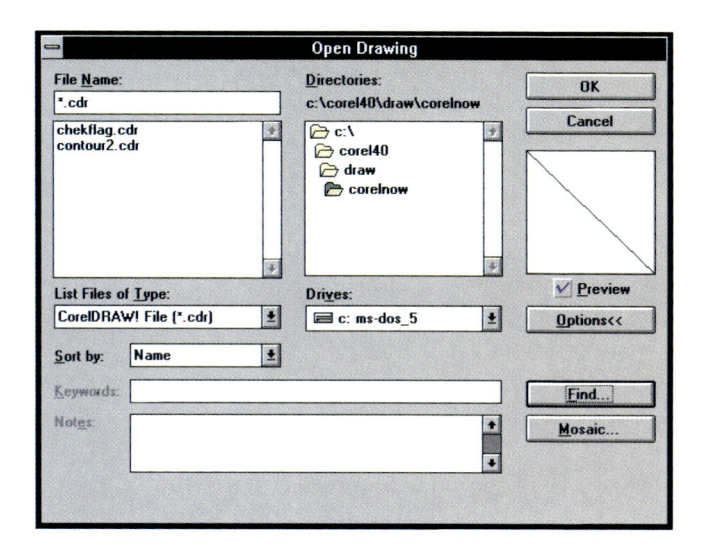

Figure 10.2
Files with the SFX keyword are displayed.

Files can have multiple keywords. The keywords must be separated by commas.

Use the Open command to edit the Keywords and Notes of existing files. When you save a new file or use the Save As command, you can enter the Keywords and Notes you want.

Importing and Exporting Files

You can use commands in the File menu to import and export files.

1. Select Import from the File menu.
2. From the List Files of Type box, select CorelDRAW!,*.CDR.

Chapter 10: Managing Files

If you are importing a Corel clip art file from the CD-ROM disk, for example, use this file setting, then change the drive to that of your CD-ROM and select the directory that contains the clip art you want. For this example, you will import a file that was previously created.

3. From the files listed, double-click on APPLE.CDR. A drawing of an apple appears, as shown in figure 10.3.

Figure 10.3
An apple drawing is imported with Import.

When you import a CorelDRAW! file, the objects in it are automatically grouped. To edit the imported file, you need to select Ungroup from the Arrange menu first.

You can import any file type for which you have installed the import filter. Open the Import dialog box by choosing Import from the File menu. Select List Files of Type and scroll through the list. These are the file types that can be imported.

If you import object-based graphics into CorelDRAW!, you can edit them as you would a CorelDRAW! file. Computer Graphic Metafile (CGM), Encapsulated PostScript (EPS), and Adobe Illustrator (AI) files all can be edited after import. If you import a bit-map file like Targa (TGA), TIFF (TIF), or PC Paintbrush (PCX), do all your editing to the bit-map before you import it, because it cannot be edited in CorelDRAW!. Or use CorelTRACE! to convert the bit map to a vector-based image, which then can be edited.

Exporting Files (Vector Based)

If you want to incorporate a graphic that you have created into another program, you will have to convert the file into a format that the other program understands. This conversion process is called *exporting*. To use a graphic in a desktop publishing program, for example, you would export it as an EPS file.

Importing and Exporting Files

1. Click on **O**pen from the **F**ile menu. Select ACES.CDR.
2. From the **F**ile menu, select **E**xport.
3. From the Export dialog box, select Encapsulated PostScript (*.EPS) as the file type.
4. The file name currently appears as ACES. Leave it unchanged, and the resulting file will be ACES.EPS.
5. You also can select the drive and directory to which this file will be exported. Set it for the Programs subdirectory of COREL40. Click on OK.

Normally, you would export the file into the directory of the program that will use this new file.

6. The Export EPS dialog box appears (see fig. 10.4), displaying the options available for this file format:

   - **Text A̲s Curves.** All text in the graphic is converted to curved objects.
   - **Text As T̲ext.** All text in the graphic remains as text objects using the CorelDRAW! fonts.
   - **All Fonts R̲esident.** CorelDRAW! assumes that all fonts are resident in the printer and will not use CorelDRAW! fonts. When sending the file to a third party for printing, for example, Adobe versions of the fonts used will be substituted for CorelDRAW! fonts.
   - **C̲onvert Color Bitmaps To Grayscale.** This option is necessary if the file contains a color bit map and you want to print it on a black-and-white PostScript Level 1 printer.
   - **F̲ountain Steps.** This option adjusts the number of steps used to represent a fountain fill. A small number of steps decreases printing time, and a greater number of steps yields a smoother fountain fill.
   - **H̲eader Resolution.** The image header creates a screen representation of the graphic that is used for sizing, cropping, and positioning. While it does not affect output quality, you can select a higher resolution if you find it easier to work with.

7. Click on As T̲ext to select it, and check the All Fonts R̲esident box.
8. Click on H̲eader Resolution and select 300 DPI.
9. Click on OK.

Chapter 10: Managing Files

The resulting file (ACES.EPS) will print using the resident fonts of the printing device, and will have a high-resolution screen image.

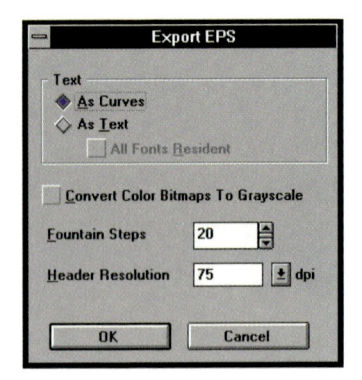

Figure 10.4
The Export EPS dialog box.

*You also can export only a portion of a file. First, select only those objects you want to export by using the Pick tool. Then, in the Export dialog box, click on the box for **S**elected Only. The exported file will contain only those objects that were selected.*

Exporting Files (Bit Maps)

1. From the **F**ile menu, open the APPLE.CDR file.
2. Again from the **F**ile menu, select **E**xport.
3. Select TIFF 5.0 Bitmap as the file type to be exported and click on OK. The Bitmap Export dialog box appears (see fig. 10.5), displaying the available options:

   - **C**olor. You can export in color or in shades of gray. Color options are 4-bit (16 colors), 8-bit (256 colors), or 24-bit (16 million colors). Gray options are 1-bit (black and white), 4-bit (16 shades), or 8-bit (256 shades).
   - **D**ithered colors. This option makes the bit map look like it has more colors than are actually available. It can be enabled for 16 and 256 colors, and 16 shades of gray.

Make sure that the program you are exporting to supports the color and dithering options you select.

   - Com**p**ressed. This enables you to significantly reduce the size of the exported bit-map file, which sometimes can be quite enormous. Some file formats automatically compress, while others give you the option.

Using Object Linking and Embedding

Some programs do not allow for use of compressed formats. Others do not deal with them well. Save the drawing in case it might have to be reexported.

- **Size.** This enables you to select the size of the bit map. If 1 to 1 is selected, you also can select the output resolution.

- **Resolution.** The higher the DPI (dots per inch), the better the visual quality of the bit map. The default setting is 300, but the custom setting can go as high as 600.

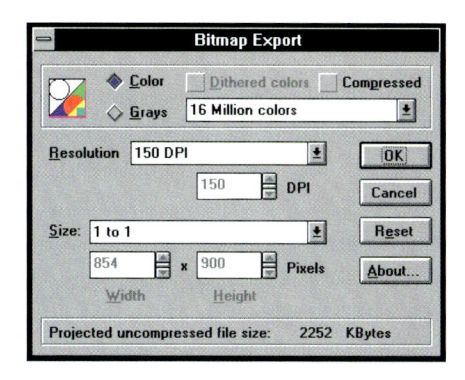

Figure 10.5
The Bitmap Export dialog box.

This file, when set at 16 million colors and sized at 1 to 1 with 300 dpi resolution, will export to a bit-map file of over 9 megabytes (9M). Files of this size can exceed the capacities of your system and can result in error messages. Reducing the resolution to 150 dpi reduces the size of the file by about 75 percent. This is a good way to reduce file size.

4. Select 256 colors and check **D**ithered colors in the color options section.

5. Click on the **S**ize menu and select 800×600 (SVGA). The size of the exported file is down to less than .5M. Click on OK.

6. The file is exported as APPLE.TIF.

Using Object Linking and Embedding

Object linking and embedding (OLE) is a Windows feature that enables you to take information created in one program and import it into another program while maintaining a connection between the two. Let's say you have created a graphic in CorelDRAW!, for example, and have exported it into a desktop publishing program using OLE. A few days later your client asks you to make changes to the graphic. By using OLE, when you make and save changes in CorelDRAW!, the changes are reflected in the graphic in the desktop program as well.

When you installed CorelDRAW! you were asked if you wanted to install SHARE. It must be installed if you wish to use OLE. If you chose not to install SHARE, refer to your DOS manual for installation instructions.

Embedding Objects

When you embed an object, you are taking information from a source application and copying it to a destination application. This is similar to using the Import command. The difference is that you can make changes to the object from within the destination application. As you are working with a copy, any changes you make from within the destination application will not affect the object in the source application. Nor will changes made in the source application affect the image in the destination application.

What you basically are doing is running both applications at once. Your system must have enough memory to support this.

Linking Objects

When you link an object in your destination application, you are not making a copy, but are sharing the original object from the source application. When you edit the object in the source application, the changes are reflected wherever it has been linked.

Chapter 13 includes an overview of CorelCHART!, in which a chart is created and imported into CorelDRAW! using OLE.

Using CorelMOSAIC!

CorelMOSAIC! enables you to visually organize and manipulate files by creating small bit-map versions of your files called *thumbnails*. CorelMOSAIC! supports other file formats besides those created in CorelDRAW! and can create compressed libraries of files as well.

You can activate Mosaic from the COREL 4 program group in the program manager or from within the program. Select Open from the File menu and choose Options, then choose Mosaic. The Mosaic display window appears, as seen in figure 10.6.

Opening a File

By displaying thumbnails, CorelMOSAIC! makes it easy to view and open files.

1. To open a file, double-click on the thumbnail of the file.
2. Scroll down until you can see STYLES.CDR. Double-click on it to open it.

Using CorelMOSAIC! 201

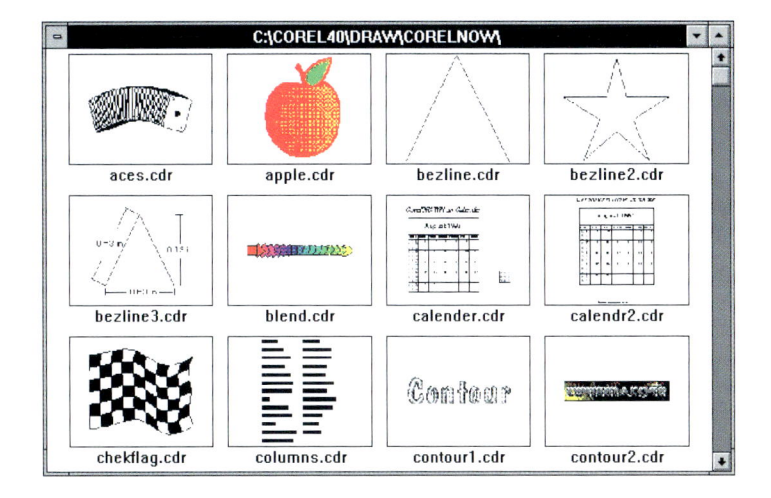

Figure 10.6
The Mosaic screen.

3. To return to Mosaic, select **O**pen from the **F**ile menu, choose **O**ptions, and choose **M**osaic.

Windows gives you a shortcut to jump between applications. Hold down the Alt key and press the Tab key. This enables you to cycle through all applications open in Windows. Release these keys when you see CorelMOSAIC!.

Creating a Library

When you save files in a library, they are automatically compressed to save hard disk space.

1. From the **F**ile menu, select **N**ew Catalog/Library.

2. List Files of **T**ype should be set to Corel Library (*.CLB), as in figure 10.7.

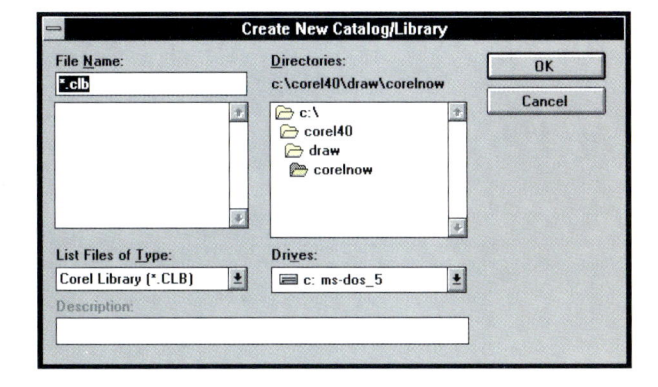

Figure 10.7
The Create New Catalog/Library dialog box, showing Corel Library (.CLB) in the List Files of **T**ype menu.*

3. In the File **N**ame window, type **SFX**. Click on OK. SFX.CLB appears in the scroll box below the File Name box.

Searching for Files

You also can use keywords to find files in CorelMOSAIC!.

1. Click on the title bar of the window containing your Corel files to make it active.

2. From the **E**dit menu, click on Select By **K**eyword.

3. In the first box, type **SFX**. Click on start search. The program highlights the files with that keyword (see fig. 10.8).

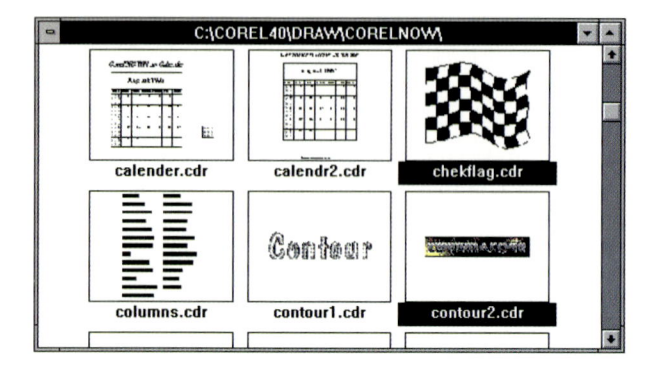

Figure 10.8
Keyword files are highlighted.

Copying Files to a Library

After a library file has been created, you can place CorelDRAW! files in it.

1. With the two files highlighted, click and drag on one of them and move the cursor to the library window (see fig. 10.9).

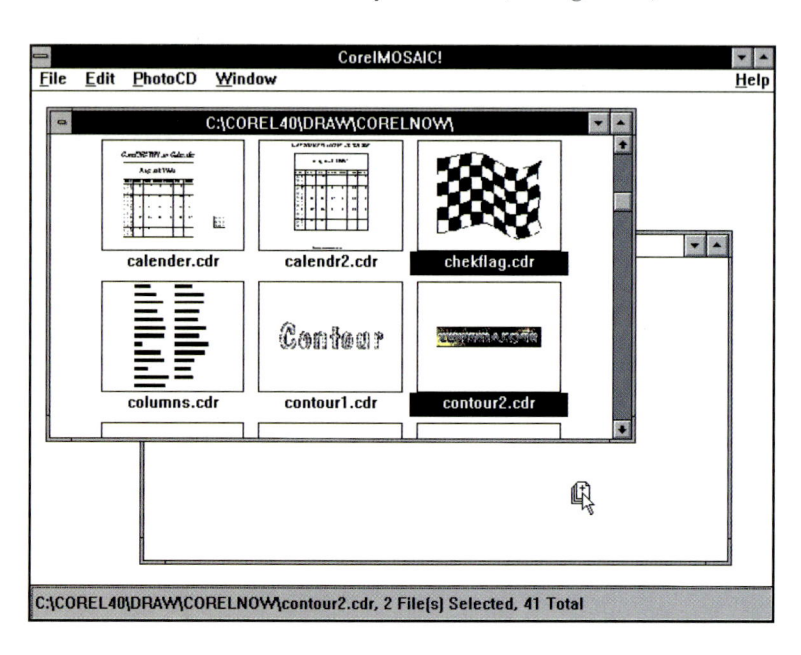

Figure 10.9
The Drag and Drop function.

Using CorelMOSAIC!

2. When prompted to confirm copy, click on Yes to All.

3. The files now are copied and compressed in the SFX library.

Creating a Catalog

A *catalog* is a group of thumbnails assembled as a sort of "photo album." It enables you to group files together without creating new subdirectories.

1. Double-click on the upper left corner of the SFX library window to close it.

2. From the File menu, select New Catalog/Library. Click on the List Files of Type menu and select Corel Catalog.

3. Name the catalog **BEZLINE**. Click on OK.

4. Click on the window containing your Corel files to make it active.

5. Select the three files created in the Bézier line examples and copy them to the catalog. Click on BEZLINE.CDR to highlight it.

6. While holding down the Ctrl key, click on BEZLINE2.CDR to highlight it as well. Repeat this once more with BEZLINE3.CDR. All three files are highlighted.

Holding down the Ctrl key enables you to make multiple selections of files. If you want to select a large group of files in succession, click on the first file to highlight it, hold down the Shift key, and click on the last file you want. This selects those two files and all the files between them.

7. With the three files selected, click on one of them, drag the files to the catalog window, and release the mouse button.

8. When prompted to confirm copy, click on Yes to All.

Unlike a library, a catalog does not copy the file. It is used only to organize files, not to archive them.

Chapter 11
Printing Files

With CorelDRAW! you can output your work on PostScript and non-PostScript printers, Linotronics, and film recorders, as long as the device is supported by Windows. You can output files by using the **P**rint command in the **F**ile menu.

Preparing Your Printing Device

Before you begin printing, there are a number of options to consider and adjustments to make.

Print Setup

1. From the **F**ile menu, select P**r**int Setup. The Print Setup dialog box appears (see fig. 11.1).

2. The printer that is currently selected is displayed as the **D**efault Printer. If you need to use a different printer (or print driver), select Specific **P**rinter and click on the menu arrow to display the printers and drivers that are available. Choose your printer or print driver, and click on OK.

Print Dialog Box

To execute the print command, there must be objects present to print. Use one of the previously created files for this example.

1. From the **F**ile menu, select **O**pen and click on CONTOUR2.CDR.

FEATURES COVERED

This chapter covers the following topics:

- Preparing your printing device
- Printing a file
- Batch printing

Chapter 11: Printing Files

2. From the File menu, select Print. The Print dialog box appears, as in figure 11.2.

You can select Portrait or Landscape orientation from Print Setup. If a file selected for printing does not match the marked orientation, the program automatically will prompt you to correct it.

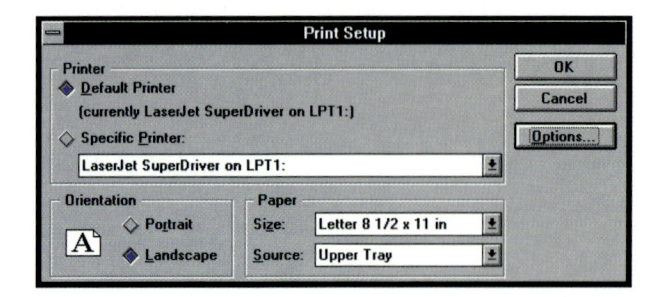

Figure 11.1
The Print Setup dialog box.

The Options button enables you to adjust options specific to your printing device. For that reason, setting options cannot be discussed.

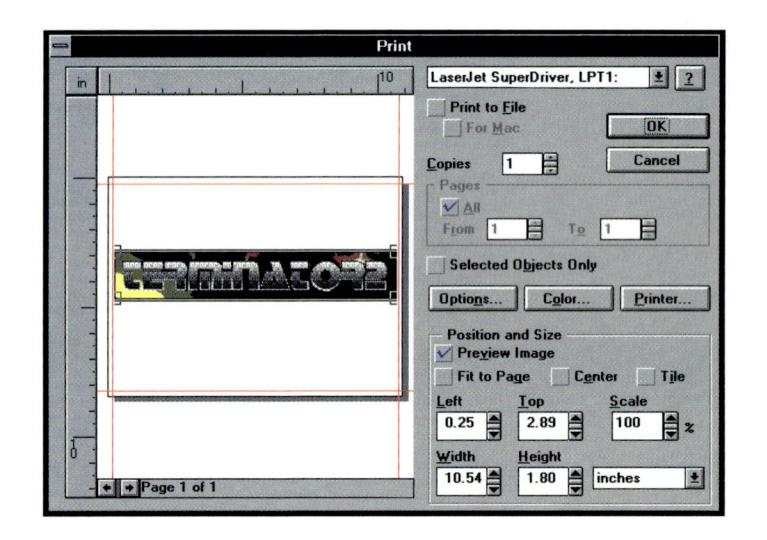

Figure 11.2
The Print dialog box.

The keyboard shortcut for the Print command is Ctrl+P. The Print command is used often, so commit this shortcut to memory!

The Print dialog box options are as follows:

- **Printer Selection Box.** Enables you to change the printer device or driver. It displays the currently selected printer or driver.
- **Print to File.** This creates an image and saves it as a file, instead of sending it to your printing device. It is useful when you need to send an image to a third-party printer or service bureau.
- **Copies.** Enter a value for the number of copies to print.
- **Pages.** If the file has multiple pages, you can print all of them by checking All, or uncheck All and enter page numbers for From and To. To print a single page of a multiple page document, enter that page number for both values.
- **Selected Objects Only.** With this option checked, only objects currently selected by the Pick tool will be printed.
- **Printer.** Clicking here displays the Windows Printer dialog box.
- **Preview Image.** With this box checked, the window to the left displays the graphic. You might want to uncheck this if you are printing complex files and don't want to wait for them to redraw.
- **Fit to Page.** This function scales down the entire image to fit the paper size of the printer currently selected. If you create an image that is larger than your printer's paper, this will reduce the image to fit on the page. It does not have any effect on the original file—only on the way it is printed.
- **Center.** This takes the entire image and centers it on the page. Again, this does not affect the original file—only the way it is printed.
- **Tile.** If portions of your image exceed the page boundaries, this option prints them on additional pages.
- **Scale.** This increases or reduces the size of your image when printed. This option can help you in proofing small objects without having to make changes in the original file.

Options Dialog Box

You can access the Options dialog box by selecting the Options button in the Print dialog box (see fig. 11.3).

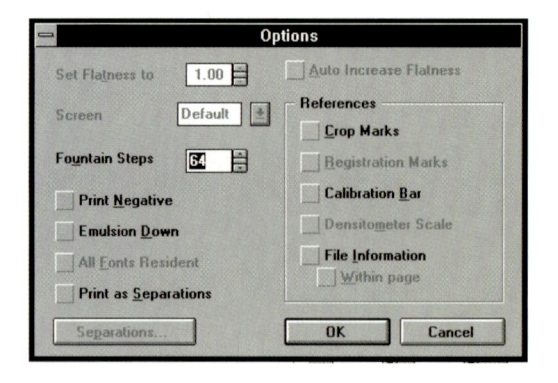

Figure 11.3

The Options dialog box.

The Options dialog box contains the following choices:

- **Set Fla**t**ness to.** This applies only to PostScript devices. Sometimes when printing a complex object you get a "limitcheck error" and the printer stops printing. Increasing the value of the Flatness simplifies the way the curves of an object are drawn, making it easier to print.

- **Screen.** This applies to PostScript devices. When set at default, your file prints at your printer's default screen setting. To change the setting, click on the menu arrow and choose a frequency from the list.

- **Fo**u**ntain Steps.** This sets the number of steps that are printed when rendering a fountain fill. For proofing purposes, a low number (like 20) is good because the image will print faster. For final output, a higher number (like 200) will render the fountain fills much smoother.

At some point the step value will max out. What that means is, as you increase the value, the image will take longer to print, but its quality will not improve. A little experimentation with your particular device may be necessary to find the max-out point.

- **A**uto Increase Flatness. With this box checked, the program automatically increases the flatness value until the file prints.

- **Print N**egative. This causes the file to print as a negative image; it enables you to print directly to film.

- **Emulsion D**own. This causes the file to print as a mirror image of itself.

- **All F**onts Resident. With a PostScript device, the program uses the fonts resident in the printer rather than the CorelDRAW! fonts.

- **Print as S**eparations. With this option checked, the program prints each color component on a separate page. If you are using Process colors (CMYK), for example, the image will print on four pages: cyan, magenta, yellow, and black. Also, when Print as **S**eparations is selected, the program automatically checks the boxes for **C**rop Marks, Densito**m**eter Scale, **R**egistration Marks, and File **I**nformation.

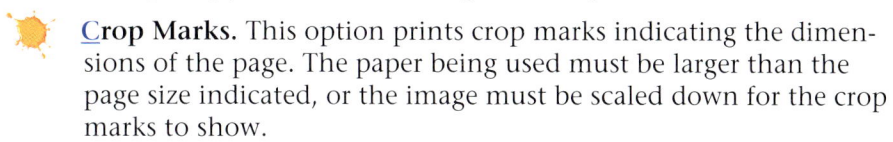

- **Se**p**arations.** This option is available only when Print for **S**eparations is selected. Clicking here brings up the Separations dialog box, giving you access to the separation options.

- **C**r**op Marks.** This option prints crop marks indicating the dimensions of the page. The paper being used must be larger than the page size indicated, or the image must be scaled down for the crop marks to show.

- **R**e**gistration Marks.** This prints small registration lines on the graphic to help align negatives. It is available only if you are printing separations.

- **Calibration B**a**r.** With this option selected, a calibration bar of six colors plus a gray scale is printed. You can use this to check the color output of your printing device against the colors on your computer screen.

- **Densito**m**eter Scale.** This prints a densitometer scale with your graphic. A *densitometer scale* shows the intensity of each color ink as a grid to help you check accuracy and consistency of the output.

- **File I**n**formation.** This option prints the file name and current date outside the page border. The image might need to be scaled down for the information to fit on the page. When printing to separation, the color separation information is printed as well.

- **W**it**hin Page.** When File **I**nformation is checked, this option is available. When checked, the file information is printed within the printed page. If necessary, the program will automatically scale the image size.

Printing a File

Now that you have explored the printing options, you can output the file to the printer.

1. To start from scratch, click on Cancel in the current dialog box. Repeat this until you return to the drawing screen.
2. Press Ctrl+P to bring up the Print dialog box.
3. If the Pre**v**iew Image box is not checked, click on it now to check it.
4. Click on the Optio**n**s button to bring up the Options dialog box.
5. Set Fo**u**ntain Steps to 64.
6. Click on the boxes for **C**rop Marks, Calibration **B**ar, and File **I**nformation so that they all are checked. Click on OK.

Chapter 11: Printing Files

7. Looking at the preview window, nothing seems to have changed. Reduce the **S**cale value from 100% to 75%. Now you can see the effects of the options settings (see fig. 11.4).

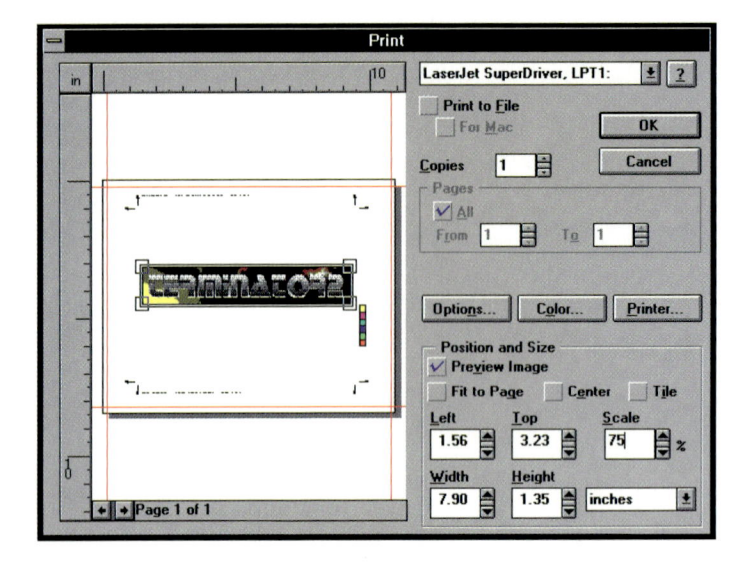

Figure 11.4
The Print dialog box displays options selected.

8. As a final touch, click on C**e**nter in the Position and Size section so that the image is perfectly centered.

9. To output the image to your printer, click on OK.

Printing Tips

Use the following tips to improve printing quality and to save time on print jobs.

- **Printer memory.** The internal memory of your printing device can affect the quality of your output. For example, an HP LaserJet printer can print at 300 dpi. However, it may be configured with only 500K or 1M of internal memory. This severely limits the size and complexity of an image to be printed, and might force you to print at 75 or 150 dpi. Adding additional memory to the printer will solve this problem.

- **Bit maps, bit-map fills, and pattern fills.** These can tax your system and greatly increase printing time. To save printing time when proofing work, use the Selected O**b**jects Only option in the Print dialog box, and unselect objects that will take a long time to print. Also, reducing the size of a bit-map image in the drawing will improve print time.

*To unselect unwanted objects, first use the Select **A**ll command from the **E**dit menu. Then, with the Pick tool, click on those objects you want to exclude from printing while pressing the Shift key. This unselects those objects while leaving the others unaffected.*

- **Fountain fills.** To reduce time when printing images with many fountain fills, reduce the number of Fo**u**ntain Steps when printing proofs. A value of 20 probably will show a good improvement in printing time. Also, radial fills put more stress on the system than do linear fills, so you might want to use them sparingly.

- **Masks.** When two objects are combined to create a window mask, the resulting object can be a very complex one for the program to image. If you have trouble printing an image, try printing everything but the mask and see how that affects output.

Batch Printing

You have created a series of drawings and want to print them. Opening each file one at a time and executing the **P**rint command could take forever. To save time, use the batch printing function of CorelMOSAIC!.

1. Select **O**pen from the **F**ile menu. Click on Options and select **M**osaic. The Mosaic screen appears.

2. Select one or more files that you want to print using any of these methods:

    - Choose Select by **K**eyword from the **E**dit menu.

    - Select **A**ll—also from the **E**dit menu—highlights every file in this directory.

    - Click on thumbnails using the Ctrl key—this enables you to select a group of individual files from throughout the directory.

    - Click on thumbnails using the Shift key—this enables you to select a group of successive thumbnails by clicking on the first and last of a group.

3. From the **F**ile menu, select **P**rint Files.

4. The Print dialog box appears. Click on the Optio**n**s button.

5. Click on the boxes to uncheck **C**rop Marks, File **I**nformation, and Calibration **B**ar. Click on OK.

6. Uncheck the box for C**e**nter.

7. Return the Scale value to 100%.

8. Click on OK to print the files.

Chapter 12
CorelTRACE!

CorelTRACE! is a fast and versatile file conversion program. It enables you to take bit-map files and convert them into vector format (object-oriented) files, which then can be edited in CorelDRAW!. If you own a scanning device supported by the program, CorelTRACE! gives you direct access to it.

Tracing an Image

Scenario: You are creating a document for your client (or yourself), and you need to incorporate an existing logo. You could try to re-create it in CorelDRAW!, but that might not be practical. The solution: scan it with a scanning device, convert it in CorelTRACE!, and import it into CorelDRAW!. For this example, you will edit a previously created file and use that as your logo.

1. Open the CorelDRAW! program and open the CHEKFLAG.CDR file.

2. Select Align from the Arrange menu and click on the box for Center on Page. Click on OK.

3. Using the Artistic Text tool, enter the text string **Corel Race Team** below the flag art. Edit the text as Switzerland, Bold-Italic, 40 point, center alignment. Position it under the flag art.

4. Using the Rectangle tool, draw a rectangle around the flag and text string.

FEATURES COVERED

This chapter covers the following:

- Tracing an image
- Tracing options
- Tracing a text image
- Importing a traced image
- Tracing multiple files

214   Chapter 12: CorelTRACE!

5. With the Outline tool, edit the rectangle thickness to 8 points. Your logo should resemble figure 12.1.

Figure 12.1
The finished logo.

6. Save the file as LOGO.CDR.
7. Select **E**xport from the **F**ile menu to bring up the Export dialog box.
8. For the type of file, select TIFF 5.0 Bitmap. In the directory box, make CORELNOW the directory to which the file will be exported. Click on OK.
9. In the Bitmap Export dialog box, click on **G**rays. From the drop-down menu for colors, select Black & White. Set **R**esolution at 300 dpi, and size at 1:1. Click on OK.

    You now have a TIFF file of the logo, exactly as you would if you had scanned it from a logo sheet.

If you are not familiar with scanners, the scan file is always a bit-map image, and the TIFF format is a common file format.

10. Minimize the CorelDRAW! screen and bring up the Program Manager. From the Corel 4.0 group, double-click on CorelTRACE. The CorelTRACE! screen appears, including the menu bar shown in figure 12.2.

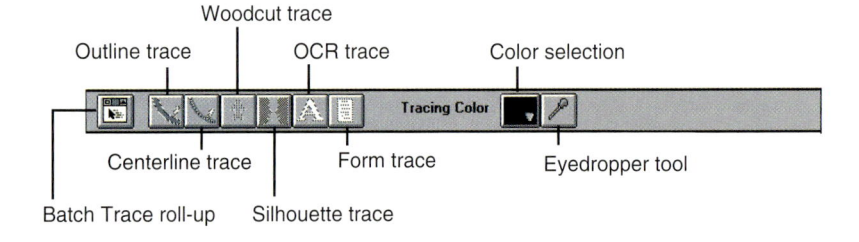

Figure 12.2
The CorelTRACE! menu bar.

11. From the **F**ile menu, select **O**pen; the Open dialog box appears. Select TIFF Bitmap for the type of file. The file box will display LOGO.TIF as the only TIF file available. Double-click on it to open it. The image appears in the source window, as in figure 12.3.

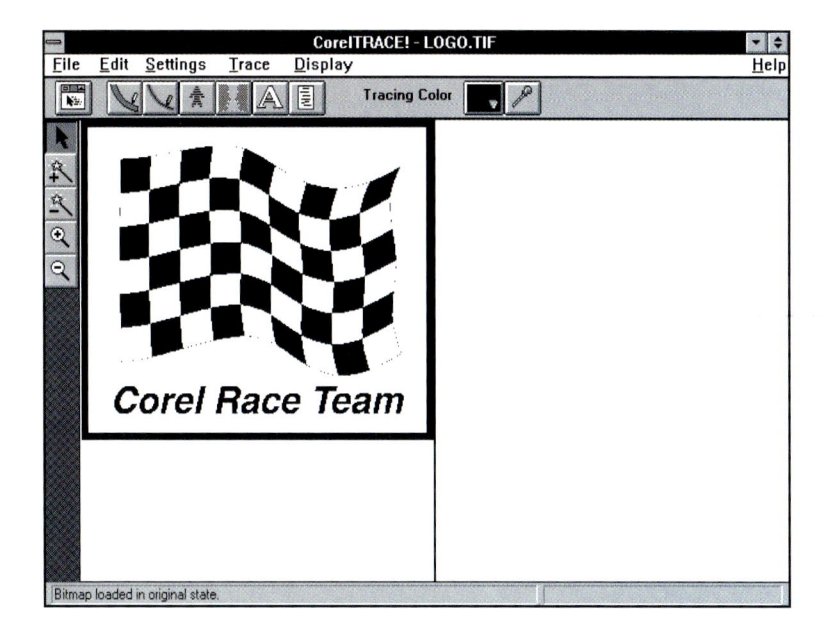

Figure 12.3
The TIFF file is displayed in the source window.

The image is ready to be traced. There are six tracing methods in all:

- **Outline method.** This method traces the outline of each element of the image and fills the resulting object with respect to the original. It is used to trace images with solid shapes, like the Corel Race Team logo.

- **Centerline method.** This method is for tracing an image with thin lines, as opposed to a solid object. An example might be an electronic schematic or an illustration drawn with a fine-tipped pen.

- **Woodcut method.** This method creates a woodcut special effect of the image. The angle and thickness of the woodcut are adjustable.

- **Silhouette method.** Used when tracing a portion of an image, it creates a single object filled with a specified color.

- **Optical Character Recognition (OCR).** Use this method to scan text when you want it to remain as text in the resulting file. You then can edit it as text and apply any and all text attributes to it.

- **Form method.** This traces text with the OCR method, then traces any remaining objects as objects. As the name implies, you might use it to trace a form.

Use the Outline method to trace the logo.

1. Select Outline from the Trace menu, or click on the Outline icon. The program traces the image and displays the trace image, as in figure 12.4.

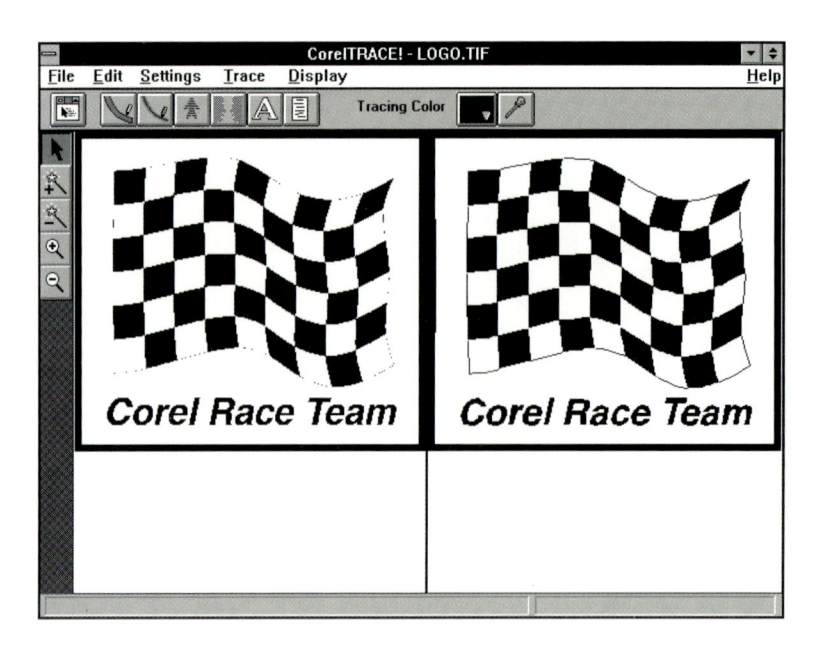

Figure 12.4
The trace image is displayed.

2. To save the trace image, select Save from the File menu. From the Save fly-out menu, choose Trace As. In the Save Trace As dialog box, name the file LOGO and click on OK. CorelTRACE! will save it in PostScript format as LOGO.EPS.

Using the Tracing Options

CorelTRACE! offers a number of options for how an image is traced.

Tracing with the Pick Tool

You might scan an entire page but need only a portion of it. The Pick tool selects the area to be traced. In this example, you might want to trace only the flag art and then add the type and surrounding rectangle in CorelDRAW!.

1. Select Open from the File menu, and double-click on LOGO.TIF to reopen it.

2. Select the Pick tool and marquee-select only the flag art in the source image. Click on the Outline icon.

3. The resulting trace image contains only those objects within the marquee-select box, as in figure 12.5.

Using the Tracing Options   217

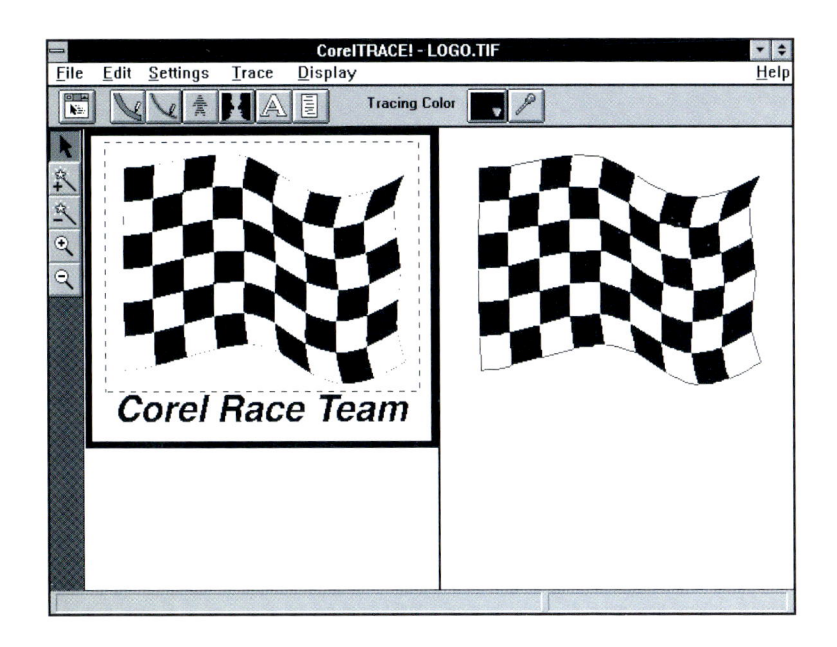

Figure 12.5
Tracing selected objects only.

Selecting only the objects you need to trace greatly reduces the time it takes to trace an image, and saves you the work of having to delete unwanted objects later.

Click in the source window below the logo image. This clears the marquee box around the flag.

Tracing with the Magic Wand

The Magic Wand enables you to select areas of similar color and trace them.

1. Select the Zoom In (+) tool. Draw a marquee box around the word *Corel*.

2. Select the Magic Wand Selection (+) tool. Place the point of the wand inside the letter *C* in *Corel* and click. The letter is selected and surrounded by a marquee line, as shown in figure 12.6.

When you click the Magic Wand on an area, it pans out in all directions from the point where you clicked, and defines the area to be traced by the color of the spot where you clicked.

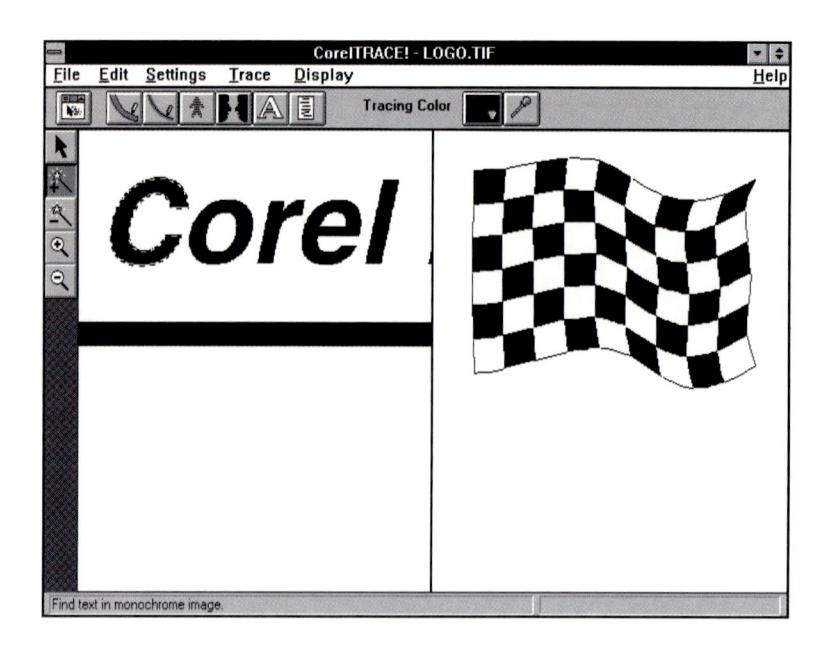

Figure 12.6
Selecting areas with the Magic Wand.

Using the Silhouette Method

The Silhouette method is used in conjunction with the Magic Wand to select areas to be traced by color. It also enables you to select the resulting fill color in the trace image.

1. The source image still is a close-up of the word *Corel*. Select the Magic Wand (+) tool and click on the letter *o* in *Corel*. Hold down the Shift key and click on the letter *r*. Repeat this for *e* and *l* so that all four letters are selected.

> *Just as in CorelDRAW!, holding down the Shift key enables you to multi-select items. You will find that this sort of consistency occurs whenever possible.*

2. Click on the Tracing Color button and select Blue.

3. Click on the Silhouette icon. As you should see, the objects are shown in blue, but the letters have filled in.

4. Using the Magic Wand (+) tool, click in the white area inside the letter *o* to select it. Hold the Shift key down and select the white area inside the letter *e* too.

5. Click on the Trace Color button and select White. Click on the Silhouette icon. The white areas are added, and the text now should look correct.

Setting the Custom Tracing Options

CorelTRACE! has certain default settings that control the way an image is traced. The **S**ettings menu gives you access to these controls.

From the **S**ettings menu, choose **M**odify. From the fly-out menu, select **L**ine Attributes. The Line Attributes dialog box appears, as in figure 12.7.

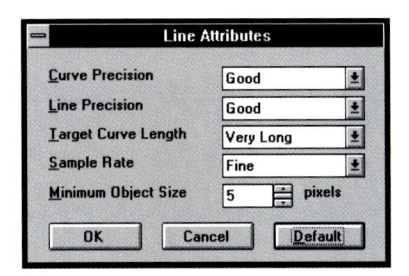

Figure 12.7
The Line Attributes dialog box.

This dialog box displays the five parameters you can adjust.

> *The parameters currently are set at default, and they can be returned to these settings after being changed by clicking on the **D**efault button.*

The parameters are:

- **Curve Precision.** This determines how tightly the curves of the original image are followed.

- **Line Precision.** This determines whether a straight section of a curve is converted to a line.

- **Target Curve Length.** This determines the limit for the length of individual curves in the trace image. A shorter curve length setting will result in a more detailed tracing by creating more nodes, but also will create a larger trace file.

- **Sample Rate.** This determines how closely the program follows the shapes it traces. The Medium setting is best for most images. The Coarse setting might help eliminate jaggies along some lines.

- **Minimum Object Size.** CorelTRACE! counts the number of pixels in an object. If that number is less than the Minimum Object Size set, the object is not traced. A low number setting yields a traced image of greater detail.

> *There are no set answers as to the way you should adjust these parameters. The best procedure is to trace an object using the default settings, save it, and examine it closely in CorelDRAW!. From there on, it's trial and error. Change one setting at a time and save it for comparison.*

Tracing a Text Object

To trace text so that it remains as a text object, use the OCR method. You will create a simulated scan object as in the first example, then trace it as text.

1. Return to CorelDRAW!. Choose New from the File menu if another file currently is open.

2. Select Text Roll-Up from the Text menu. Edit the text as Courier, 12 point, normal, left align. (This will simulate scanning a page of typewriter copy.) Click on Apply. The Text Attributes dialog box appears. Check the box for Paragraph Text only, and click on OK.

3. Select the Paragraph Text tool and draw a paragraph box 1 1/2 inches high and 3 inches wide in the middle of the page.

4. Enter the following text:

   ```
   This is for tracing purposes only. This is for tracing purposes
   only. This is for tracing purposes only.
   ```

   Click on the Pick tool to leave Paragraph Text mode. Use the Zoom In tool to check that the text is correct, as shown in figure 12.8.

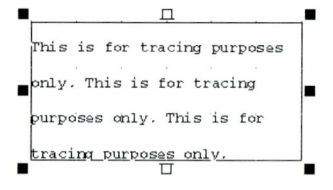

Figure 12.8
The text should appear like this.

5. From the File menu, select Export. The file type should still be the same as TIFF, and the directory should still be set as CORELNOW. Name the file TRACETXT and click on OK. The Bitmap Export dialog box appears.

6. The settings in the dialog box are those from the previous example and will work fine for this image as well. Click on OK.

7. Return to CorelTRACE!. From the File menu select Open, and double-click on TRACETXT. The image appears in the source window, as in figure 12.9.

8. To trace the text image as text, click on the OCR trace button.

9. To save the traced text, you have two options. You can save it as a CorelTRACE file (EPS), as you did in the previous example. However, save it here as a TXT file (ASCII), which will retain the paragraph text attributes. Select Save from the File menu, and click on Text As from the fly-out.

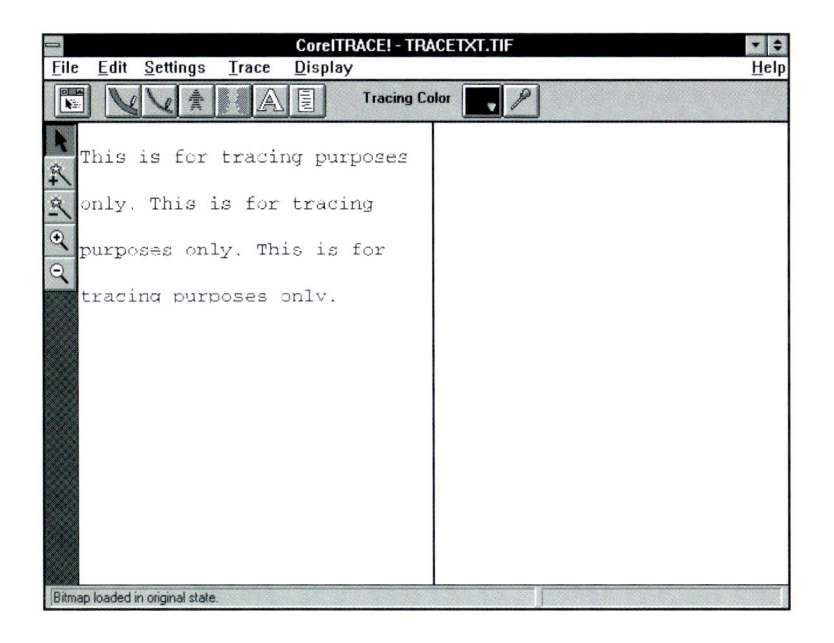

Figure 12.9
The text as it appears in the source window.

10. In the Save Text As dialog box, name the file TRACETXT. Make sure the directory selected is CORELNOW. Click on OK. The text is saved as an ASCII file in the CORELNOW directory.

Importing a Traced Image

After an image has been traced, you can bring it into CorelDRAW! and treat it as you would any other object.

1. Return to CorelDRAW!. Choose New from the File menu.

2. Select Import from the File menu. Click on CORELTRACE.EPS for the type of file to be imported. Make sure CORELNOW is the current directory.

3. LOGO.EPS will be the only file name displayed. Double-click on it to import it. It appears in the center of the page, as in figure 12.10.

Figure 12.10
The trace image appears in the center of the page.

Chapter 12: CorelTRACE!

4. Use the Zoom In tool and make the logo as large as possible. Select **E**dit Wireframe from the **D**isplay menu (or use the shortcut, Shift+F9). As you should see, the lines of the surrounding box are not perfectly straight.

5. Use the Zoom In tool again and show a close-up of the word *Corel*. Notice that the text characters did not trace that smoothly.

> *What are your options to improve the traced logo?*
>
> - *Go back to CorelTRACE! and make changes in the parameters to see if you can improve the tracing.*
>
> - *In this case, you have the font available in CorelDRAW!. You can replace the traced text by using the text tool. If this were a custom font designed for this logo, you wouldn't have this option.*
>
> - *Assuming this is the best trace you can achieve, and that the font was not available, you can clean up the image with the Shape tool.*

6. The logo currently is grouped together. Use the **U**ngroup command from the **A**rrange menu to ungroup the objects.

> *Trace images that are imported into CorelDRAW! are always grouped together.*

7. Choose the Shape tool and double-click on the letter *C* in *Corel*. This selects the letter and brings up the Node Edit roll-up menu. You now can select nodes and curve segments and smooth them out by hand.

> *Trying to fix up traced images (especially text) is an excellent way to learn the Node Edit tools.*

8. Click on the Zoom tool and select the Full Page icon. From the **E**dit menu, choose Select **A**ll, then press Del.

9. From the **F**ile menu, select **I**mport again. Change the type of file to import to TEXT.*.TXT. The TRACETXT.TXT file is the only one available. Double-click on it to import it. As in figure 12.11, the text appears in Paragraph Text mode.

> *Notice that the multiple page number appears in the bottom left corner. The program imported the full page area of the text file, so it continues it on a second page. Notice the + sign in the bottom control handle. Remember, that means that it is connected to another paragraph box. If you were to add text*

Importing a Traced Image 223

to the paragraph on Page 1, it would automatically flow to the paragraph box on Page 2.

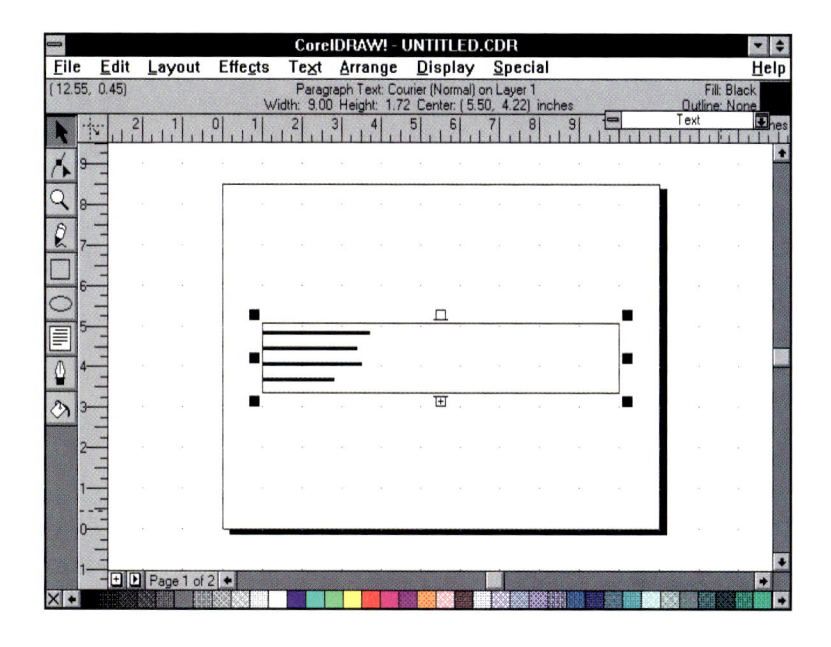

Figure 12.11

The text is imported in Paragraph mode.

10. Use the Zoom In tool to view the text as large as possible. As figure 12.12 shows, the text was not interpreted correctly.

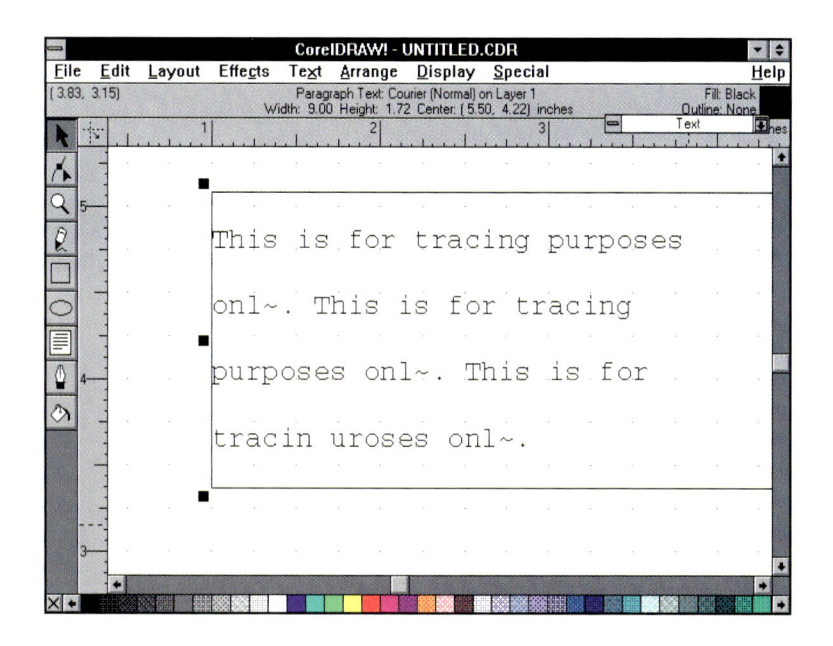

Figure 12.12

Some characters have been replaced, or are missing entirely.

224 Chapter 12: CorelTRACE!

When you use the OCR method to trace text, be sure to proof the resulting image carefully. As shown here, even a small amount of text can have many errors in it.

Tracing Multiple Files

You might have a number of bit-map files that need to be traced. CorelTRACE! enables you to batch process them.

1. Return to CorelTRACE!. Click on the Batch Trace roll-up button. The Batch Trace roll-up menu appears, as in figure 12.13.

Figure 12.13
The Batch Trace roll-up menu.

The roll-up menu displays the currently open file, TRACETXT.

2. If the file displayed is not one to be traced, click on it to highlight it, and then click on the delete button.

This does not delete the file, it just removes it from the list.

Leave it on the list to be traced.

3. Click on the Add button in the roll-up menu; the Open Files dialog box appears. You can add any files displayed to the batch list by double-clicking on them. Double-click on LOGO.TIF. As shown in figure 12.14, LOGO.TIF is added to the batch list.

Figure 12.14
LOGO.TIF is added to the batch list.

Tracing Multiple Files   225

4. You would now click on one of the icons in the roll-up menu to select the tracing method. To trace all the files listed, click on Trace All.

*If any files on the batch list have been traced before, you might be prompted to replace existing files. To override the prompting, select **M**odify ... Batch Output from the **S**ettings menu. In the Batch Output dialog box, check the box for **R**eplace old versions, as shown in figure 12.15.*

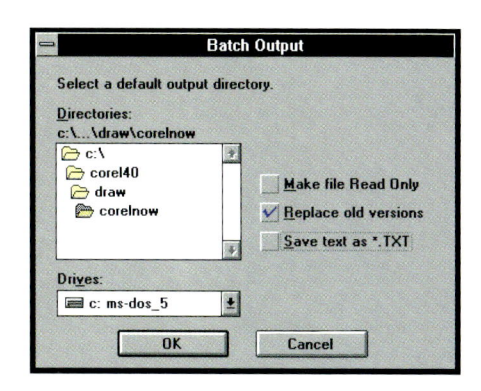

Figure 12.15
The Batch Options dialog box.

When batch tracing images, all options such as tracing method or tracing parameters can be selected, but they will be applied to every image.

To use different options for files when batch processing, use the Trace Selected command. You can highlight selected flies on the list by holding down the Ctrl key and clicking on the files you want. Set the options for those files and click on Trace Selected. The highlighted files are traced with the options currently set.

Chapter 13
CorelCHART!

CorelCHART! is the first of the "bonus programs" bundled with CorelDRAW!. Were CorelCHART! to be judged as a stand-alone product, it could hold its own against many of the chart programs currently on the market.

This chapter offers a quick overview of the charting program and points out some of Chart's features. As promised earlier, a chart is included to demonstrate object linking and embedding (OLE) with CorelDRAW!.

Exploring the CorelCHART! Screen

When you click on the CorelCHART! icon in Program Manager, the CorelCHART! screen appears. As you can see in figure 13.1, it is not unlike the CorelDRAW! screen.

It has a menu bar at the top, a toolbox on the left, and a working page area in the center of the screen. The on-screen color palette at the bottom is a little different from CorelDRAW!'s. An addition of note is the Text Ribbon, the row of icons just below the menu bar. Now, to take a close look at the screen elements.

The CorelCHART! Toolbox

Figure 13.2 shows the CorelCHART! toolbox.

From top to bottom, the tools are:

- **The Data Manager/Chart View button.** It enables you to switch between Chart view (where the actual chart appears) and the Data Manager window (where you find the text and chart data).

The chapter covers the following:

- The CorelCHART! screen
- The Data Manager
- Creating a chart
- Chart styles
- OLE

Chapter 13: CorelCHART!

- **The Pick tool.** As you might expect, you use the Pick tool to select objects on-screen for moving, editing, and so on.

- **The Pop-Up Menu tool.** The Pop-Up Menu tool enables you to directly access menus that pertain to specific objects in a chart. Clicking on a bar in a 3D Riser bar chart, for example, brings up a menu of 3D Riser options (see fig. 13.3).

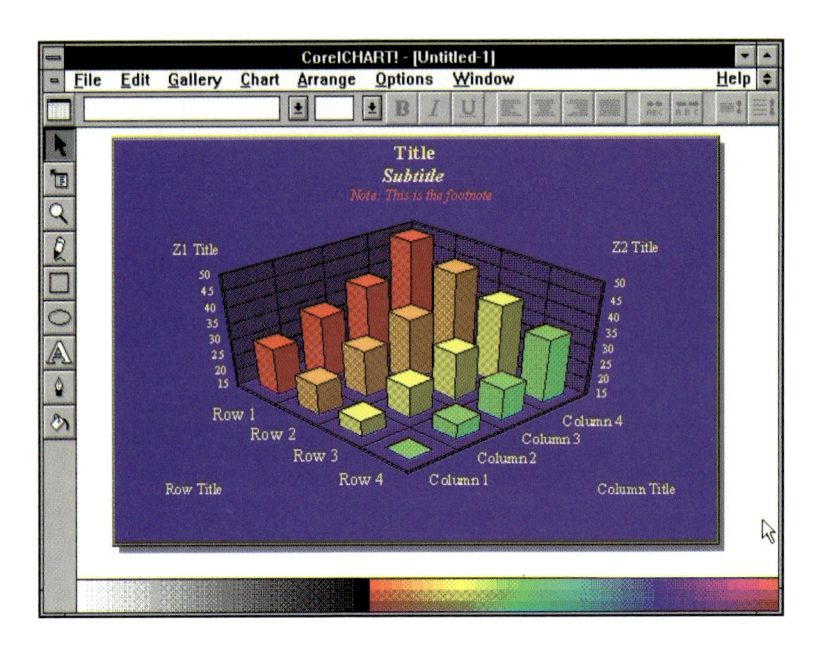

Figure 13.1
The CorelCHART! screen displays a 3D Riser chart.

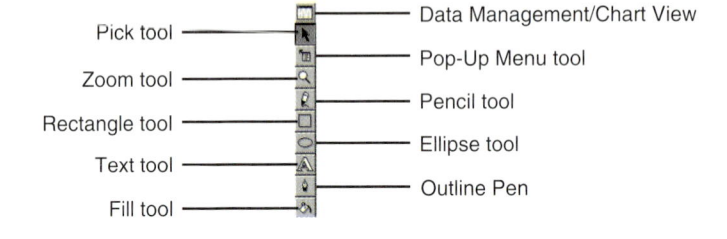

Figure 13.2
The CorelCHART! toolbox.

Figure 13.3
A pop-up menu displays specific options.

For quick access to the pop-up menu of an object in a chart, click on that object with the secondary mouse button.

Exploring the CorelCHART! Screen

- **The Zoom tool.** The Zoom tool performs the same function as it does in CorelDRAW!, but in a slightly different fashion. Clicking on the Zoom tool brings up the fly-out menu shown in figure 13.4.

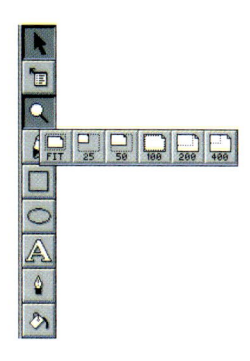

Figure 13.4
The Zoom tool fly-out menu.

You select how much you want to zoom in or out (25%, 50%, 200%, and so on), and the screen view is resized accordingly.

- **The Pencil tool.** As shown in figure 13.5, this tool also has a fly-out menu.

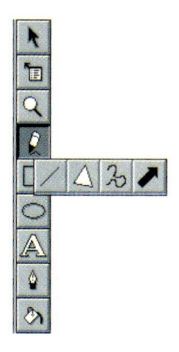

Figure 13.5
The Pencil tool fly-out menu.

The first tile is used to draw straight lines by clicking and dragging on the page. The second tile is for drawing polygons (closed objects of three or more sides). Click on the screen to define each corner of the polygon, and click on the starting point to complete the object. The third tile is for drawing freehand curves, and works much the same as the freehand pencil in CorelDRAW!. The last tile is for drawing arrows. Click and drag the cursor on-screen, and the point at which you release the mouse button gets the arrowhead.

- **The Rectangle tool.** Much like CorelDRAW!, you use the Rectangle tool to draw rectangular objects.

- **The Ellipse tool.** As in CorelDRAW!, you use the Ellipse tool to draw ellipses and circles.

Chapter 13: CorelCHART!

The constrain control from CorelDRAW! (the Ctrl key) works the same in CorelCHART!. Use it with the Rectangle and Ellipse tools as you learned earlier.

- **The Text tool.** The Text tool in CorelCHART! is primarily used to add annotations to charts. It also is used to select and edit titles, subtitles, and footnotes in a chart.

- **The Outline Pen.** As shown in figure 13.6, the Outline Pen fly-out menu, as well as its functions, are much the same as in CorelDRAW!.

Figure 13.6
The Outline Pen fly-out menu.

- **The Fill tool.** As shown in figure 13.7, the Fill tool also is similar to its CorelDRAW! counterpart.

Figure 13.7
The Fill tool fly-out menu.

The CorelCHART! Fill tool has two basic differences from the CorelDRAW! Fill tool. A selection of preset pattern fills is available in CorelCHART!, as opposed to the solid gray fills in CorelDRAW!. Second, the last tile on the right accesses the roll-up menu for Pictographs (see fig. 13.8).

Figure 13.8
The Pictograph roll-up menu.

As figure 13.8 shows, the Pictograph roll-up menu currently displays the apple graphic created previously. The Pictograph enables you to use graphical images (like the apple, a coin, or a dollar sign) rather than a solid bar. Any file created in CorelDRAW!, or any type of file supported by CorelDRAW!, can be used as a pictograph.

The Text Ribbon

The Text Ribbon is the row of buttons and drop-down menus found just below the menu bar, as shown in figure 13.9.

Figure 13.9
The Chart screen Text Ribbon.

The following list is an explanation of the functions of the Text Ribbon items (from left to right):

- **Typeface box.** Displays the currently selected font. Click on the drop-down menu button to its right for access to all currently installed Windows fonts.

- **Point size box.** Enables you to select the point size of type by value. Click on the drop-down menu button to its right to access the values.

- **Bold, italic, underline.** The next three buttons modify the selected text. The buttons act as toggle switches, so clicking on a button again reverses the effect.

- **Text alignment.** The next four buttons are for aligning multiple lines of text. They are Left-Align, Center-Align, Right-Align, and Left/Right-Align.

- **Spacing.** The last four buttons control spacing. As illustrated by the icons, the first two buttons decrease or increase the spacing between letters, and the last two buttons decrease or increase the space between lines of text.

Anatomy of a Chart

A chart is comprised of specific objects. A 3D Riser bar chart is shown in figure 13.10, with these objects labeled.

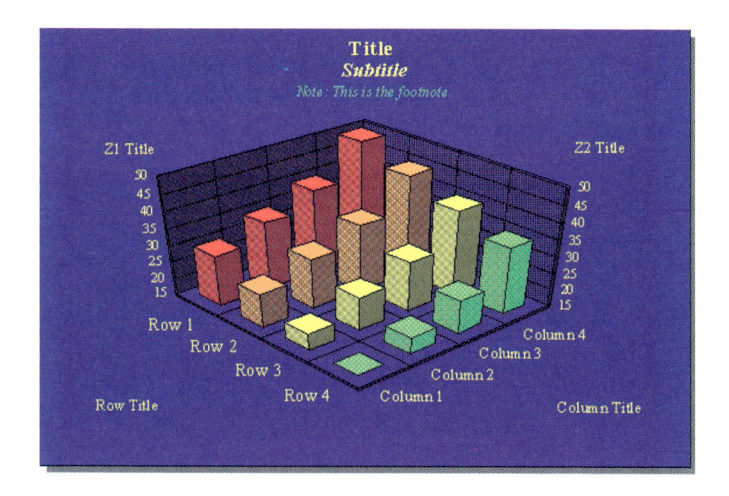

Figure 13.10
A 3D Riser bar chart.

Chapter 13: CorelCHART!

In CorelCHART! you can choose from a great number of chart types and styles. You then can plug text and data in the appropriate positions (the actual title where it says *Title,* for example). You also can modify the look of the chart and save it as a template to use later.

The Chart Menu Bar

Most commands common to both CorelDRAW! and CorelCHART! are in the same place in the menu bar (the File menu is almost identical in both programs, for example). Two new menu titles in CorelCHART! are Gallery and Chart.

Gallery. The Gallery menu displays the selection of charts available, and the fly-outs show further selections with each chart type (see fig. 13.11).

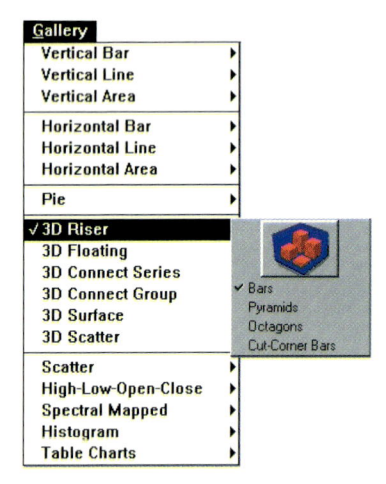

Figure 13.11

The Gallery menu, showing the 3D Riser fly-out menu.

Chart. As shown in figure 13.12, this menu offers commands specific to CorelCHART!, with fly-out menus indicated by the right-facing arrows.

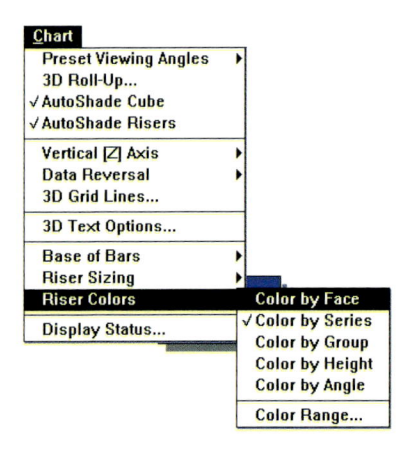

Figure 13.12

The Chart menu, showing the Riser Colors fly-out menu.

Exploring the Data Manager

Think of the Data Manager as a form you fill out with all the information for your chart. If you have any experience with spreadsheets, you should feel like you are in familiar territory.

Click on the Data Manager/Chart View button to bring up the Data Manager. The data for the 3D Riser bar chart in figure 13.10 appears in figure 13.13.

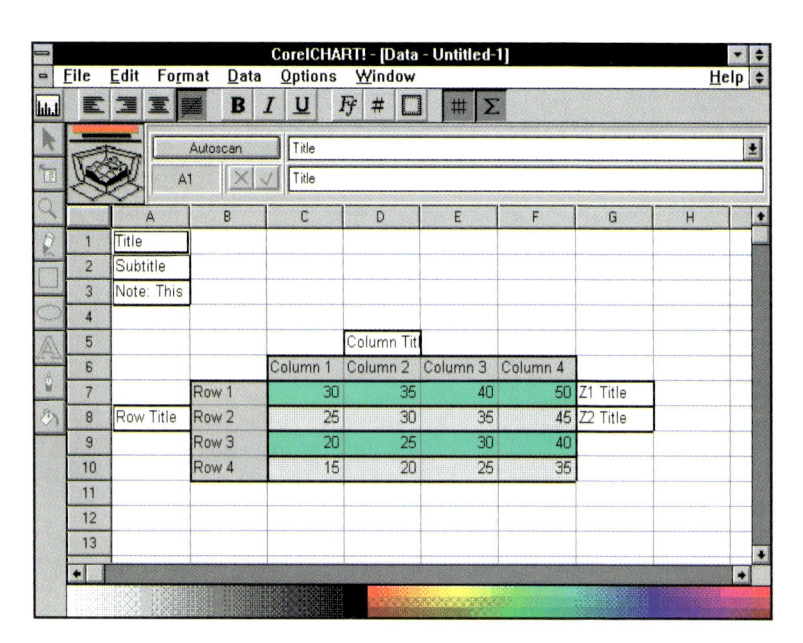

Figure 13.13

The Data Manager, showing the data for the 3D Riser bar chart.

Although the control functions layout is similar to that of Chart view, it has a few differences worth noting:

- **The Toolbox.** In the Data Manager, the Toolbox serves no function, so it is grayed out.

- **The Menu bar.** Two new menu titles appear, Format and Data. These offer commands specific to the Data Manager.

- **The Text Ribbon.** It appears here, but in a somewhat different configuration. The first seven icons (from the left) are type controls found in Chart View.

    Clicking on the next icon (*Ff*) displays the Font dialog box.

    Clicking on the # icon brings up the Numeric Format dialog box, which is used to modify the way numeric data is represented (dollar value, percentage, month-day-year, and so on).

    Clicking on the next icon (third from the right) displays the Border Format dialog box. Border Format enables you to emphasize selected cells (boxes with text or data) in the data set by editing the borders or the cell fill.

The next icon (second from the right) is the grid control, which controls whether the grid pattern appears in the data set.

The last icon is for Auto Recalc. With this option selected, the program automatically recalculates formulas in the chart when data is edited.

- **The Data Set.** The main window of the Data Manager contains the data set, rows and columns of cells containing text, and data information. The data set contains all the information you want to convey to your audience.

CorelCHART! takes that information and puts it in chart form. The reason you display information in chart form is not so software companies can sell you programs. The reason is that a graphic display of information (a chart) is a powerful means of communicating data and facilitates understanding for your audience.

Creating a Chart

Creating a simple chart will give you an idea of how CorelCHART! works.

1. Select New from the File menu. The New dialog box appears (see fig. 13.14).

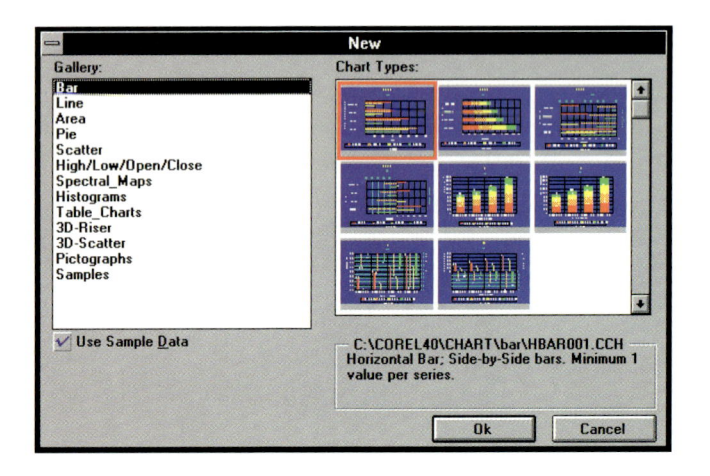

Figure 13.14
The New dialog box.

The Gallery window displays the different available chart styles. The Chart Types window shows what type of chart is available for the selected chart style. A group of thumbnails is displayed to give you an idea what the chart will look like. If you click on a thumbnail, it is highlighted with a bounding box, and a verbal description of the chart appears just below.

Creating a Chart   235

2. Click on the box for Use Sample Data. In the Gallery window, click on Bar. Double-click on the first chart, Horizontal Bars - Side by Side, to select it. The bar chart appears in the chart page, as in figure 13.15.

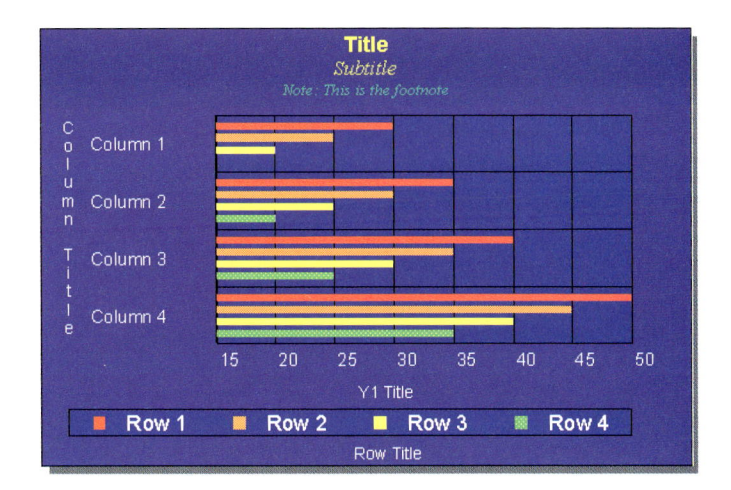

Figure 13.15
The horizontal bar chart.

Now, to edit the chart with your data.

3. Click on the Data Manager/Chart View button to bring up the Data Manager, as shown in figure 13.16.

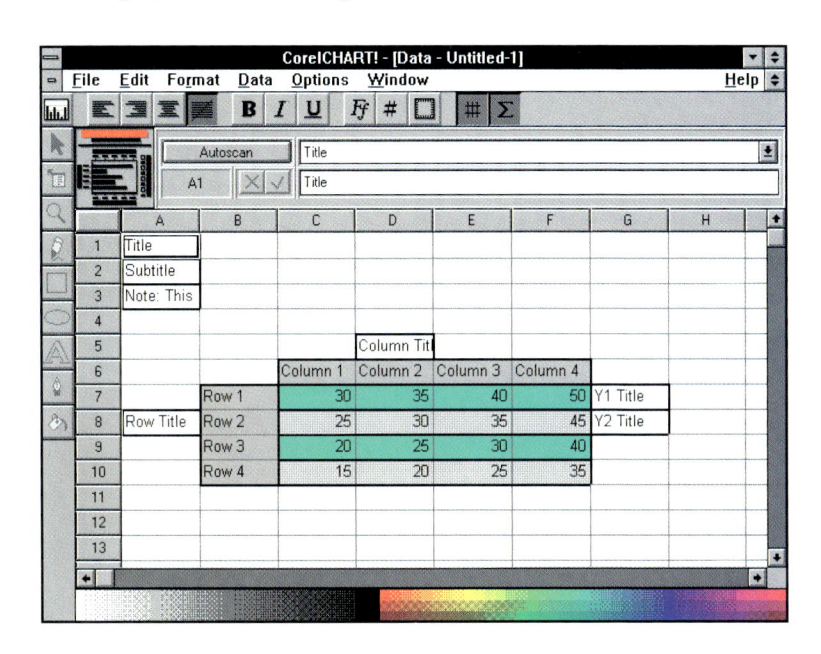

Figure 13.16
The Data Manager for your chart.

4. First, enter the title of the chart. Click in the A1 cell (column A, row 1), and place the cursor in the title box above the Column letters (the formula bar). The pointer changes to a text cursor.

Chapter 13: CorelCHART!

5. Click on the formula box, and a text cursor appears next to the word Title. Press the Backspace key to delete it, and type **CorelDRAW! NOW!**. Click on the check mark icon; this tells the program you are done editing the cell and to make the change.

If you want to cancel the edit, click on the X icon.

The text in the cell reflects the edit, as shown in figure 13.17.

Figure 13.17
The A1 cell is edited.

Notice that after you accept the cell edit, the next cell is automatically highlighted.

6. Click on the A1 cell again. Look at the box above the Formula bar (this is the Tag List menu box). This menu tags a cell, meaning that it labels the cell as to what type of chart element it is. In this case, cell A1 contains the chart title.

7. Click on cell A2 to select it. This is the Subtitle cell, as indicated by the tag list. Click on the formula bar to get the text cursor. Delete the current copy and enter **Fruit Sales**.

To delete the text, click and drag the text cursor from right to left over the copy to highlight it. Then type the new copy to replace it.

Click on the check mark icon to accept the change.

8. Cell A3 (footnote) now is highlighted. Click in the Formula Bar and replace the copy with **Note: All data is estimated**. Click on the check mark to accept the change.

9. Click on cell D5 (column title). In the Formula Box, change the title to **Fruits Sold**. Click on the check mark to accept the change.

Creating a Chart   237

10. Click on cell G7 (Y1 title). Change the text to read **Sales in $Millions**. Click on the check mark to accept.

11. The G8 cell (Y2 title) is the next cell, and is automatically selected. Click on the menu button for the Tag list and the tag selections appear, as in figure 13.18.

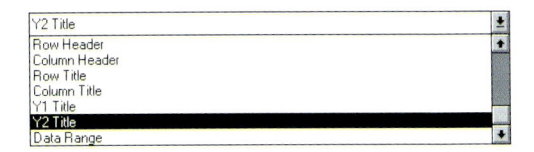

Figure 13.18
The Tag List drop-down menu.

Scroll up the list and select (none).

Label a cell none if you do not want it to appear in the chart. You can delete the cell entirely, but this way enables you to add an additional title later by relabeling the cell from the Tag list.

12. You don't need `Row Title` (cell A8) either, so change its tag to (none) as well.

13. You need only two rows for the data, so delete the other two rows. Place the cursor in cell B9. Click and drag it to cell F10. All ten cells in the two rows are selected, as in figure 13.19.

Figure 13.19
Selecting multiple cells.

With the ten cells selected, press the Del key. The Cut and Clear Options dialog box appears, as shown in figure 13.20.

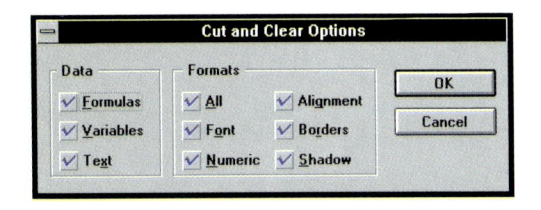

Figure 13.20
The Cut and Clear Options dialog box.

Chapter 13: CorelCHART!

Leave all the options checked and click on OK. The data is deleted.

14. With the ten cells still selected, click on the Tag List and select (none). Click on the Chart View button to see the changes in the chart, as shown in figure 13.21.

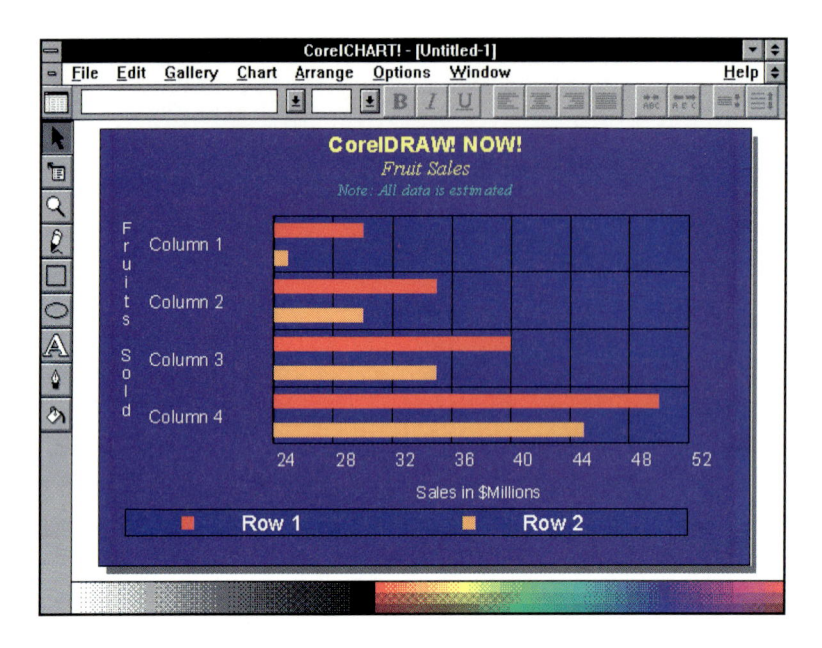

Figure 13.21

The chart begins to take shape.

15. Make the following text changes:

Cell B7 (Row 1): **Apples**
Cell B8 (Row 2): **All Others**

16. In the following cells, enter the values shown:

C7: **22**
D7: **31**
E7: **45**
F7: **63**
C8: **40**
D8: **55**
E8: **60**
F8: **76**

17. Make the following changes to cells C6–F6 (column headers):

Column 1: **1990**
Column 2: **1991**
Column 3: **1992**
Column 4: **1993**

18. Click on the Chart View button. You have all the necessary text and data changes, so now you can edit the chart graphically. Click on one of the grid boxes of the chart to select the entire grid rectangle.

Control handles appear around the rectangle. Click and drag the left-center control handle and stretch the grid rectangle to the left, as shown in figure 13.22.

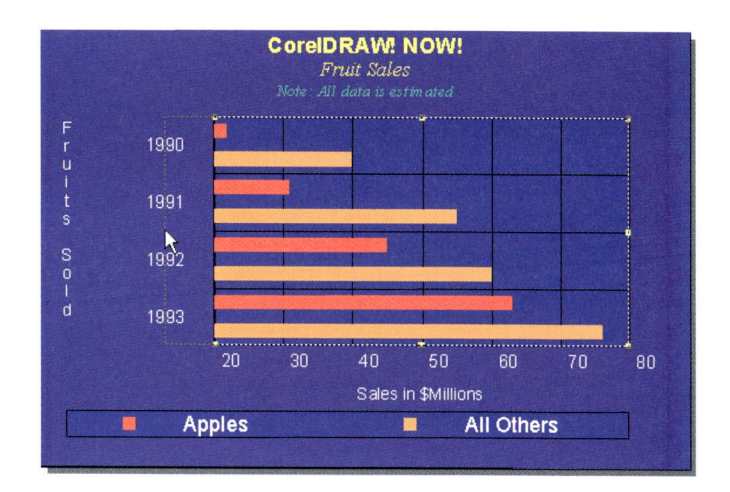

Figure 13.22
Editing the grid rectangle.

19. Click on the rectangle that has the chart legend. Click and drag the left- or right-center control handle while holding down the Shift key. Drag toward the center of the legend to reduce its size by about one-third. Click on the legend and drag it to the right until it is centered under the grid rectangle.

20. Other things can be done to improve the chart visually (changing fonts types, style, and position, for example), but consider the chart finished for now. From the File menu, choose Save. In the File Name box, type **NOWCHART**. Change the directory to the CORELNOW that you created to store your CorelDRAW! files. Click on OK.

Exploring Chart Types

CorelCHART! offers enough chart types and styles to address almost every need. Take a quick look at some of the formats available, and apply them to the chart you just created.

> *You might have a tendency to select a particular chart style because you find it visually appealing. First and foremost, a chart style should be chosen because it best illustrates the information you want to communicate. Three-dimensional bar charts shown in a perspective view can look very dramatic and yet do little as far as communication is concerned. Try to keep this in mind when creating a chart presentation.*

Chapter 13: CorelCHART!

1. With NOWCHART still the active file, select **G**allery from the menu bar. Click on Horizontal Bar (notice it has a check mark) to display the fly-out menu. The Side-by-Side option is checked because the current chart is in that style. Click on Stacked. The chart style changes, as shown in figure 13.23.

Figure 13.23
The horizontally stacked bar chart.

The bars in the chart now are stacked on one another, instead of displayed side by side.

TIP: You might select Stacked vs. Side-by-Side if the chart contains many columns. This keeps the chart from looking too crowded.

2. From the **G**allery menu, select 3D Riser. In the fly-out menu, click on Pyramid. The chart now is displayed in 3-D, as shown in figure 13.24.

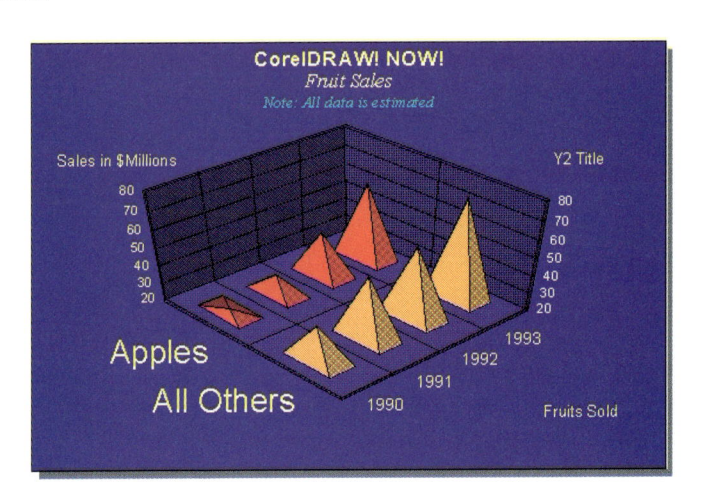

Figure 13.24
The chart as a 3-D riser-pyramid.

Exploring Chart Types 241

The chart has an interesting look to it, but does it convey the information as well as the original bar chart?

3. Select the Gallery menu and click through the chart styles to get an idea of what is available. Many of the charts probably do not make sense; that is because the data does not conform to the particular chart style.

4. After you finish reviewing the Gallery, select Vertical Bar/Side-by-Side from the Gallery menu. The resulting chart is shown in figure 13.25.

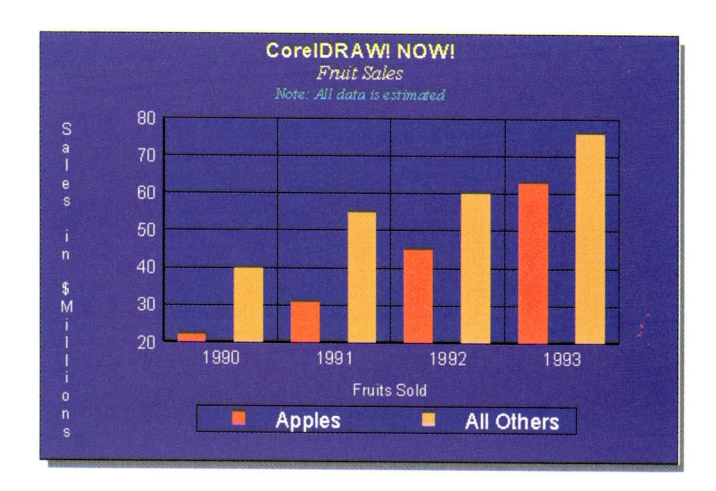

Figure 13.25
A vertical bar/side-by-side chart.

5. Click on the Fill tool in the Toolbox, and select the Pictograph roll-up (the last icon on the top row). The roll-up menu appears, as shown in figure 13.26.

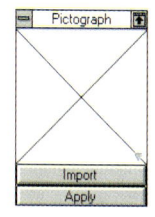

Figure 13.26
The Pictograph roll-up menu.

6. Click on Import in the roll-up, and the Import File dialog box appears. If the current directory is not CORELNOW, change to it.

7. You want to import the apple art you created, so double-click on the file name APPLE.CDR to import it. It appears in the Pictograph roll-up, as shown in figure 13.27.

242   Chapter 13: CorelCHART!

Figure 13.27
The apple art in the Pictograph roll-up.

8. To use the apple art in the chart, you must tell the program that you want to. From the **C**hart menu, click on Show as Pictograph.

9. Before you apply the art, thicken up the bars. From the **C**hart menu, click on Bar Thickness and change the setting from Default to Major.

10. From the Pictograph roll-up, click on Apply. The bars representing apple sales now are stacks of apples, as shown in figure 13.28.

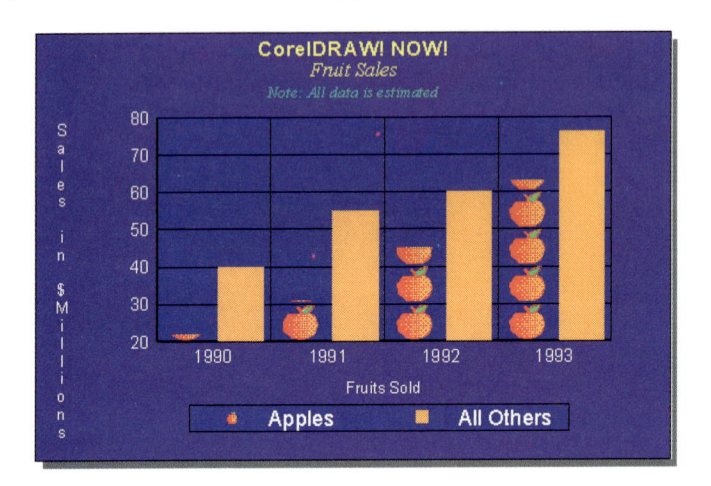

Figure 13.28
The bar chart as a pictograph.

11. Choose **S**ave from the **F**ile menu to save this version of the chart.

Importing a Chart with OLE

Object linking and embedding (OLE) enables you to import a file from one program into another while retaining a connection between the two programs. Look at OLE using the chart you created.

1. With the chart still active in CorelCHART!, click on the **E**dit menu and select Copy Ch**a**rt to copy the entire chart to the Windows clipboard.

2. Click on the minimize button to reduce CorelCHART! to an icon.

3. From Program Manager, open CorelDRAW!.

Importing a Chart with OLE 243

Depending on your system and the memory available, you might have problems running both programs.

4. Use the Rectangle tool to draw a rectangle the full size of the page.

5. Press F11 (Fountain Fill) and select a radial fill From black To white. Click on OK.

6. From the Edit menu, select Paste Special; the Paste Special dialog box appears, as shown in figure 13.29.

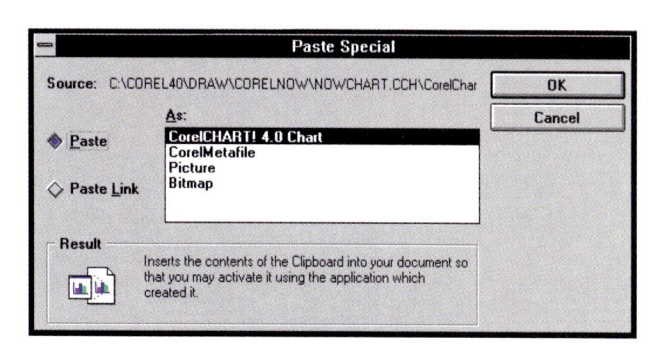

Figure 13.29
The Paste Special dialog box.

The Paste Special dialog box presents the following two options:

- **Paste.** Enables you to access the native program of the pasted object from within the current program. What this means is that you can click on the chart to access CorelCHART! from within CorelDRAW!, make changes to the original chart, and return to CorelDRAW! with the changes in effect.

- **Paste Link.** Links the file between the two programs. You can update the chart in CorelCHART! at any time, and when you open the CorelDRAW! file containing the chart, the chart reflects those updates.

7. Choose Paste Link.

8. The As box displays `CorelCHART! 4.0 Chart`, which is correct, so click on OK.

9. After the chart is drawn on-screen, select a control handle with the Pick tool and stretch it while holding down the Shift key until the chart is about 9 inches wide (see fig. 13.30).

244   Chapter 13: CorelCHART!

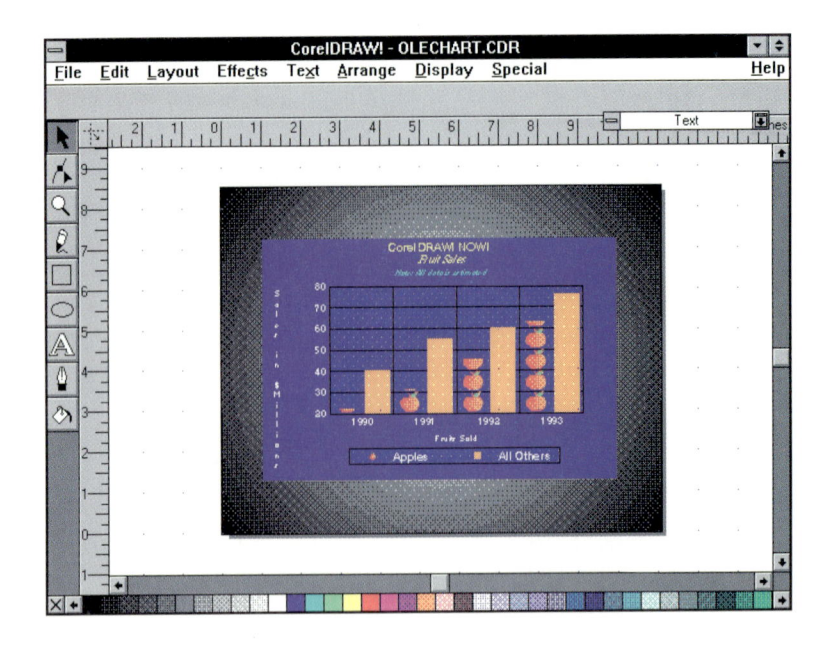

Figure 13.30
The chart is pasted onto a CorelDRAW! file.

10. Select **S**ave from the **F**ile menu, name the file OLECHART, and click on OK.

11. Minimize CorelDRAW! and open CorelCHART!. Click on the Data Manager button.

12. Edit the value in cell C7 to **60**. Edit the value in cell F8 to **30**. Select **S**ave from the **F**ile menu.

13. Minimize CorelCHART! and open CorelDRAW!. As shown in figure 13.31, the data changes are reflected in the chart.

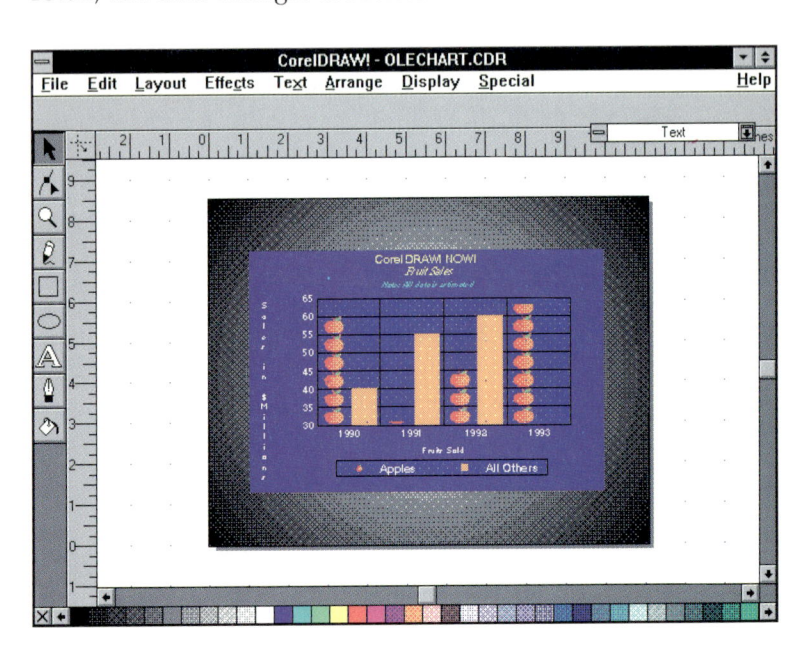

Figure 13.31
OLE updates changes in chart data.

Chapter 14
CorelPHOTO-PAINT!

CorelPHOTO-PAINT! is a painting and photo-retouching program with some fairly impressive capabilities. If you find you have extensive need for this type of program, you might want to look into some of the stand-alone products that are on the market. But don't dismiss Photo-Paint yet. You might find it offers more than enough power and versatility for your projects. And when you consider the cost of the program (it comes free with CorelDRAW!), you'll be hard-pressed to find a better value.

Why would you need this program? Unlike CorelDRAW!, the images you work on here are bit maps. You can scan in full-color photographs, for example, make subtle enhancements, or do some heavy retouching, and then export them into CorelDRAW! or any program that supports bit-map images.

Exploring the Photo-Paint Screen

Clicking on the Photo-Paint icon in the program manager loads the program and brings up the CorelPHOTO-PAINT! screen, as shown in figure 14.1.

Like the other Corel programs, it has the title bar at the top and the menu bar just below the title bar. Here's a quick look at the menus:

- **File and Edit.** These contain pretty much what you'd expect, from opening and saving files to copying and pasting

- **Image.** Contains the image enhancement controls, which enable you to brighten or darken an image, enhance the detail, diffuse or soften it, and much more

- **Effects.** Contains the effects filters, with which you can give an image an embossed look, a solarized or posterized effect, or make it look like an Impressionist painting.

FEATURES COVERED

This chapter offers a brief overview of the program, and covers these topics:

- The Photo-Paint screen
- The Toolbox
- The roll-up menus
- Image enhancement
- Effects

Chapter 14: CorelPHOTO-PAINT!

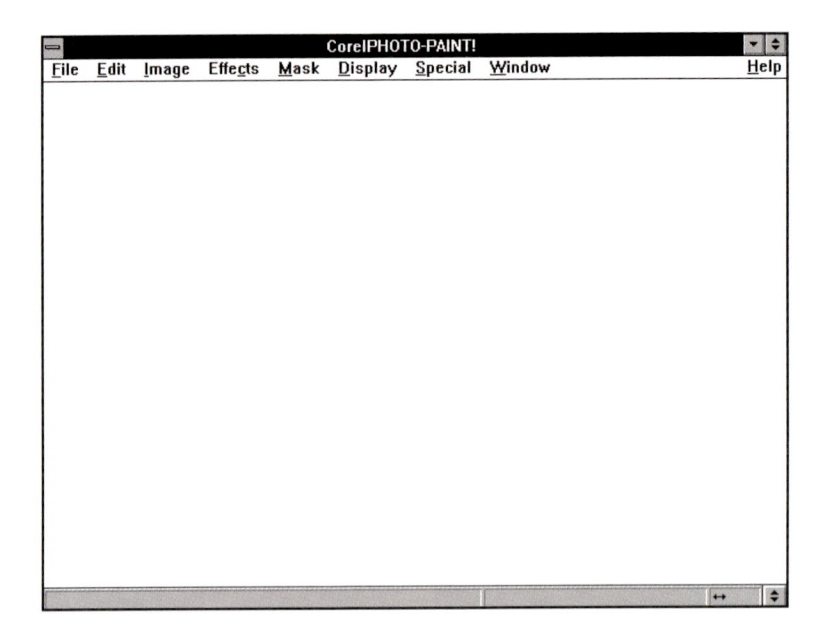

Figure 14.1
The CorelPHOTO-PAINT! screen.

- **Mask.** Contains masks, which you use to define an area of an image you want to edit, which in turn protects the rest of the image from inadvertent changes

- **Display.** Gives you access to the Zoom controls, as well as the various Photo-Paint roll-up menus

- **Special.** Contains the Preferences and Color Tolerance commands

- **Window.** Contains commands that control the way windows are displayed on the screen

The Photo-Paint program and its functions can eat up a lot of memory. Depending on your system configuration, you might get Out Of Memory warnings when you try to execute certain commands.

Exploring the Toolbox

The Toolbox gives you quick access to commands for selecting areas, painting, drawing, retouching, and manipulating images.

1. Before you can open the Toolbox, you must have a file active in Photo-Paint. Select **O**pen from the **F**ile menu. The dialog box for Load a Picture from Disk appears, as shown in figure 14.2.

   Go to the Samples subdirectory indicated, and double-click on APPLE.PCX. When the image window appears, just press its minimize button for now.

Exploring the Toolbox 247

2. From the **D**isplay menu, select **T**oolbox to check it. The Toolbox appears as shown in figure 14.3.

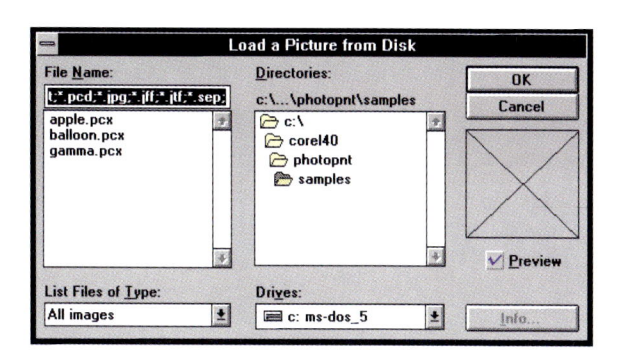

Figure 14.2
The Load a Picture from Disk dialog box.

Figure 14.3
The Photo-Paint Toolbox.

It contains some icons that look familiar, but they function quite differently here. It uses fly-out menus, like the other toolboxes you've seen, but also gives you the option of viewing all the tools at once.

3. Click on the control bar (in the upper left corner) on the Toolbox. The drop-down menu appears as shown in figure 14.4.

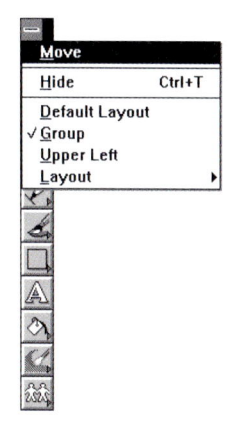

Figure 14.4
The Toolbox control menu.

248 Chapter 14: CorelPHOTO-PAINT!

4. Click on the control bar of the Toolbox and choose <u>U</u>pper Left to uncheck it if it is checked. This enables you to move the Toolbox from the default position in the upper left corner to anywhere on the screen you want.

5. Click on the control bar of the Toolbox and choose <u>G</u>roup to uncheck it. This displays all the icons from the various fly-out menus.

6. Click on the control bar of the Toolbox and choose <u>L</u>ayout. From the drop-down menu, choose 4 Columns. All the icons of the Toolbox now appear, as shown in figure 14.5.

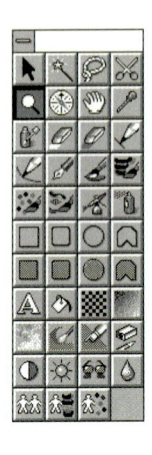

Figure 14.5
The expanded Toolbox.

The tools are listed as follows, accompanied by a brief description of their function. They are divided into five groups: Selection tools, Display tools, Painting tools, Drawing tools, and Retouching tools.

> *After you work with the program for a while, you learn which tool is which. Until then, place the cursor on any tool in the Toolbox and look at the Help bar at the very bottom of the screen. The name of a tool appears any time the cursor is placed over that tool.*

Selection Tools

Rectangle selection. Like the Pick tool, you marquee-select an area with a rectangular marquee box.

> *Remember that you are dealing with bit-map images here, not vector objects. When you marquee-select an area, all the pixels in the marquee box are selected.*

Exploring the Toolbox

Magic Wand. Enables you to select an area with similar colors, and works much the same as the Magic Wand tool in CorelTRACE!.

Lasso. Enables you to define irregular shapes. If you draw a freehand marquee shape around an area, for example, all the pixels within that area are selected.

Polygon selection. Similar to Rectangle selection, but you draw a polygon marquee box rather than a rectangle.

Display Tools

Zoom. Has a set of preset magnifications. Click the mouse button to zoom in to the next interval. Click the secondary mouse button to zoom out to the next interval.

*Click on **Z**oom in the **D**isplay menu to see the list of preset magnifications.*

Locator. Use to display a similar area on an image in a duplicate copy of that image in a different magnification. If you work in a high-zoom magnification, it enables you to see exactly where you are in a second window at normal magnification.

Hand. Enables you to move your image vertically, horizontally, or diagonally.

Painting Tools

Paintbrush. Simulates the strokes of a standard art paintbrush, and uses the selected outline color.

Artist Brush. Simulates the strokes of an oil paintbrush, and offers a variety of brush styles.

Impressionist Brush. Enables you to paint with multicolored brush strokes, and offers extensive editing options as to color, width, and so on.

Pointillist Brush. Enables you to create clusters of dots. Extensive editing options are available.

Airbrush. Enables you to shade an area with a soft spray.

Spraycan. Simulates the effect of spraying paint with a spraycan.

Flood Fill tool. Fills an enclosed area with a solid fill color.

Tile Fill tool. Fills an enclosed area with a repeating tile pattern.

Gradient Fill tool. Fills an enclosed area with a gradient fill.

Texture Fill tool. Fills an enclosed area with a bit-map texture.

Clone. Enables you to use an area of an image to paint in another area of an image. If you are retouching a portrait, for example, you might clone an area of smooth skin and paint over wrinkles or blemishes to remove them.

Impressionist Clone. Enables you to clone an area of an image and apply it elsewhere using an Impressionistic brush stroke.

Pointillist Clone. Enables you to clone an area of an image and apply it somewhere else using a Pointillist brush stroke.

Drawing Tools

Line tool. Enables you to draw single or joined straight lines.

Curve tool. Enables you to draw single or joined curves.

Pen tool. Enables you to draw freehand shapes as you would with a pen.

Text tool. Enables you to add text to an image. Any Windows fonts installed in your system are supported.

Hollow Box. Draws a hollow rectangle (meaning just the outline is drawn) in the selected outline color.

Hollow Rounded Box. Draws a rectangle with rounded corners in the selected outline color.

Hollow Ellipse. Draws a hollow ellipse or circle in the selected outline color.

Hollow Polygon. Draws a hollow polygon in the selected outline color.

Filled Box. Draws a rectangle filled with the currently selected fill color.

Filled Rounded Box. Draws a rectangle with rounded corners filled with the currently selected fill color.

Filled Ellipse. Draws an ellipse or circle filled with the currently selected fill color.

Filled Polygon. Draws a filled polygon with the currently selected fill color.

Retouching Tools

Freehand Contrast tool. Enables you to brighten or darken selected areas of an image.

Freehand Brighten tool. Enables you to increase or decrease the intensity of colors in a selected area of an image.

Freehand Tint tool. Enables you to apply the selected outline color as a tint to an area of an image.

Freehand Blend tool. Use to soften or smooth specific areas of an image, somewhat like adding water to a watercolor painting.

Freehand Smear tool. Use to spread or smear colors in an image, not unlike smearing colors in an oil painting.

Freehand Smudge tool. Use much as you would use the Smear tool. It mixes the color dots of an area, like mixing colors with pastels or chalk.

Exploring the Roll-Up Menus   251

Freehand Sharpen tool. Use to sharpen areas of an image. You might sharpen an object in the foreground to help separate it from the background.

Eyedropper. Enables you to pick up a color in an image. Clicking the left mouse button selects it as the outline color. Clicking the secondary mouse button selects it as the fill color.

> *Pressing the Shift key with any tool (except the selection tools) activates the Eyedropper.*

Local Undo. Undoes the last command performed on a specific area of an image. Double-clicking the Local Undo tool performs the Undo command as if you selected it from the **E**dit menu.

> *Photo-Paint does not offer multiple levels of Undo. Only one Undo level!*

Eraser. Works like an eraser by replacing areas with the background color of the image.

Color Replacer. Use to replace the outline color with the fill color.

That's the Toolbox. The best way to get an understanding of the tools is to experiment. Open one of the sample files, or start a new one, then test them.

> *Ideally, you should have a 24-bit (photo-realistic) color display for your monitor when retouching. You can work in SVGA (8-bit, 256 colors), but you can't fully appreciate the Retouch tools.*

Exploring the Roll-Up Menus

In addition to the Toolbox, Photo-Paint has four roll-up menus that can be accessed from the **D**isplay menu. They all are shown in figure 14.6.

- **The Canvas roll-up.** You can use the supplied Canvas patterns, or you can create custom patterns. When a canvas pattern is applied, it adds a texture to the image, as if it were drawn on canvas or some other textured surface.

- **The Color Selection roll-up.** Enables you to select outline, fill, and background colors; load color palettes; and define To and From colors for gradient fills.

- **The Fill Settings roll-up.** Enables you to adjust various fill settings. When the roll-up appears and the Gradient Fill tool is selected, the roll-up displays the Gradient Fill controls. When the Tile Fill or

Chapter 14: CorelPHOTO-PAINT!

Texture Fill tools are selected, the corresponding controls are shown in the roll-up.

- **The Tool Settings roll-up.** Displays the controls for editing the Photo-Paint tools. You can edit the shape and width of brushes, the softness and spacing of a paint stroke, the opacity of the paint, or the stroke Fade Out (the rate at which the brush stroke disappears).

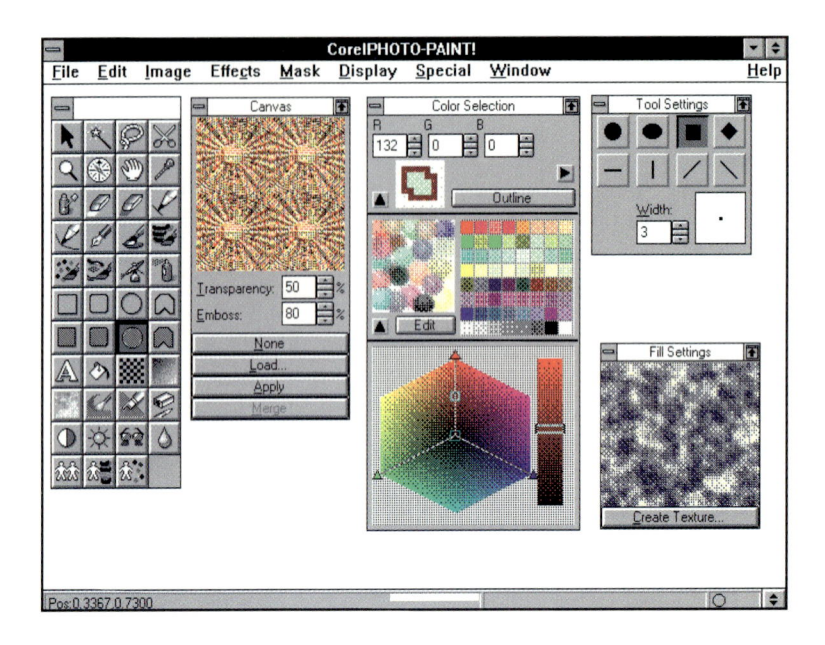

Figure 14.6
The Toolbox and roll-ups.

Tool settings are specific to selected tools. You can select different settings for different tools and not have to change settings when you change tools.

Exploring Image Enhancement

The **I**mage menu contains filters that can help you enhance an image. Many of the commands offer a Preview option that shows you how the filter affects an image before you apply it. Experiment with the filters to get an idea of how they affect images.

The **I**mage menu is shown in figure 14.7.

The first command in the **I**mage menu is **C**olor. The **C**olor command gives you access to:

- **B**rightness and Contrast. Enables you to lighten or darken an image (Brightness), adjust the distinction between light and dark areas (Contrast), and adjust the overall intensity of an image (Intensity). Intensity affects only the brighter areas on an image.

Exploring Image Enhancement 253

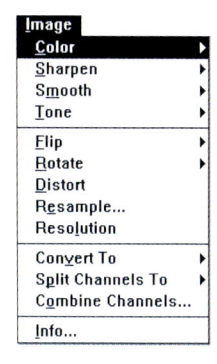

Figure 14.7
*The **I**mage menu.*

When you work on small areas of an image, use the Freehand tools for Brightness and Contrast.

- **T**hreshold. Converts an image to solid colors with no gradated shading. The amount of Threshold filtering is adjustable.
- **G**amma. Adjusts the middle tones of an image without affecting the shadow (darkest areas) or the highlight (brightest) areas.
- **H**ue & Saturation. Adjusts the hue and saturation of an image without affecting the brightness. *Hue* refers to a particular color (blue, green, red, and so on), and *saturation* refers to the amount of the color. You can use these to color-correct images or to create color effects.

The next group of commands in the menu is under **S**harpen:

- **S**harpen. Enhances the edges of areas in an image, bringing out detail and sharpening the image.
- **E**nhance Detail. Analyzes the pixels of an image to determine the amount of sharpening to apply.
- **U**nsharp Mask. Increases edge detail while sharpening the smooth areas of an image.
- **A**daptive Unsharp Mask. Increases edge detail, but doesn't affect the rest of the image.

Experiment with the sharpening tools on the same image to see the differences in effect.

The next group of filters is found under S**m**ooth:

- **S**m**ooth. Tones down the differences between adjacent pixels in an image, resulting in only a slight loss of detail.

Chapter 14: CorelPHOTO-PAINT!

*The S**m**ooth filter, as well as the other filters found in the **I**mage menu, can be applied to the entire image or just a portion of it. You can enhance the foreground of a landscape, for example, and leave the sky untouched.*

So**ften.** Adjusts the harshness of an image without losing detail.

Diffuse. Scatters the colors in an image, giving it a fuzzy, diffused look.

Blen**d.** Smoothes and softens colors in an image, producing an effect similar to adding water to a watercolor painting. Use the Freehand Blend tool for small areas.

The last filter group is **T**one:

Color/Gray Map. Enables you to adjust the lighting of an image. When selected, the Color/Gray Map dialog box appears, as in figure 14.8.

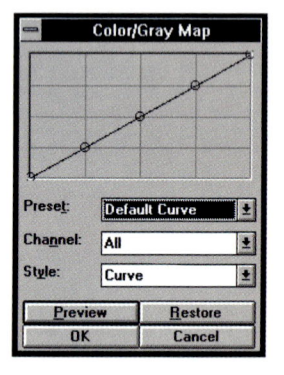

Figure 14.8
The Color/Gray Map dialog box.

You can select from the Prese**t**s to adjust midtones or shadows automatically. Use Cha**n**nel to adjust all colors or just Red, Green, or Blue. Use the St**y**le menu to select the style of color mapping (curve, freehand, or linear). Clicking on **R**estore returns you to the original values.

Equalize. Changes the way colors are distributed in an image. The darkest colors become black, the lightest colors become white, and all other colors are stretched between.

***E**qualize generally improves the appearance of a scanned image. It's a good idea to equalize an image before applying other filters.*

There are five more commands to look at in the **I**mage menu:

Flip. Enables you to do just that: flip an image or part of an image vertically or horizontally.

Exploring the Effects Menu

- **R**otate. Enables you to rotate an image or a part of an image. As in CorelDRAW!, you can input the specific amount of rotation, or you can adjust it right on the screen.

- **D**istort. The Distort filter is something like the Envelope effect in CorelDRAW!. You drag the handles of a marquee box to change the shape of an image.

- R**e**sample. Enables you to make a new image from an original image of different size and resolution.

- Res**o**lution. Enables you to adjust the resolution of an image to a specific value.

Exploring the Effects Menu

The **E**ffects menu contains a collection of special effects filters that can yield some interesting results. Some examples using the file APPLE.PCX are presented in this chapter. Figure 14.9 shows the APPLE.PCX image.

Figure 14.9
The Apple.PCX image.

- **A**rtistic. Enables you to apply an Impressionist or Pointillist look to an image. Figure 14.10 shows the apple with an Impressionist look.

Figure 14.10
The Impressionist apple.

The image shown in figure 14.10 was captured from a VGA display. To fully appreciate some of the effects, 24-bit photo-realistic display would be better.

NOTE

- **E**dge. The Edge filters are used to create outline effects. Using Edge Detect selects areas of an image to outline. Contour outlines the

256 Chapter 14: CorelPHOTO-PAINT!

edges in an image with lines. Edge Emphasis highlights edges among areas of different shades and colors. Outline creates an outline of an area of that color, and fills the shape a shade of gray. In figure 14.11, the Edge Detect and Contour filters are applied.

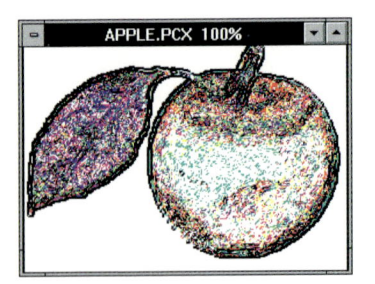

Figure 14.11

Applying the Outline effects of the Edge filter.

Emboss. Gives an image an embossed look. You can adjust the direction of the emboss, as well as the colors used. Figure 14.12 shows a gray emboss going down and right at a 45-degree angle.

Figure 14.12

The Emboss effect.

Invert. Inverts the colors of an image, giving it the look of a photo negative.

Jaggy Despeckle. Scatters colors in an image, creating a diffused look. The degree of diffusion can be adjusted.

Motion **B**lur. Gives the effect of movement. The direction and degree of blur are adjustable. An example is shown in figure 14.13.

Figure 14.13

The Motion Blur effect.

Exploring the Effects Menu 257

The blur effect is not something you normally would use for an apple, but a photo of a car or a runner can be greatly enhanced by using Motion Blur.

- **N**oise. The Noise filters create a granular effect that add texture to an image. The remaining Noise filters are used to reduce noise in an image, which soften it and reduce the speckled look sometimes created when you scan an image.

- **P**ixelated. Creates a block-like effect with an image. You've probably seen it used on television to obscure someone's identity. An example is shown in figure 14.14.

Figure 14.14
The Pixelated effect.

- **Po**sterize. Re-creates an image using only a preselected number of colors. In figure 14.15, the apple has been posterized, giving it the look of an Andy Warhol graphic.

Figure 14.15
The Posterize effect.

- **P**sychedelic. Gives an image a 1960s look by randomly changing its colors. The percentage of change is adjustable, and an example is shown in figure 14.16.

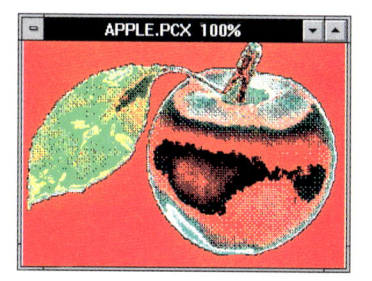

Figure 14.16
The Psychedelic effect.

Solarize. Works much the same as the Invert filter, in that it creates a photo-negative image. Solarize enables you to determine which pixels (by value) are converted to a negative.

That's a quick overview of some of the Photo-Paint functions. Theyz require a good deal of trial-and-error experimentation, but the rewards can be well worth your time.

Chapter 15
CorelMOVE!

It probably is impossible to be alive in this century and not be familiar with animation. From the cartoons we watched as children, to the sophisticated movie and television graphics of today, animation has informed and entertained us for a long time. The production of animation was somewhat limited to professionals until recently, when computer animation programs were made available for the PC.

Which brings us to CorelMOVE!, Corel's animation program. CorelMOVE! takes the traditional approach to animation: individual cels are created with objects changing in shape and position, and the cells then are shown in sequence to create the illusion of movement.

If you are interested in producing high-tech, commercial-quality animations, CorelMOVE! probably will not be up to the challenge. But Move is a good way to get your feet wet, and it is capable of producing some simple yet effective animated presentations.

Exploring the CorelMOVE! Screen

To start CorelMOVE!, click on its icon in the Corel 4 group of the Program Manager. The program loads and the initial screen appears, as shown in figure 15.1.

Only the title and menu bars are displayed, with the File menu the only one available now. A file must be opened, or a new one created, before the rest of the menus, tools, and controls become available. For the full display, select Open from the File menu and open the SAMPLE.CMV file from the Samples directory of CorelMOVE!, as shown in figure 15.2.

This chapter examines:

- The CorelMOVE! screen
- Creating a simple animation
- Using CorelSHOW!

260 Chapter 15: CorelMOVE!

Figure 15.1
The initial CorelMOVE! screen.

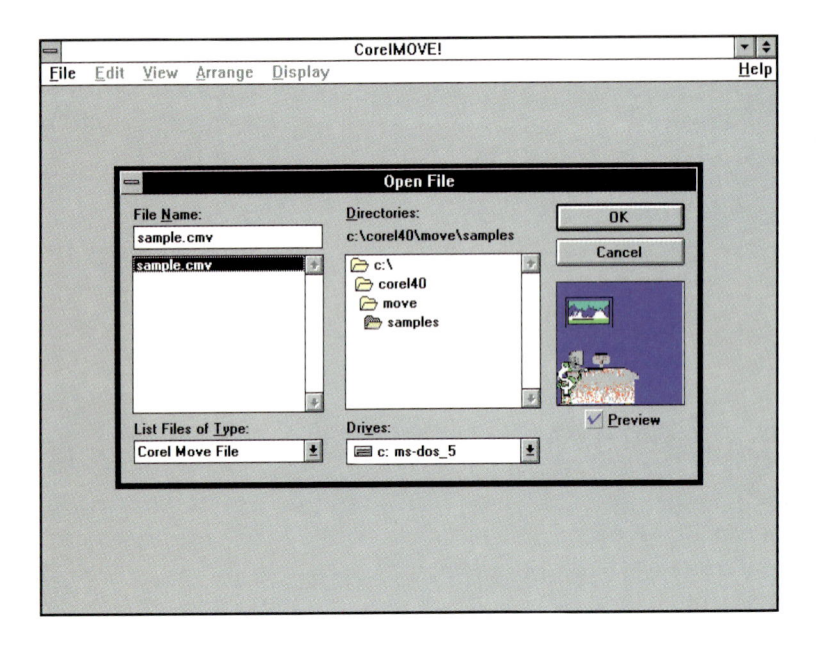

Figure 15.2
Opening an animation file with the Open File dialog box.

NOTE

CorelMOVE! files are saved with the file extension CMV.

CorelMOVE! opens the file and displays the first frame of the animation as well as the tools and controls, as shown in figure 15.3.

Exploring the CorelMOVE! Screen   **261**

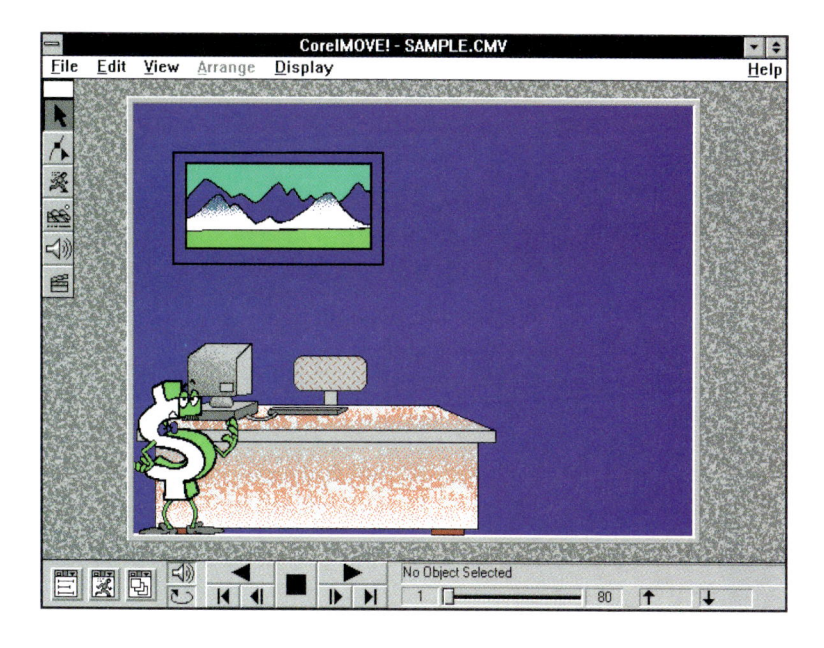

Figure 15.3
The CorelMOVE! screen with an animation file open.

The menu bar is not as extensive here as in the other Corel programs because most of the controls are accessible on-screen. (You will see how to use them shortly.) To play the animation sequence, choose **P**lay from the **V**iew menu, or use the shortcut key—F9. Choose one and play the sequence. To stop it, just press the Esc key.

> While the animation is playing, look at the bottom of the screen to see the Frame Counter in action. It displays the total number of frames and the frame currently being displayed.

The Toolbox

Now to examine the screen, starting with the Toolbox. The Toolbox is found on the left side of the CorelMOVE! screen, and the description of its tools is from top to bottom.

- **The Pick tool.** Its main function is to select objects and move them on-screen. If you double-click on any object with the Pick tool, it brings up a dialog box with information on that object.

- **The Path tool.** Objects that move on-screen are called *actors*. The Path tool enables you to create or edit the path an actor follows on the screen. When the Path tool is selected, the Path Edit roll-up menu appears, as shown in figure 15.4.

Figure 15.4
The Path Edit roll-up menu.

- **The Actor tool.** This enables you to add a new actor to an animation sequence. Clicking on this tool accesses the New Actor dialog box, from which you select an actor source.

- **The Prop tool.** This tool enables you to create and place props in an animation sequence. A *prop* is a single-cel object that appears in an animation but will not show any movement. In the sample animation you looked at, there were 11 prop objects: the background, desk, and picture; four bullets; and four text objects. As demonstrated in the animation, a prop can be made to appear at any time during an animation.

- **The Sound tool.** In addition to actors and props, CorelMOVE! enables you to record and add sound to an animation.

To use the Sound tool, your system must have a microphone and a sound capturing board, such as a Sound Blaster.

You also can incorporate existing sound files (.WAV) into an animation by using the Import command in the File menu.*

- **The Cue tool.** This tool enables you to add cues to an animation sequence. A *cue* is an action that takes place at a certain time or under certain circumstances. In the sample animation, for instance, a cue is set for frame 9 for the first bullet and text object to appear. When the animation is played and reaches frame 9, the bullet and text appear, and, in this case, remain on the screen until the last frame is shown.

The Control Panel

The other set of on-screen controls appears at the bottom of the screen, in the Control Panel. The various controls are shown in figure 15.5.

Figure 15.5
The CorelMOVE! Control Panel.

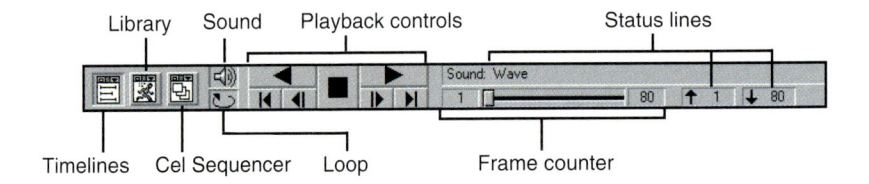

Following is a brief explanation of the Control Panel functions.

Timelines

Clicking on the Timelines icon accesses the Timelines dialog box. Clicking on the expand arrow in the dialog box displays the Timelines of the animation, as shown in figure 15.6.

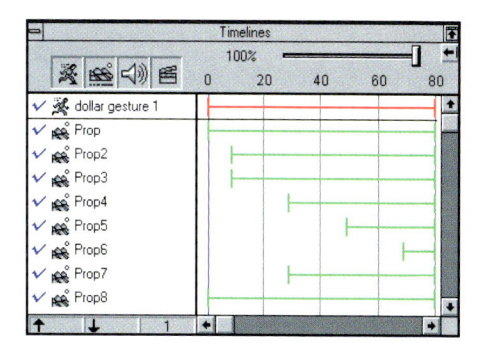

Figure 15.6

The Timelines dialog box, showing the Timelines of an animation.

The Timelines dialog box graphically represents when an actor appears in the animation and when it leaves. For instance, the dollar sign actor from the previous example appears in the first frame and remains throughout the sequence. The Timelines chart in figure 15.6 shows it starting at frame 0 and going until frame 80 (the last frame).

> *If you click on the name of an actor or prop in the Timeline dialog box, that line is highlighted, and the object (or its position) is indicated by a marquee box. Click on each line in the dialog box and see the corresponding object highlighted on the screen.*

Library

Clicking on the Library icon brings up the Library roll-up menu, as shown in figure 15.7.

Figure 15.7

The Library roll-up menu.

Chapter 15: CorelMOVE!

The Library is where you keep actors, props, and sounds before placing them into animations. It enables you to group them as you see fit and preview them in the roll-up before you import them to the animation.

Cel Sequencer

Clicking on the Cel Sequencer icon accesses the Cel Sequencer roll-up menu, as shown in figure 15.8.

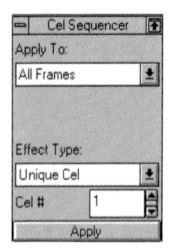

Figure 15.8

The Cel Sequencer roll-up menu.

Let's say you create an actor of a man walking across the screen. The actual animation might be comprised of ten movements (or cels). To show fluid motion, you would display the cels in order (1, 2, 3, 4, 5, 6, 7, 8, 9, 10). If the man were walking on hot coals, his movement would be anything but fluid. The Cel Sequencer enables you to show the cels in any order you want—3, 6, 1, 8, 2, 7, 9, 4, 10, 5, for example, which creates a jerky motion, as someone walking on hot coals might have.

Cel Sequencer also enables you to change the size of a cel. By selecting and editing a range of cels, you can give the impression that the actor is moving closer by making it increase in size.

Sound

When this icon is selected the animation will play any sounds that have been added to the animation. The icon acts as a toggle switch—when you click it to unselect it, the animation plays, but without sound.

Loop

When this icon is selected, the animation returns to its first frame upon completion and plays again. When the icon is unselected, the animation plays until the last frame and stops.

Playback Controls

The seven playback control buttons are similar to those found on a VCR or CD player. The square is the stop button, the right and left triangles play the animation in forward or reverse, and the triangles with lines enable you to move one frame at a time or jump to the first or last frame of the animation.

Frame Counter

The number to the left is the frame currently displayed, and the number to the right is the total number of frames in the sequence. Between them is the slider. Click and drag the slider left or right to quickly jump to any frame in the animation.

Status Lines

The line above the slider displays the name of the object currently selected, as well as what type of object it is. The boxes to the right (with arrows) indicate at what frame the selected object enters the animation and at what frame the object exits the animation.

Menu Bar Controls

The last controls discussed here are accessed from the menu bar: Animation Info and Playback Options commands in the Display menu, the Import command in the File menu, and the Insert New Object command in the Edit menu.

Animation Info

Choosing Animation Info (Ctrl+A) from the Display menu accesses the Animation Information dialog box, as shown in figure 15.9.

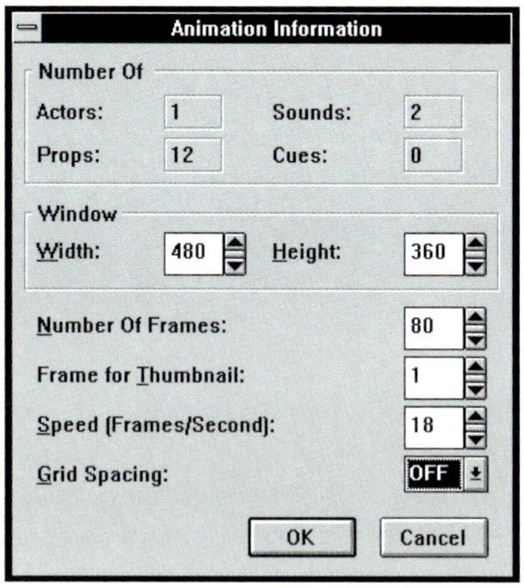

Figure 15.9
The Animation Information dialog box.

The dialog box displays general information about the animation (number of actors, props, cues, and so on), and enables you to make certain changes in the animation (frames per second, total frames in the animation, and so on).

The number of frames per second is dependent on the processor speed and memory in your system. If a value of 18 frames per second (fps)—the maximum—is selected, your computer might not have the power to support that speed. As a result, the animation would run slower.

Playback Options

Choosing Playback Options (Ctrl+K) from the Display menu brings up the Playback Options dialog box, as shown in figure 15.10.

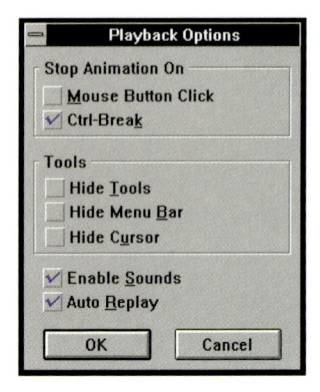

Figure 15.10
The Playback Options dialog box.

The dialog box enables you to choose the action that stops the playing of an animation, whether any of the tools are displayed during playback, whether the sound files are heard, and whether the animation will loop.

Regardless of the settings chosen, the Esc key always stops the play of an animation. The Enable Sounds and the Auto Replay options perform the same functions as the Sound and Loop icons in the Control Panel.

Import

Choosing Import from the File menu enables you to use graphics and sounds not created in the CorelMOVE! program. You can import a variety of bit-map files to be used as actors or props. You also can import sound files (*.WAV) that you have created previously or purchased on disk.

Insert New Object

Choosing Insert New Object from the Edit menu inserts CorelDRAW! (*.CDR) files into an animation. This command uses the capabilities of object linking and embedding (OLE) when inserting a CDR file into CorelMOVE!.

Creating a Simple Animation

Now that you are familiar with CorelMOVE! commands, you can create a simple animation by creating a couple of actors and a prop.

1. From the File menu choose New. Name the animation file CORELNOW.

2. Start by creating a background. Click on the Prop tool icon to access the New Prop dialog box. Name this prop BKGD1. With the Create New box checked and CorelMOVE 4.0 the selected Object Type, click on OK.

3. The Paint window and its toolbox appear now, as shown in figure 15.11.

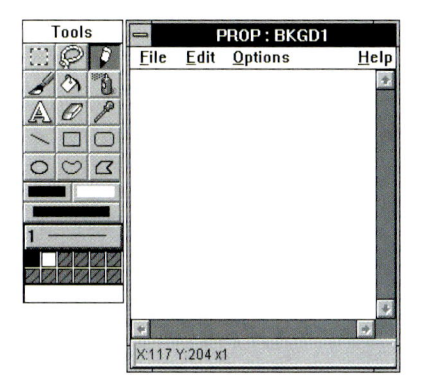

Figure 15.11
The Paint window and toolbox.

The size of the Paint window is the maximum size of the prop. Because the Paint window is smaller than the animation window, you can not create a background that would fill the screen. The Paint window must be resized.

4. From the File menu of the Paint window, select Page Setup. In the Set Size dialog box, set the horizontal value to 480 and the vertical value to 360. Click on OK. The Paint window now has the same dimensions as the animation window.

5. From the toolbox, click on the foreground color box, as shown in figure 15.12. The color palette appears.

   Slide the cursor over to the blue square and release the mouse. The foreground color box changes to blue.

The left color box is the foreground color, the right color button is background color, and the box below them is for a pattern fill. The terms foreground *and* background *refer to the ways in which the colors are used in the pattern*

Chapter 15: CorelMOVE!

fills. When you draw an object or use the Fill tool, the foreground color is used. By pressing the secondary mouse button when using a drawing or Fill tool, the background color is used.

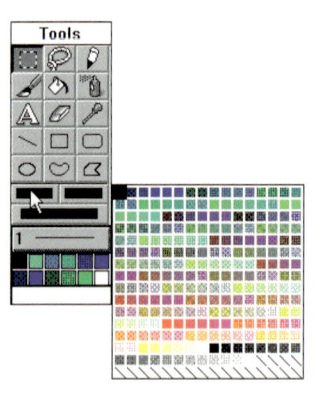

Figure 15.12

Selecting colors from the toolbox color palette.

6. Select the Paint Bucket tool, and click in the center of the Paint window. The screen is filled in blue.

7. From the File menu of the Paint window, choose Apply Changes (this is the equivalent to the Save command), then choose Exit. You are returned to the main screen, but as shown in figure 15.13, the background prop is a little out of position.

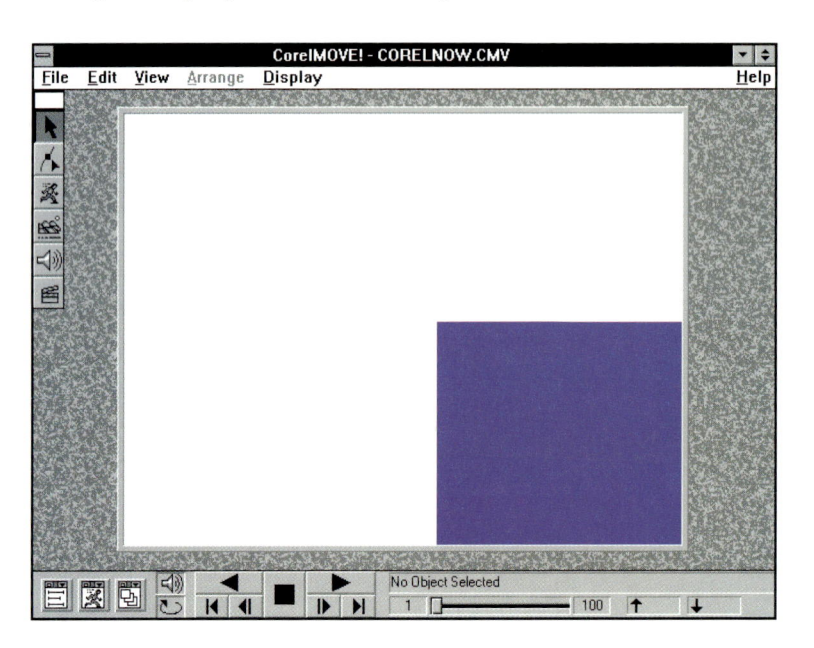

Figure 15.13

The prop appears on the screen, but it needs to be positioned.

8. Select the Pick tool and click on the background prop. The prop is surrounded by a marquee box, and the cursor now is a four-pointed arrow. Click and drag the cursor on the prop, and the marquee box moves with it, indicating the new position.

Creating a Simple Animation   269

9. Drag the marquee box so that it fits to the frame of the animation window. Release the mouse, and the entire screen now is blue.

10. Click on the Actor tool to access the New Actor dialog box. Select CorelMOVE 4.0 for Object Type, click on the Create New box, name the actor **BOX1**, and click on OK.

11. In the Paint window, select Page Setup from the File menu again and reset the values to 480 and 360, as you did before.

12. Click on the foreground color box and choose green. Click on the Rectangle tool and draw a rectangle to the approximate size and shape as shown in figure 15.14.

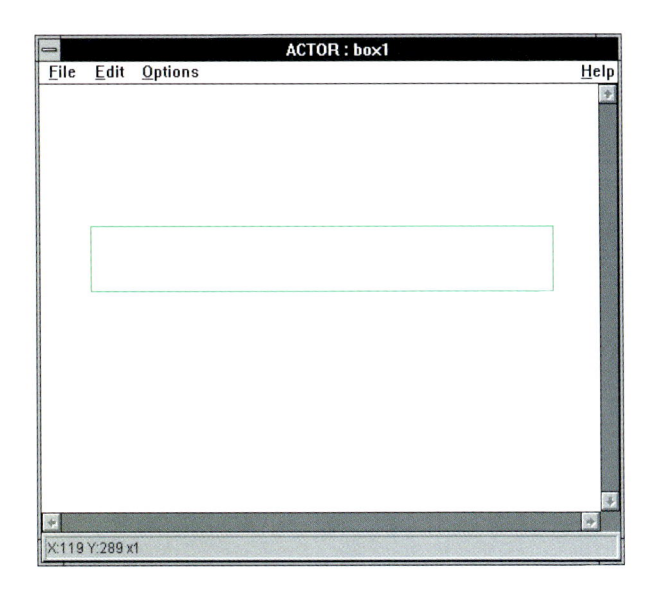

Figure 15.14

Draw a rectangle approximately this size.

13. Select the Paint Bucket tool and click inside the rectangle. It fills to a solid green.

14. Choose Apply Changes in the File menu, then choose Exit. You return to the main screen.

15. Select the green rectangle with the Pick tool and drag it to the center of the animation window.

16. Select the Actor tool again. With Create New and CorelMOVE 4.0 selected, name the actor **TYPE1** and click on OK.

17. Select Page Setup from the File menu, and as done before, change the settings to 480 and 360. Click on OK.

18. Choose yellow for the foreground color.

19. From the Options menu, select Font; the Font dialog box appears. Select Switzerland for the Font, Bold Italic for the Style, and 26 point for the Size.

Chapter 15: CorelMOVE!

20. Select the Text tool and click anywhere on the left side of the Paint window; a text cursor appears. Enter the following text on the screen: **CorelDRAW! NOW!** (see fig. 15.15).

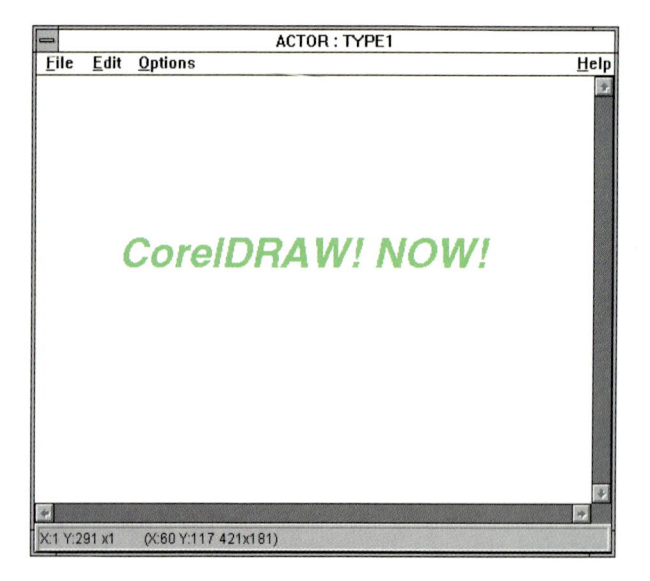

Figure 15.15
Adding text in the Paint window.

21. From the File menu, choose Apply Changes, then Exit.

22. Click on the text actor with the Pick tool and move it so it is centered in the green rectangle, as shown in figure 15.16.

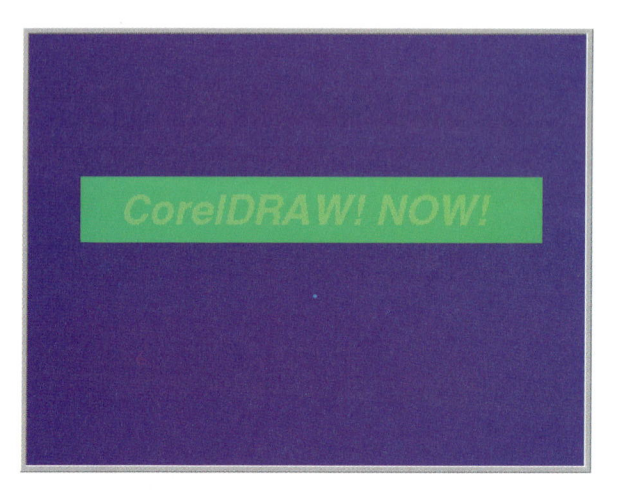

Figure 15.16
Actors are created and positioned on-screen.

Now that you have your actors, define their movement.

23. Click on the green rectangle with the Pick tool to select it. Drag it to the upper left corner of the screen, until the marquee box is completely outside the animation window, and release the mouse button.

Creating a Simple Animation   271

24. Click on the Path tool; the Path Edit roll-up menu appears. Click the mouse to the left of the text actor. A path line is drawn, as shown in figure 15.17.

Figure 15.17
A path line for the actor is drawn.

The rectangle actor (BOX1) currently is made up of two frames: the first has the box in the upper left corner, and the second has it in the middle of the screen. The box in the second frame needs to be positioned so that it aligns with the text actor.

25. In the playback controls section of the Control Panel, click on the button to advance the animation one frame. The BOX1 actor appears in the middle of the screen, and the frame counter displays 2.

If the display counter shows 100, you pressed the advance button to jump to the last frame. Click the reverse button to go back to 1 and advance one frame to frame 2.

26. Click on BOX1 with the Path tool and position the marquee box so that it is centered around the text actor.

27. From the Path Edit roll-up menu, click on the +/– button to access the Scale Path dialog box, as shown in figure 15.18.

Chapter 15: CorelMOVE!

Figure 15.18
The Scale Path dialog box.

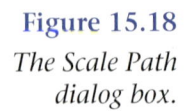

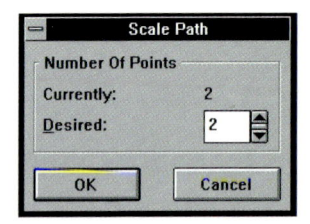

This dialog box enables you to set the number of points of an actor's path. Each point corresponds to one frame in the animation. Enter a Desired value of 50, and click on OK.

28. Press the play button in the playback controls to run the animation you have created so far. Press the stop button and using the slider control, set the frame number to 50. This puts BOX1 in its final position.

You now will perform a similar procedure with the text actor, using a more accurate method of positioning.

29. Select the text actor (TYPE1) with the Pick tool. Click on the Path tool to bring up the Path Edit dialog box. Click on the Point Information icon (it is the only one in the top row that is not grayed out). The Point Information dialog box appears, as shown in figure 15.19.

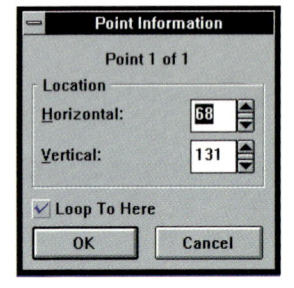

Figure 15.19
The Point Information dialog box.

This box displays the exact position of the actor in terms of pixel position. Record the values on paper, and click on Cancel.

Your position values probably will differ from those in the example, but that is to be expected.

30. With the Pick tool, click on the text actor (TYPE1) to select it. Click and drag it to the bottom right corner, until the marquee box is outside the animation window.

Creating a Simple Animation 273

31. Select the Path tool and click it just below the lower left corner of BOX1 to create a path, as shown in figure 15.20.

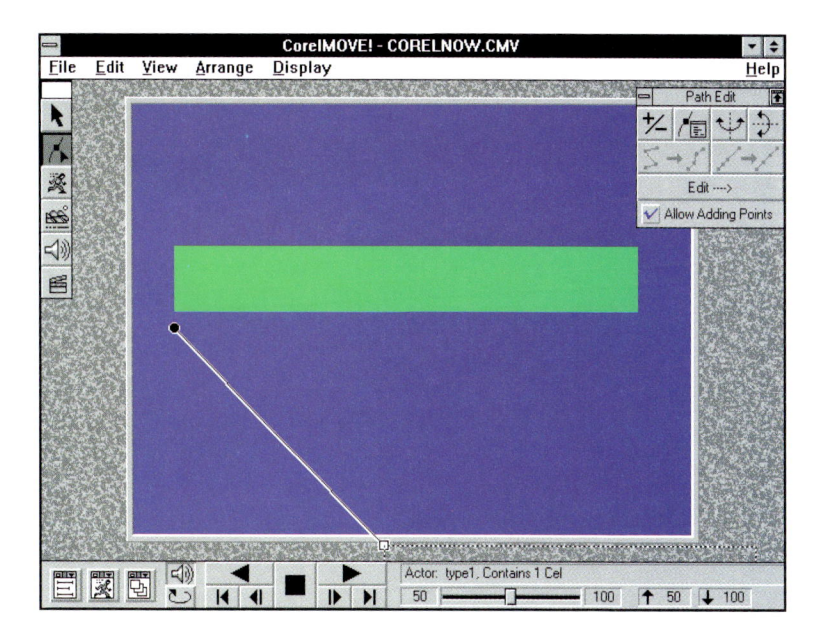

Figure 15.20
Creating a path for the TYPE1 actor.

32. Using the playback controls, advance to frame 51. TYPE1 now appears in the middle of the screen, but needs to be in the center of BOX1.

33. Click on the Point Information icon again and enter the values you recorded earlier. Click on OK. TYPE1 now is repositioned in the center of BOX1.

34. Click on the Scale Path icon (+/-) and change the Desired number of points to 50. Click on OK.

35. From the Control Panel, bring the animation back to frame 1 and click on the play button. BOX1 animates down from the top, and then TYPE1 animates up from the bottom. Click on the stop button.

36. Click on the Timelines icon from the Control Panel; the Timelines dialog box appears. Click on the expand arrow so that the entire Timelines graph is visible, as shown in figure 15.21.

37. Place the cursor on the left end of the graph line for TYPE1. Click and drag it to the left until it starts at the 0 mark, as shown in figure 15.22. Close the dialog box when done.

Chapter 15: CorelMOVE!

Figure 15.21

The Timelines graph displays the elements of the animation.

Figure 15.22

TYPE1 is edited in the Timeline graph.

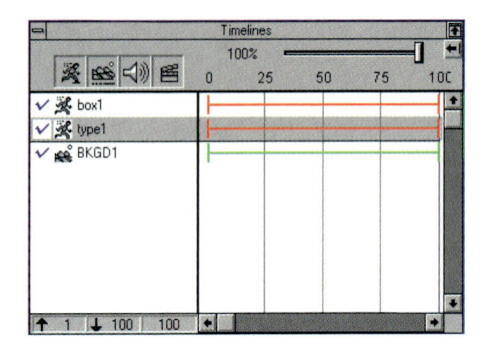

38. Click back to frame 1 and press play. The two actors now animate onto the screen simultaneously.

39. Now for one last touch: click on the Pick tool and select TYPE1 (you might have to advance the animation so that it is visible on-screen).

40. With TYPE1 selected, click on the Cel Sequencer icon in the Control Panel. Its roll-up menu appears, as shown in figure 15.23.

Figure 15.23

The Cel Sequencer roll-up menu.

41. Click on the drop-down menu for Apply To and select Frame Range. Enter values From: **1** To: **50**. This will apply the effect to the entire animation sequence.

42. Click on the drop-down menu for Effect Type and choose Scale Sequence. Click on the drop-down menu that appears just below Scale Sequence and choose Small to Large. Click on Apply.

43. Use the playback controls to return to frame 1 and press the play button. Now the TYPE1 actor grows in size as it animates on.

Using CorelSHOW!

You can use CorelSHOW! to show your CorelMOVE! animation (or any other Corel file). Working with CorelSHOW! is like putting a slide show together. Instead of slides, you use animations, CDR files, charts, bit maps, or files from any program that is OLE supported. In CorelSHOW! each frame of the presentation is referred to as a *slide*.

Clicking on the CorelSHOW! icon in Program Manager brings up the CorelSHOW! welcome screen. Select Start a New Presentation, and click on OK. The Welcome dialog box disappears, and the full working CorelSHOW! screen is displayed.

> *The CD-ROM discs that come with CorelDRAW! contain some generic Autodesk Animation files. Think of them as computer-animated clip art, and feel free to use them as you wish.*

> *The CorelSHOW! documentation in the manual is extremely limited. However, there is a great deal of information available through on-line help.*

INDEX

Index

Symbols

3-D effects, applying to objects, 170-176
3D Riser bar charts, 231

A

Absolute Coordinates option, 73-74
actions
    constraining, 73
    undoing, 37
Actor tool, 262, 269
actors, 261
    Timelines chart representations, 263
Adaptive Unsharp Mask filter (CorelPHOTO-PAINT!), 253
Add Perspective command (Effects menu), 167-169
adding pages, 139-142
airbrush effects, 185-188, 249
Airbrush tool, 249
Align command (Arrange menu), 89, 117-118, 213
Align dialog box, 117-118

Align to Baseline command (Text menu), 67-68
alignment, 47
    objects, 117-119
        with guidelines, 119-120
    pattern fills, 102-104
    text, 49
    vanishing points, 168-169
All Fonts Resident option (Export EPS dialog box), 197
All Fonts Resident option (Options dialog box), 208
animation, 3
    backgrounds, 267
    inserting files, 266
    creating, 267-274
    opening files, 260-261
Animation Info command (Display menu, CorelMOVE!), 265
Animation Information dialog box, 265
Apply Changes command (File menu, CorelMOVE!), 268-270
applying styles, 155-157
arcs, drawing, 39-41
Arrange menu commands, 16
    Align, 89, 117-118, 213
    Break Apart, 129-130, 186

Combine, 128
Convert to Curves, 36
Group, 121-122
Move, 73
Order, 126
Ungroup, 222
Weld, 132-133
arrows
dragging, 50
moving objects on-screen, 13
Artist Brush tool, 249
Artistic filter (CorelPHOTO-PAINT!), 255
Artistic text
alignment, 47
entering, 43-45
Artistic Text dialog box, 44-45
editing text, 52-53
fonts, selecting, 47
selecting text attributes, 47
Artistic Text tool, 43-44, 53, 63, 69, 213
attributes
character, modifying, 53-55
copying, 112-113
text
copying, 68-69
editing, 46-47
Auto Increase Flatness option (Options dialog box), 208
Auto-Pan box, 13
AUTOEXEC.BAT file, modifying at installation, 6
automatic scrolling, 13

B

Back/Front extrusions, 170
background, 267-268
bar charts, 242

Batch Output dialog box, 225
batch printing, 211
batch tracing, 224-225
Bézier mode
curves, drawing, 24
lines, drawing, 22-23
Big/Small extrusions, 170
bit maps, 210
exporting, 198-199
bit-map files, importing (CorelMOVE!), 266
bit-map fills, 100-107, 210
applying from Fill roll-up menu, 110-111
Bitmap Export dialog box, 198-199, 214, 220
Blend filter (CorelPHOTO-PAINT!), 254
blend groups
fusing, 182-183
splitting, 182
Blend roll-up command (Effects menu), 179-181
Blend roll-up menu
color controls, 183
Splitting/Fusing icon, 182
borders, displaying, 11
bounding boxes, drawing, 49
Break Apart command (Arrange menu), 129-130, 186
breaking apart objects, 129-130
brightness, 92
Brightness and Contrast filter (CorelPHOTO-PAINT!), 252
bullets, 149-150

C

Calibration Bar option (Options dialog box), 209

calligraphic pens, drawing outlines, 89
Canvas roll-up menu (CorelPHOTO-PAINT!), 251
catalogs, creating, 203
CD-ROM drives, 4
  fonts, installing, 7-8
  installation option, 4
CDs (compact discs), 4
Cel Sequencer roll-up menu, 264, 274
cels, sizing, 264
center of rotation, 78
Center option (Print dialog box), 207
centering rectangles, 89
centerline tracing method, 215
Character Attributes dialog box, 54-55
characters
  attributes, modifying, 53-55
  special, 70
Chart menu (CorelCHART!), 232
charts
  3D Riser bar charts, 231
  bar charts, 242
  creating, 2, 234-239
  deleting text, 236
  horizontal bar charts, 235
  importing, 242-244
  selecting cells, 237
  types, 239-242
  vertical bar/side-by-side charts, 241
  see also CorelCHART! utility
checkered flag, creating, 159-168
chrome type, creating, 177-179
circles
  creating, 37-39
  floating text around, 65-66
  placing text inside, 66
Clear Perspective command (Effects menu), 169

Clear Transformations command (Effects menu), 75-76, 163-169
clicking mouse, 18
clip art, installing, 6
Clipboard. copying text, 45
Clone tool, 249
cloning objects, 12-13, 83-84
closing roll-up menus, 28
CMYK Color Model, 91
color
  adding to color palette, 92-93
  HSB Color Model, 92
  line color, editing, 25-28
  object fill color, editing, 90
  options
    Blend roll-up menu, 183
    Extrude roll-up menu, 172
  outline color
    editing, 90
    setting, 87-88
  paper, setting, 11
  RGB Color Model, 92
  selecting, 92
Color command (Image menu), 252
Color option (Bitmap Export dialog box), 198
Color Palette command (Display menu), 12
Color Palette menu, 12
color palettes, 10, 91
  adding colors, 92-93
  optimizing, 14
  rearranging colors, 93-94
  selecting colors, 92
Color Replacer tool, 251
Color Selection roll-up menu (CorelPHOTO-PAINT!), 251
color separations, 208
Color/Gray Map filter (CorelPHOTO-PAINT!), 254

INDEX

columns - commands

columns, formatting, 150-151
Combine command (Arrange menu), 128
combining objects, 127-131
commands
   accessing, 44
   Arrange menu, 16
      Align, 89, 117-118, 213
      Break Apart, 129-130, 186
      Combine, 128
      Convert To Curves, 36
      Group, 121-122
      Move, 73
      Order, 126
      Separate, 174
      Ungroup, 222
      Weld, 132-133
   Display menu, 17
      Animation Info, 265
      Color Palette, 12
      Edit Wireframe, 12, 133, 222
      Playback Options (CorelMOVE!), 266
      Show Preview, 17
      Show Rulers, 12
      Show Status Line, 10
   Edit menu
      Clone, 83
      Copy, 16, 45
      Copy Attributes From, 69
      Cut, 16
      Delete, 16, 82
      Duplicate, 16, 82
      Insert New Object (CorelMOVE!), 266
      Paste, 16, 45
      Redo, 16, 37
      Repeat, 16, 83
      Select All, 16, 128, 211
      Select by Keyword (CorelMOSAIC!), 211
      Undo, 16, 30, 37
   Effects menu
      Add Perspective, 167-169
      Blend, 179-181
      Clear Perspective, 169
      Clear Transformations, 75-76, 163-169
      Contour, 176-178
      PowerLine, 190
      Rotate & Skew, 79-81
      Stretch & Mirror, 76-77, 164, 188
   File menu
      Apply Changes (CorelMOVE!), 268-270
      Export, 197-199, 220
      Import, 195-196, 221-222, 262
      New, 16, 45
      New From Template, 154
      Open, 16, 71
      Print Files, 211
      Print Setup, 10, 205
      Save, 16, 31
      Save As, 16, 31
   Image menu (CorelPHOTO-PAINT!)
      Color, 252
      Distort, 255
      Flip, 254
      Resample, 255
      Resolution, 255
      Rotate, 255
      Sharpen, 253
      Smooth, 253-254
      Tone, 254
   Layers roll-up menu
      Grid, 134
      Locked, 137
      Move To, 135
      New, 134

Layout menu, 16
  Delete Page, 143-144
  Grid Setup, 11, 123-124
  Guidelines Setup, 120
  Insert Page, 139-140
  Page Setup, 11
  Snap To, 118
Object menu (Select Master), 84
Preferences submenu
  Constrain Angle, 13
  Cross Hair Cursor, 13
  Interruptible Display, 13
  Miter Limit, 13
  Nudge, 13
  Place Duplicates and Clones, 12-13
  Undo Levels, 13
Settings menu
  Modify, 219
  Modify...Batch Output, 225
Special menu (Preferences), 12, 74, 78
Text menu
  Align to Baseline, 67-68
  Edit Text, 16
  Fit Text to Path, 16, 63
  Spell Checker, 57-58
  Straighten Text, 67-68
  Thesaurus, 59-60
Trace menu (Outline), 215
transformation, 85-86
comments, *see* notes
Compatibility Message box (Preferences submenu), 14
Compressed option (Bitmap Export dialog box), 198
conserving memory, 127-128
Constrain Angle command (Preferences submenu), 13
Contour effect, 176-179
Contour roll-up menu, 176-178
contrast, adjusting, 252
control bar (CorelPHOTO-PAINT!), 247-251
control handles, 75-76, 162
Control Panel (CorelMOVE!), 262-265
control points, editing, 28-30
Convert Color Bitmaps To Grayscale option (Export EPS dialog box), 197
Convert To Curves command (Arrange menu), 36
Copies option (Print dialog box), 207
Copy Attributes dialog box, 69, 112-113
Copy Attributes From command (Edit menu), 69
Copy command (Edit menu), 16, 45
copying
  attributes, 68-69, 112-113
  effects, 169-170
  files to libraries, 202
  objects between pages, 141-142
  shapes, 164-165
CorelCHART! utility, 2, 227-244
  Chart menu, 232
  chart types, 239-242
  creating charts, 234-239
  Data Manager, 233-235
  Gallery menu, 232
  importing charts, 242-244
  menu bar, 232
  Text Ribbon, 230-231
  toolbox, 227-230
  see also charts

CorelDRAW! 4.0
  components, 2-3
  installation, 3-8
    CD-ROM, 4
    hardware requirements, 3-4
    user requirements, 4
CorelMOSAIC! utility, 2, 200-203
  catalogs, creating, 203
  copying files to library, 202
  installing, 6
  libraries, creating, 201
  opening files, 200-201
  searching for files, 202
CorelMOVE! utility, 3
  animations, creating, 267-274
  Control Panel, 262-265
  starting, 259-261
  toolbox, 261-263
CorelPHOTO-PAINT! utility, 3
  Effects menu, 255-258
  Image menu, 252-255
  roll-up menus, 251-252
  screens, 245-246
  toolbox, 246-251
CorelSHOW! utility, 3
  CorelMOVE! animation, showing, 275
CorelTRACE! utility, 2
  installing, 6
  opening, 214
  tracing
    methods, 215
    options, 216-219
    text objects, 220-221
corners, rounding, 35
Crop Marks option (Options dialog box), 209
Cross Hair Cursor command (Preferences submenu), 13
Ctrl key
  actions, constraining, 73
  holding down when dragging, 50
  squares, drawing, 35
Cue tool, 262
cursors, 43
Curve tool, 250
curves
  color, editing, 25-28
  converting objects to, 36-37
  drawing, 23-24
    Bézier mode, 24
    Freehand mode, 23-24
  extending, 24
  thickness, editing, 25-28
Curves dialog box, 14
custom installation, 5
custom tracing options (CorelTRACE!), 219
Customize menu, 6
Cut and Clear dialog box (CorelCHART!), 237
Cut command (Edit menu), 16

D

Data Manager (CorelCHART!), 233-235
default
  fills, setting, 107-108
  outlines, setting, 107-108
  screen, setting, 10-15
Definitions window (Thesaurus), 60
Delete command (Edit menu), 16, 82
Delete Page command (Layout menu), 143-144

deleting
- pages, 143-144
- text from charts, 236

Densitometer Scale option (Options dialog box), 209

Desktop layer, *see* **Master layer**

dialog boxes
- Align, 117-118
- Animation Information, 265
- Artistic Text, 44-47, 52-53
- Batch Output, 225
- Bitmap Export, 198-199, 214, 220
- Character Attributes, 54-55
- Copy Attributes, 69, 112-113
- Curves, 14
- Cut and Clear (CorelCHART!), 237
- Dimension Preferences, 15
- Export EPS, 197-198
- Fit Text to Path Offsets, 65
- Fountain Fill, 95
- Grid Setup, 11-12
- Insert Page, 139-140
- Layer Options, 134
- Line Attributes, 219
- Load a Picture from Disk, 246-247
- Move, 73
- New (CorelCHART!), 234
- New Actor, 269
- New Prop, 267
- Open Drawing, 71-72
- Open Files, 224, 260
- Options, 62, 207-209
- Outline Color, 26
- Outline Pen, 28, 87-88, 107
- Paste Special (CorelCHART!), 243
- Path Edit, 271
- Playback Options, 266
- Point Information, 271
- Preferences, 74-78
- Preferences-Display, 14
- Preferences-Mouse, 15
- Preferences-roll-ups, 15
- Print, 205-211
- Print Setup, 10, 205
- Printer, 207
- Rotate & Skew, 79
- Save Style As, 152-154
- Save Text As, 221
- Save Trace As, 216
- Scale Path, 271-272
- Separations, 209
- Spacing, 51-52
- Spelling Checker, 57-59
- Text, 51-52, 56
- Text Attributes, 220
- Text Edit, 167
- Texture Fill, 105
- Thesaurus, 59-60
- Timelines, 263, 273-274
- TrueType Font Selector, 7-8
- Uniform Fill, 90-91, 178

dictionaries, creating, 58-59

Diffuse filter (CorelPHOTO-PAINT!), 254

dimension lines, 15
- drawing, 30-32

Dimension Preferences dialog box, 15

Display menu (CorelPHOTO-PAINT!), 246

Display menu commands, 17
- Animation Info, 265
- Color Palette, 12
- Edit Wireframe, 12, 133, 222
- Show Preview, 17
- Show Rulers, 12
- Show Status Line, 10

display tools (CorelPHOTO-PAINT!), 249
displaying layers, 134
Distort command (Image menu), 255
Dithered colors option (Bitmap Export dialog box), 198
dithering, 14
documents
   adding pages, 139-142
   deleting pages, 143-144
double-clicking mouse, 18
dragging mouse, 18, 72-73
   arrows, 50
drawing
   arcs, 39-41
   bounding boxes, 49
   curves, 23-24
      Bézier mode, 24
      Freehand mode, 23-24
   ellipses, 37-38
   lines, 19-23
      Bézier mode, 22-23
      dimension lines, 30-32
      Freehand mode, 19-21
   outlines with calligraphic pen, 89
   rectangles, 33-34, 89
   squares, 34-35
   wedges, 39-41
drawing tools (CorelPHOTO-PAINT!), 250
drivers, installing, 6
drives, CD-ROM, 4
   fonts, installing, 7-8
   installation option, 4
Duplicate command (Edit menu), 16, 82
duplicating objects, 12-13, 81-83
   see also copying

E

Edge filters (CorelPHOTO-PAINT!), 255-256
Edit menu commands
   Clone, 83
   Copy, 16, 45
   Copy Attributes From, 69
   Cut, 16
   Delete, 82
   Duplicate, 16, 82
   Paste, 16, 45
   Redo, 16, 37
   Repeat, 16, 83
   Select All, 16, 128, 211
   Select by Keyword, 211
   Undo, 16, 30, 37
Edit Text command (Text menu), 16
Edit Wireframe command (Display menu), 12, 133, 222
editing
   control points, 28-30
   envelope types, 161-162
   nib shapes, 191
   nodes, 28-30
   object fill color, 90
   objects within group, 122-123
   outline color, 90
   parts of text strings, 53-55
   pattern fill alignment, 102-104
   perspective views, 167-170
   text, 48-49, 52-53
      attributes, 46-47
      Text roll-up menu, 67
editing window, 9
effect filters, 245

effects
   airbrush, 185-188
   copying, 169-170
   lighting, adding to extruded objects, 175-176

Effects menu, 16
   CorelPHOTO-PAINT!, 245, 255-258

Effects menu commands
   Add Perspective, 167-169
   Blend, 179-181
   Clear Perspective, 169
   Clear Transformations, 75-76, 163-169
   Contour, 176-178
   Rotate & Skew, 79-81
   Stretch & Mirror, 76-77, 164, 188

ellipse envelope, preset, 163

Ellipse tool, 16, 37-39
   CorelCHART!, 229

ellipses
   converting to curves, 36-37
   creating, 37-39

embedding objects, 200

Emboss filter (CorelPHOTO-PAINT!), 256

Emulsion Down option (Options dialog box), 208

Enhance Detail filter (CorelPHOTO-PAINT!)), 253

entering paragraph text, 56

envelope modes, 161

Envelope roll-up menu, 160-161

Envelope tool, 159-163

envelopes
   changes, canceling, 162
   mapping options, 164
   paragraph text, 166-167
   preset, adding, 163-164
   shapes, copying, 164-165

Equalize filter (CorelPHOTO-PAINT!), 254

Eraser tool, 251

errors, limitcheck, 208

Export command (File menu), 197-199, 220

Export EPS dialog box, 197-198

exporting files, 195-199
   bit maps, 198-199
   vector-based, 196-198

extending curves, 24

extrude groups, ungrouping, 174

Extrude roll-up menu, 170
   color options, 172

Extrude Rotator tool, 172-173

extruding by specific value, 171

extrusions
   creating, 170-176
   dynamic linking, 173-174
   rotating, 172-173
   types, 170

Eyedropper tool, 251

F

File Information option (Options dialog box), 209

File menu commands
   Export, 197-199, 220
   Import, 195-196, 221-222, 262
   New, 16, 45
   New From Template, 154
   Open, 16, 71
   Print Files, 211
   Print Setup, 10, 205
   Save, 16, 31
   Save As, 16, 31

files
   copying to libraries, 202
   exporting, 195-199
      bit maps, 198-199
      vector-based, 196-198

importing, 195-196, 266
keywords, attaching, 194-195
naming, 32
notes, attaching, 194-195
opening, 14, 71-72
   animation files, 260-261
   CorelMOSAIC!, 200-201
previewing, 72
printing, 208-210
scan, 214
searching in CorelMOSAIC!, 202
sorting, 193-194
sound, importing for animation, 262
tracing, 224-225

Fill roll-up menu, 108-111
   bit-map fills, applying, 110-111
   fountain fills, applying, 108-109
   two-color patterns, applying, 109-110

Fill Settings roll-up menu (CorelPHOTO-PAINT!), 251

Fill tool, 16

Filled Box tool, 250

Filled Ellipse tool, 250

Filled Polygon tool, 250

Filled Rounded Box tool, 250

fills
   bit-map fills, 100-107
      applying from Fill roll-up menu, 110-111
   color, editing, 90
   defaults, setting, 107-108
   fountain, 94-99
      angling fill direction, 96
      applying from Fill roll-up menu, 108-109
      custom, creating, 97-99
      preset, creating, 96-97

   pattern fills, 100-107
      alignment, editing, 102-104
      creating, 101-102
      full-color fills, 104
      sizes, 101
      two-color patterns, 100-101
   PostScript textures, 107
   practical uses, 114-115
   with solid color, 89-91

filters
   effect, 245
   Effects menu (CorelPHOTO-PAINT!), 255-258
   Image menu (CorelPHOTO-PAINT!), 252-254
   installing, 6

Fit Text to Path command (Text menu), 16, 63

Fit Text to Path Offsets dialog box, 65

Fit to Page option (Print dialog box), 207

Flip command (Image menu), 254

Flood Fill tools, 249

fonts
   installing, 6-8
   selecting, 47
   sizes, modifying, 47-48

Fonts window, 47

foreground, 267-268

form tracing method, 215

formatting paragraph text, 147-150

Fountain Fill dialog box, 95

fountain fills, 94-99, 211
   angling fill direction, 96
   applying from Fill roll-up menu, 108-109
   custom, creating, 97-99
   preset, creating, 96-97
   steps, printed, 208

Fountain Steps option (Export EPS dialog box), 197
Fountain Steps option (Option dialog box), 208
frame counter control (CorelMOVE! control panel), 265
frames, advancing, 271
frames per second, 266
Freehand Blend tool, 250
Freehand Brighten tool, 250
Freehand Contrast tool, 250
Freehand mode
    curves, drawing, 23-24
    lines, drawing, 19-21
Freehand Pen tool, 189
Freehand Pencil tool, 165
Freehand Sharpen tool, 251
Freehand Smear tool, 250
Freehand Smudge tool, 250
Freehand Tint tool, 250
Front/Back extrusions, 170
full-color pattern fills, 104
    applying from Fill roll-up menu, 110
full-color view, 12
fusing blend groups, 182-183

G

Gallery menu (CorelCHART!), 232
Gamma filter (CorelPHOTO-PAINT!), 253
Gradient Fill tool, 249
Greek Text Below option, 14
grid, 11-12
    changing, 123-125
    sizing, 124-125
    spacing lines, 11

Grid command (Layers roll-up menu), 134
Grid Frequency option, 11
Grid layer, 133
Grid Origin option, 11
Grid Setup command (Layout menu), 11, 123-124
Grid Setup dialog box, 11-12
Group command (Arrange menu), 121-122
grouping objects, 120-123
guidelines, 119-120
Guidelines Setup command (Layout menu), 120
Guides layer, 133

H

Hand tools, 249
handles, control, 162
hardware requirements, 3-4
Header Resolution (Export EPS dialog box), 197
Help menu, 18
hiding Master Layer, 143
highlighting text, 46
Hollow Box tool, 250
Hollow Ellipse tool, 250
Hollow Polygon tool, 250
Hollow Rounded Box tool, 250
horizontal
    arrow, dragging, 50
    bar charts, 235
    scroll bars, 10HSB Color Model, 92
HSB Color Model, 92
hue, 92
Hue & Saturation filter (CorelPHOTO-PAINT!), 253

I

image controls, adjusting, 191-192
Image menu (CorelPHOTO-PAINT!), 245, 252-255
images
  scanned, converting, 2
  tracing, 213-216
Import command (File menu), 195-196, 221-222, 262
importing
  charts, 242-244
  files, 195-196
    bit-map, 266
  symbol sets, 61
  traced images, 221-223
Impressionist Brush tool, 249
Impressionist Clone tool, 250
indents, 148-149
Ink Flow option (Image Controls), 191
input terminology, 18
Insert New Object command (Edit menu, CorelMOVE!), 266
Insert Page command (Layout menu), 139-140
Insert Page dialog box, 139-140
installation, 5-8
  CD-ROM, 4
  hardware requirements, 3-4
  options, 5
  user requirements, 4
Interruptible Display command (Preferences submenu), 13
Invert filter (CorelPHOTO-PAINT!)), 256

J–K

Jaggy Despeckle filter (CorelPHOTO-PAINT!), 256
Keep Lines option, 164
keyboard shortcuts
  Alt+Enter (Redo), 37
  Ctrl+A (Animation Info, CorelMOVE!), 265
  Ctrl+C (Copy), 16
  Ctrl+D (Duplicate), 16, 82
  Ctrl+J (Preferences), 12
  Ctrl+L (Combine), 128
  Ctrl+P (Print), 206
  Ctrl+PgDn (Send Back One), 157
  Ctrl+R (Repeat), 16, 83
  Ctrl+T (Edit text), 44
  Ctrl+V (Paste), 16
  Ctrl+X (Cut), 16
  Ctrl+Y (Snap to Grid), 12
  Ctrl+Z (Undo), 16, 37
  Del key, 16, 82
  F9 (Play, CorelMOVE!), 261
  F9 (Show Preview), 17
  F11 (Fountain Fill), 95
  Shift+F9 (Edit Wireframe), 222
  space bar (Pick tool), 15
keyboards, moving objects with, 74
keywords, 194-195

L

landscape orientation, selecting, 206
Lasso tool, 249
Layer Options dialog box, 134
layers, 133-138
  adding, 134
  adding objects, 135
  displaying, 134
  distinguishing between, 136-137
  Grid layer, 133
  Guides, 133
  locking, 137
  Master, 134

Layers roll-up menu - models

moving objects between, 135
printing, 138
reordering, 136
Layers roll-up menu, 133
Grid command, 134
Locked command, 137
Move To command, 135
New command, 134
Layout menu commands, 16
Delete Page, 143-144
Grid Setup, 123-124
Guidelines Setup, 120
Insert Page, 139-140
Page Setup, 11
Snap To, 118
leading, reducing, 51
libraries
copying files to, 202
creating in CorelMOSAIC!, 201
Symbol, 60-61
Library roll-up menu (CorelMOVE!), 263-264
lighting effects, adding to extruded objects, 175-176
lightness, 92
limitcheck errors, 208
Line Attributes dialog box, 219
Line tool, 250
lines
color, editing, 25-28
drawing, 19-23
Bézier mode, 22-23
dimension lines, 30-32
Freehand mode, 19-21
multisegment lines, 20-21
thickness, editing, 25-28
linked objects, ungrouping, 174
linking objects, 200

Load a Picture from Disk dialog box, 246-247
Local Undo tool, 251
Locator tool, 249
Locked command (Layers roll-up menu), 137
locking layers, 137
Loop icon (CorelMOVE! control panel), 264

M

Magic Wand, tracing, 217
Magic Wand Selection (+) tool, 217
Magic Wand tool, 218, 249
mapping options, envelopes, 164
marquee-selecting, 29, 72
Mask menu (CorelPHOTO-PAINT!), 246
masks, 211
creating, 130-132
master clones, identifying, 84
Master layer, 134
creating, 142-143
hiding, 143
memory
conserving, 127-128
printer, 210
menu bars, 9, 16-18
CorelCHART!, 232
CorelMOVE!, 261, 265-266
CorelPHOTO-PAINT!, 245-246
CorelTRACE!, 214
menus, see **commands; roll-up menus**
mirroring, 77-78
Miter Limit command (Preferences submenu), 13
models, Wireframe, 12

modes - objects

modes
- Bézier
  - curves, drawing, 24
  - lines, drawing, 22-23
- envelope, 161
- Freehand
  - curves, drawing, 23-24
  - lines, drawing, 19-21
- Paragraph Text, 222-223
  - exiting, 220
- Rotate & Skew, 84
- Skew, 85
- Snap to Grid, 12
- text edit, quitting, 53

Modify command (Settings menu), 219

Modify...Batch Output command (Settings), 225

Mosaic command (Options menu), 211

motion, controlling, 13

Motion Blur filter (CorelPHOTO-PAINT!), 256-257

mouse, 15, 18
- moving objects, 72-73
- rotating objects, 78-79
- skewing objects, 80
- stretching objects, 74-76

Move command (Arrange menu), 73

Move dialog box, 73

Move To command (Layers roll-up menu), 135

moving objects between layers, 135

multimedia presentations, 3

multiple files, tracing, 224-225

multiple objects, creating, 183-185

N

naming files, 32

negative images, printing, 208

New Actor dialog box, 269

New command (File menu), 16, 45

New command (Layers roll-up menu), 134

New dialog box (CorelCHART!), 234

New From Template command (File menu), 154

New Prop dialog box, 267

nib shapes, adjusting, 191

Node Edit roll-up menu, 28-30, 37, 222

Node Edit tool, 169

nodes, 19-21
- control handles, 162
- editing, 28-30
- picking out, 54

Noise filter (CorelPHOTO-PAINT!), 257

notes, 194-195

Nudge command (Preferences submenu), 13

nudging, 13, 74

O

object linking and embedding, *see* OLE

Object menu, 84

object-oriented drawing programs, 2

objects
- adding to layers, 135
- aligning, 117-119
  - with guidelines, 119-120
- blending, 179-181
- breaking apart, 129-130
- cloning, 12-13, 83-84
- combining, 127-131
- constraining, 38
- converting to curves, 36-37
- copying between pages, 141-142

deselecting, 211
duplicating, 12-13, 81-83
dynamically linked, 173-174
editing within group, 122-123
embedding, 200
filling, *see* fills
grouping, 120-123
linked, ungrouping, 174
linking, 200
mirroring, 77-78
motion, controlling, 13
moving, 13, 72-74, 135
multiple, creating, 183-185
reordering, 125-126
rotating, 78-79
scaling, 76
selecting, 64, 121
skewing, 80-81
stretching
    from center out, 75-76
    with mouse, 74-76
    with Stretch & Mirror command, 76-77
viewing, 12
welding, 132-133

OCR (optical character recognition) tracing method, 2, 215, 220, 224
OLE (object linking and embedding), 199-200
    charts, importing, 242-244
On-line Help, installing, 5
one-point perspective, 167-168
Open command (File menu), 16, 71
Open Drawing dialog box, 71-72
Open Files dialog box, 224, 260
opening
    files, 71-72
        CorelMOSAIC!, 200-201
    templates, 154

optical character recognition (OCR) tracing method, 215, 220, 224
Optimized Palette option, 14
Options dialog box, 62, 207-209
Options menu commands, 211
Order command (Arrange menu), 126
order of objects, changing, 125-126
orientation
    selecting, 206
    text options, 64
Outline Color dialog box, 26
Outline command (Trace menu), 215
Outline Pen dialog box, 28, 87-88, 107
Outline Pen fly-out menu (CorelCHART!), 230
Outline tool, 16, 214
outline tracing method, 215
outlines
    color
        editing, 90
        setting, 87-88
    default, setting, 107-108
    drawing with calligraphic pen, 89
    practical uses, 114-115
    width, setting, 87-88
overlapping objects, combining, 128-129

P

Page Setup command (Layout menu), 11
pages
    adding, 139-142
    copying objects between, 141-142
    deleting, 143-144
Pages option (Print dialog box), 207
Paint Bucket tool, 268-269

Paint window (CorelMOVE!), 267
Paintbrush tool, 249
painting tools (CorelPHOTO-PAINT!), 249-250
palettes,
  optimizing, 14
  see also color palettes
paper size, setting, 11
paragraph text
  entering, 56
    Envelope commands, 166-167
    formatting, 147-150
      bullets, 149-150
      columns, 150-151
      indents, 148-149
      tabs, 147
    multiple text frames, 144-147
Paragraph Text mode, 222-223
Paragraph Text tool, 56, 60, 144-151, 167, 220
Parallel extrusions, 170
Paste command (Edit menu), 16, 45
Paste Special dialog box (CorelCHART!), 243
pasting text, 45
Path Edit dialog box, 271
path lines, linking to blend groups, 181
Path tool, 261
paths, fitting text to, 63-66
pattern fills, 100-107, 210
  alignment, editing, 102-104
  applying from Fill roll-up menu, 109-110
  creating, 101-102
  full-color fills, 104
  sizes, 101
  symbol, see tiling
  two-color patterns, 100-101

Pen roll-up menu, 26-28
  outlines, editing, 87-88
Pen tool, 250
  outlines, editing, 87-88
Pencil tool, 16
  CorelCHART!, 229
perspectives
  editing, 167-170
  one-point, 167-168
  two-point, 168
photo retouching tools, 3
Pick tool, 15, 33, 36, 52, 63, 261
  CorelCHART!, 228
  jumping to, 82
  text strings, selecting, 47
  tracing, 216-217
Pixelated filter (CorelPHOTO-PAINT!), 257
Place Duplicates and Clones command (Preferences submenu), 12-13
playback controls (CorelMOVE! control panel), 264
Playback Options command (Display menu, CorelMOVE!), 266
Playback Options dialog box, 266
Point Information dialog box, 272
Pointillist Brush tool, 249
Pointillist Clone tool, 250
Polygon selection tool, 249
Pop-Up Menu tool (CorelCHART!), 228
portrait orientation, selecting, 206
Posterize filter (CorelPHOTO-PAINT!), 257
PostScript textures, 107
PowerLine Roll-Up command (Effects menu), 190
PowerLine roll-up menu, 190
  image controls, adjusting, 191-192
  nib shapes, adjusting, 191

PowerLine tools, 188-192
predefined shapes, 35
Preferences command (Special menu), 12, 74, 78
Preferences dialog box, 74, 78
Preferences submenu commands, 12-14
Preferences-Display dialog box, 14
Preferences-Mouse dialog box, 15
Preferences-roll-ups dialog box, 15
presentations, multimedia, 3
preset envelopes, adding, 163-164
Preview Colors option, 14
Preview Fountain Steps option, 14
Preview Image option (Print dialog box), 207
previewing files, 72
Print as Separations option (Options dialog box), 208
Print dialog box, 205-211
Print Files command (File menu), 211
Print Negative option (Options dialog box), 208
Print Setup command (File menu), 10, 205
Print Setup dialog box, 10, 205
Print to File option, 207
printable page area, 10
Printer dialog box, 207
Printer option (Print dialog box), 207
Printer Selection box, 207
printers
   memory, 210
   preparing
      Options dialog box, 208-209
      Print dialog box, 206-207
      Print Setup command, 205

printing
   as mirror image, 208
   batch, 211
   defaults, setting, 10
   files, 209-210
   layers, 138
   tips, 210-211
program installation options, 5
Prop tool, 262
Psychedelic filter (CorelPHOTO-PAINT!), 257-258

Q–R

quadrants, applying text to, 65-66
rainbow effect, 183
RAM (random-access memory) requirements, 4
rectangle selection tool (CorelPHOTO-PAINT!), 248
Rectangle tool, 16, 33-36, 213
   CorelCHART!, 229
rectangles
   centering, 89
   converting to curves, 36-37
   creating, 33-35
   drawing, 89
   modifying, 35
Redo command (Edit menu), 16, 37
Registration Marks option (Options dialog box), 209
reordering layers, 136
Repeat command (Edit menu), 16, 83
Resample command (Image menu), 255
Resolution command (Image menu), 255
Resolution option (Bitmap Export dialog box), 199

retouching tools (CorelPHOTO-PAINT!), 250-251
RGB Color Model, 92
roll-up menus, 15, 18
   closing, 28
   CorelPHOTO-PAINT!, 251-252
   Fill, 108-111
   Layers, 133
   Node Edit, 28-30
   Pen, 26-28
   Styles, 152-157
Rotate & Skew command (Effects menu), 79-81
Rotate & Skew dialog box, 79
Rotate & Skew mode, 84
Rotate command (Image menu), 255
rotating
   extrusions, 172-173
   objects
      Rotate & Skew command, 79
      with mouse, 78-79
rulers, 9
   displaying, 12

S

SAMPLES, 5
saturation, 92
   adjusting (CorelPHOTO-PAINT!), 253
Save As command (File menu), 16, 31
Save command (File menu), 16, 31
Save Style As dialog box, 152-154
Save Text As dialog box, 221
Save Trace As dialog box, 216
saving trace images, 216
Scale option (Print dialog box), 207
Scale Path dialog box, 271-272
Scale with Image option (Image Controls), 192
scales
   densitometer, 209
   specifying, 11
scaling objects, 76
scan files, 214
scanned images, converting, 2
scanners, installing, 6
screen
   components, 9-10
   CorelCHART!, 227-232
   CorelMOVE!, 259-266
   CorelPHOTO-PAINT!, 245-246
   defaults, setting, 10-15
   redraw, halting, 13
screen method, entering Artistic text, 43-44
Screen option (Option dialog box), 208
scroll bars, 10
scrolling, 13
searching files in CorelMOSAIC!, 202
secondary buttons (mouse), 18
Select All command (Edit menu), 16, 128, 211
Select by Keyword command (Edit menu, CorelMOSAIC!), 211
Select Master command (Object menu), 84
Selected Only option (Export EPS dialog box), 198-199
selecting
   colors, 92
   objects from group, 121
selection tools (CorelPHOTO-PAINT!), 248-249
Separate command (Arrange menu), 174
Separations dialog box, 209
Separations option (Options dialog box), 209

Set Flatness to option (Option dialog box), 208
Settings menu commands
   Modify, 219
   Modify...Batch Output, 225
shadow effect, 85-86
   skewing, 86
Shape tool, 16, 39-40, 50
   corners, rounding, 35
   editing objects, 28-30
   node positions, changing, 37
   nodes, picking out, 54
shapes
   constraining, 35
   envelopes, copying, 164-165
   predefined, 35
   rectangles, defining, 34
SHARE.EXE program, installing, 6
Sharpen command (Image menu), 253
Shift key, drawing rectangles, 34
Show Font Sample in Text Roll-Up option, 14
Show Preview command (Display menu), 17
Show Rulers command (Display menu), 12
Show Status Line command (Display menu), 10
silhouette tracing method, 215, 218
Single Arc mode, 161
Single Line mode, 161
Size option (Bitmap Export dialog box), 199
sizes
   fonts, modifying, 47-48
   grid, 124-125
   paper, setting, 11
   rectangles, defining, 34
   text, expanding to fill frame, 56

Skew mode, 85
skewing
   objects, 80-81
   shadows, 86
Small/Big extrusions, 170
Smooth command (Image menu, CorelPHOTO-PAINT!), 253-254
Smooth filter (CorelPHOTO-PAINT!), 254
Snap To command (Layout menu), 118
Snap to Grid mode, 12
Soften filter (CorelPHOTO-PAINT!), 254
Solarize filter (CorelPHOTO-PAINT!), 258
sorting files, 193-194
sound files, importing for animation, 262
Sound icon (CorelMOVE!), 264
Sound tool, 262
spacing
   grid lines, 11
   text, 49-52
Spacing dialog box, 51-52
special characters, 70
special effects tools, 159-192
Special menu, 17-18
   CorelPHOTO-PAINT!, 246
   Preferences command, 12, 74
Speed option (Image Controls), 191
Spell Checker, 16, 56
Spell Checker command (Text menu), 57-58
Spelling Checker dialog box, 57-59
spelling dictionaries, creating, 58-59
splitting
   blend groups, 182
   text strings, 48

Spraycan tool, 249
Spread option (Image Controls), 191
squares, drawing, 34-35
status lines, 9-10
status lines control (CorelMOVE! control panel), 265
step values, "maxing out," 208
Straighten Text command (Text menu), 67-68
Stretch & Mirror command (Effects menu), 76-77, 164, 188
stretching objects
　from center out, 75-76
　with mouse, 74-76
　with Stretch & Mirror command, 76-77
styles, 152-157
　applying, 155-157
Styles roll-up menu, 152-157
Symbol library, 60-61
symbol patterns, *see* tiling
symbol sets
　importing, 61
　installing, 6
SYMBOLS, 6
Symbols roll-up menu, 61-62
Synonyms window (Thesaurus), 60
system requirements, 3-4

T

tabs, 147
templates, 152-157
　creating, 152-154
　opening, 154
text
　alignment, 49
　converting to curves, 36-37
　copying attributes, 68-69
　deleting from charts, 236
　displaying, 14
　editing, 46-53
　　attributes, 46-47
　　Text roll-up menu, 67
　entering, 43-45
　fitting to path, 63-66
　floating around circles, 65–66
　font size, modifying, 47-48
　highlighting, 46
　orientation options, 64
　paragraph text
　　entering, 56
　　Envelope commands, 166-167
　　formatting, 147-150
　　multiple text frames, 144-147
　pasting, 45
　placing inside circles, 66
　size, expanding to fill frame, 56
　spacing, 49-52
　strings, splitting, 48
　tracing, 224
　viewing, 14
Text As Curves option (Export EPS dialog box), 197
Text As Text option (Export EPS dialog box), 197
Text Attributes dialog box, 220
text cursor, 43
Text dialog box, 51-52, 56
Text Edit dialog box, 167
text edit mode, quitting, 53
Text menu commands
　Align to Baseline, 67-68
　Edit Text, 16
　Fit Text to Path, 16, 63
　Spell Checker, 57-58
　Straighten Text, 67-68
　Thesaurus, 59-60

text objects, tracing, 220
Text Ribbon (CorelCHART!), 230-231
Text roll-up menu, 16, 67
Text tool, 16, 43, 56, 250
    CorelCHART!, 230
Texture Fill dialog box, 105
Texture Fill tool, 249
Thesaurus command (Text menu), 59-60
Thesaurus dialog box, 59-60
Thesaurus utility, 16, 59-60
thickness (of lines), editing, 25-28
Threshold filter (CorelPHOTO-PAINT!), 253
thumbnails, 200, 211
TIFF format, 214
Tile Fill tools, 249
Tile option (Print dialog box), 207
Tile option (Symbols roll-up menu), 62
tiling, 62
Timelines dialog box, 263, 273-274
title bars, 9
Tone command (Image menu), 254
Tool Settings roll-up menu, 252
toolbox, 9, 15-16
    CorelCHART! utility, 227-230
    CorelMOVE!, 261-263
    CorelPHOTO-PAINT!, 246-251
tools
    Actor, 262, 269
    Airbrush, 249
    Artist Brush, 249
    Artistic Text, 43-44, 53, 63, 69, 213
    Clone, 249
    Color Replacer, 251
    Cue, 262
    Curve, 250
    display (CorelPHOTO-PAINT!), 249
    drawing (CorelPHOTO-PAINT!), 250
    Ellipse, 16, 37-39
        CorelCHART!, 229
    Envelope, 159-163
    Eraser, 251
    Extrude Rotator, 172-173
    Eyedropper, 251
    Fill, 16
    Filled Box, 250
    Filled Ellipse, 250
    Filled Polygon, 250
    Filled Rounded Box, 250
    Flood Fill, 249
    Freehand Blend, 250
    Freehand Brighten, 250
    Freehand Contrast, 250
    Freehand Pen, 189
    Freehand Pencil, 165
    Freehand Sharpen, 251
    Freehand Smear, 250
    Freehand Smudge, 250
    Freehand Tint, 250
    Gradient Fill, 249
    Hand, 249
    Hollow Box, 250
    Hollow Ellipse, 250
    Hollow Polygon, 250
    Hollow Rounded Box, 250
    Impressionist Brush, 249
    Impressionist Clone, 250
    Lasso, 249
    Line, 250
    Local Undo, 251
    Locator, 249
    Magic Wand, 218, 249
    Magic Wand Selection (+), 217
    Node Edit, 169
    Outline, 16, 214
    Paint Bucket, 268-269

Paintbrush, 249
painting (CorelPHOTO-PAINT!), 249-250
Paragraph Text, 56, 60, 144-151, 167, 220
Path, 261
Pen, 250
   editing outlines, 87-88
Pencil, 16
   CorelCHART!, 229
photo retouching, 3
Pick, 15, 33, 47, 52, 63, 82, 261
   CorelCHART!, 228
   tracing, 216-217
Pointillist Brush, 249
Pointillist Clone, 250
Polygon selection, 249
Pop-Up Menu (CorelCHART!), 228
PowerLine, 188-192
Prop, 262
Rectangle, 16, 33-36, 213
   CorelCHART!, 229
retouching (CorelPHOTO-PAINT!), 250-251
selection tools (CorelPHOTO-PAINT!), 248-249
Shape, 16, 35-40, 50, 54
   editing objects, 28-30
Sound, 262
special effects, 159-192
Spraycan, 249
Text, 16, 43, 56, 250
   CorelCHART!, 230
Texture Fill, 249
Tile Fill, 249
Zoom, 16, 49-50, 249
   CorelCHART!, 229
Zoom In, 217, 222-223

traced images
   importing, 221-223
   saving, 216
tracing
   images, 213-216
   Magic Wand, 217
   methods, 215
   multiple files, 224-225
   options, 216-219
   Silhouette method, 218
   text, 224
   text objects, 220-221
transformation commands, 85-86
TrueType Font Selector dialog box, 7-8
TRUMATCH color palette, 91
Two Curves mode, 161
two-point perspective, 168

U

Unconstrained mode, 161-162
Undo command (Edit menu), 16, 30, 37
Undo Levels command (Preferences submenu), 13
Ungroup command (Arrange menu), 222
ungrouping objects, 174
Uniform Fill dialog box, 90-91, 178
Unsharp Mask filter (CorelPHOTO-PAINT!), 253
user requirements, 4

V

vanishing points, aligning, 168-169
vector-based files, 2
   exporting, 196-198
vertical arrow, dragging, 50

vertical bar/side-by-side charts, 241
vertical scroll bar, 10
viewing objects, 12

W–Z

wedges, drawing, 39-41
Weld command (Arrange menu), 132-133
welding objects, 132-133
width, setting outline width, 87-88
window masks, 211
Window menu (CorelPHOTO-PAINT!), 246
windows
    Definitions, 60
    editing, 9
    Fonts, 47
    masks, *see* masks
    Paint (CorelMOVE!), 267
    Synonyms, 60
Wireframe models, 12
Within Page option (Options dialog box), 209
woodcut tracing method, 215

Zoom In tool, 217, 222-223
Zoom tool, 16, 49-50, 249
    CorelCHART!, 229

WANT MORE INFORMATION?

CHECK OUT THESE RELATED TITLES:

	QTY	PRICE	TOTAL
Inside CorelDRAW! 4.0 Special Edition. This updated version of the #1 selling tutorial on CorelDRAW! features easy-to-follow lessons that quickly help readers master this powerful graphics program. Complete with expert tips and techniques—plus a bonus disk loaded with shareware—this book is everything CorelDRAW! users need. ISBN: 1-56205-164-4.	____	$34.95	_____
Inside CorelDRAW!, Fourth Edition. (covers version 3.0) Tap into the graphics power of CorelDRAW! 3.0 with this #1 best-seller. This book goes beyond providing just tips and tricks for boosting productivity. Readers also will receive expanded coverage on how to use CorelDRAW! with other Windows programs! ISBN: 1-56205-106-7.	____	$34.95	_____
CorelDRAW! Special Effects. Learn award-winning techniques from professional CorelDRAW! designers with this comprehensive collection of the hottest tips and techniques! This full-color book provides step-by-step instructions for creating over 30 stunning special effects. An excellent book for those who want to take their CorelDRAW! documents a couple of notches higher. ISBN: 1-56205-123-7.	____	$39.95	_____
CorelDRAW! for Non-Nerds. This light-hearted reference presents all the stuff readers need to know about CorelDRAW! to get things done! With quick, easy-to-find, no-nonsense answers to common questions, this book is perfect for any "non-nerd" who wants a fun and easy way to get started using this powerful graphics program. ISBN: 1-56205-174-1.	____	$18.95	_____

Name _____

Company _____

Address _____

City _____ State ____ ZIP _____

Phone _____ Fax _____

☐ Check Enclosed ☐ VISA ☐ MasterCard

Card #_____ Exp. Date _____

Signature _____

Prices are subject to change. Call for availability and pricing information on latest editions.

Subtotal _____

Shipping _____

$4.00 for the first book and $1.75 for each additional book.

Total _____

Indiana residents add 5% sales tax.

New Riders Publishing 201 West 103rd Street • Indianapolis, Indiana 46290 USA

Orders/Customer Service: 1-800-541-6789
Fax: 1-800-448-3804

CorelDRAW! Now!
REGISTRATION CARD

NRP

Fill out this card to receive information about future New Riders titles!

Name _____ **Title** _____

Company _____

Address _____

City/State/ZIP _____

I bought this book because: _____
_____

I purchased this book from:
☐ A bookstore (Name _____)
☐ A software or electronics store (Name _____)
☐ A mail order (Name of Catalog _____)

I purchase this many computer books each year:
☐ 1–4   ☐ 5 or more

I currently use these applications: _____
_____
_____
_____

I found these chapters to be the most informative: _____
_____

I found these chapters to be the least informative: _____
_____

Additional comments: _____
_____

☐ I would like to see my name in print! You may use my name and quote me in future New Riders products and promotions. My daytime phone number is: _____

New Riders Publishing 201 West 103rd Street • Indianapolis, Indiana 46290 USA

Fold Here

PLACE
STAMP
HERE

New Riders Publishing
201 West 103rd Street
Indianapolis, Indiana 46290
USA

GRAPHICS TITLES

INSIDE CORELDRAW! 4.0, SPECIAL EDITION
DANIEL GRAY

An updated version of the #1 best-selling tutorial on CorelDRAW!

CorelDRAW! 4.0
ISBN: 1-56205-164-4
$34.95 USA

CORELDRAW! SPECIAL EFFECTS
NEW RIDERS PUBLISHING

An inside look at award-winning techniques from professional CorelDRAW! designers!

CorelDRAW! 4.0
ISBN: 1-56205-123-7
$39.95 USA

THE GRAPHICS COACH
KATHY MURRAY

The "what you need to know" book about video cards, color monitors, and the many graphic file formats!

Beginning-Intermediate
ISBN: 1-56205-129-6
$24.95 USA

INSIDE CORELDRAW! FOURTH EDITION
DANIEL GRAY

The popular tutorial approach to learning CorelDRAW!...with complete coverage of version 3.0!

CorelDRAW! 3.0
ISBN: 1-56205-106-7
$34.95 USA

To Order, Call 1-800-428-5331

Are you afraid to touch your computer?

Fear no more! You no longer have to wade through mountains of computer manuals or depend on that annoying computer know-it-all geek.

The *Non-Nerds* books are the *Essential Guide* for Busy People. In today's fast-paced world, you need practical and down-to-earth explanations presented in a lighthearted manner. Join the successful ranks of computer users without being a nerd.

Windows for Non-Nerds
ISBN: 1-56205-152-0 $18.95 USA

An important figure in Washington, D.C. said, "I now have to learn how to use the computer and fast. **Windows for Non-Nerds** helped me do that without worrying that other staffers will see a book sitting around suggesting I'm a dummy."

PCs for Non-Nerds
ISBN: 1-56205-150-4 $18.95 USA

Solutions in **PCs for Non-Nerds** are easy to find because NRP stripped away all non-essential text. One woman referred to **PCs for Non-Nerds** as a "Low-fat book—all of the good stuff, just none of the fat."

DOS for Non-Nerds
ISBN: 1-56205-151-2 $18.95 USA

Demanding an increase in the availability of Non-Nerds books, a business manager in Columbus, Ohio, said, "We don't want to become Ph.D.s in Windows, DOS, PC hardware, OS/2, or any other !@%* computer subject. We just want to learn what we need without being told we're too stupid to do so! Non-Nerds books have more information, substance, and value than other books."

OS/2 for Non-Nerds
ISBN: 1-56205-153-9 $18.95 USA

A Sacremento nurse praised the Non-Nerds books for their inviting, focused, practical approach. She said, "These books teach me how to use a computer just like I learned how to be a good nurse. I wasn't forced to learn as much as a super brain surgeon or professor of neurology."